HAMPSHIRE BI
200

Editorial

Editor:	Dr Alan Cox
Co-Editor:	Martin Pitt
Production:	Mike Wall

Systematic List Writers

Alan Abbott
Keith Betton
Paul Boswell
Trevor Carpenter
Peter Carr
John Clark
John Collman
Alan Cox
Mark Edgeller

John Eyre
Peter Hutchins
Steve Keen
Nick Montegriffo
Paul Norris
Graham Osborne
Dave Pearson
Martin Pitt
Peter Raby

Matthew Shaft
John Shillitoe
Mike Wall
Keith Wills
Paul Winter
Simon Woolley
Russell Wynn

County Recorder

John Clark

4 Cygnet Court, Old Cove Road,
Fleet, Hampshire, GU51 2RL
Tel: 01252 623397
E-mail: johnclark@cygnetcourt.demon.co.uk

Records Panel

John Clark, Keith Betton (Assistant Recorder), Trevor Codlin, Jason Crook,
Mark Edgeller, John Eyre, Marc Moody

Published December 2003
by
HAMPSHIRE ORNITHOLOGICAL SOCIETY
www.hants.gov.uk/hos

Cover photograph: Stilt Sandpiper (Mike Wall)

© Hampshire Ornithological Society - December 2003
ISBN 0-9509805-4-4

HOS is pleased to acknowledge the help of Hampshire County Council, Southampton City Council and Portsmouth City Council in the publication of this Report.

Hampshire County Council

SOUTHAMPTON CITY COUNCIL

Portsmouth CITY COUNCIL

HOS again wishes to acknowledge the continued generous support of London Camera Exchange, Winchester, whose sponsorship is invaluable in assisting with the cost of producing this Report.

London Camera Exchange, Winchester, is one of Hampshire's leading suppliers for binoculars, telescopes, cameras and video equipment. Discounts are available to members of HOS.

London Camera Exchange (Winchester) Limited

15, The Square,
Winchester,
SO23 9ES
Tel: 01962 866203

The views expressed in this report are not necessarily those held by the Hampshire Ornithological Society

CONTENTS

CHAIRMAN'S REPORT FOR 2002

The more I hear about the pressures on Hampshire's countryside the more I realise that HOS has a crucial role to play. Whether it's questions about the rights and wrongs of building a new container terminal at Dibden Bay, allocating more land for new houses or ways of managing our farmland, we need to know how such activities affect the countryside and its wildlife. Biodiversity data in general, and information about birds in particular, is becoming increasingly important in the decision making process. Many will argue that birds are no more important than other forms of wildlife but, as HOS members, we recognise that birds do have some special features. For a start they are big enough and obvious enough for most people to see, hear and perhaps even to recognise. Many species are familiar companions whenever we visit the coast, walk in the countryside or even look out of our windows. Birds range over large areas so they are good indicators of the health of the environment and, thanks to long-standing monitoring programmes, we have reliable historical information about how many there are and how numbers have changed over time. In Hampshire HOS is making a major contribution to maintaining that database.

The integration of bird information with all the other biodiversity data in the county is the aim of the new Hampshire Biodiversity Information Centre (HBIC) which was opened in 2002. Most of the local authorities in the county, together with central government agencies such as English Nature and the Environment Agency, and many natural history groups including HOS support the Centre. HBIC will act as a focal point for the collection and retrieval of biodiversity information. This will make it easier for comprehensive information to be available when required for planning and conservation purposes. HOS is a member of the Centre's Strategic Management Group and will act as the hub for feeding bird records into HBIC. To achieve this we will probably need to update our recording system including the database and recording software, so there are changes ahead. The next step is to seek a grant from the Heritage Lottery Fund to help finance the investment of time and facilities required to get the new system up and running.

During 2002, HOS continued to work on the development and implementation of Hampshire's Biodiversity Action Plan. Following completion of the Species Action Plans (SAPS) for Seed-eating Farmland Birds and Birds of Wet Grassland, a third plan was drafted on Shorebirds. Plans are all very well but what really matters is putting them into practice. Here, too, HOS has been actively involved. Action items from the SAPs that have been implemented include the establishment of a Tree Sparrow nest box scheme in the north of the county and two surveys, one of wintering birds on farmland and another of river valley birds.

In November 2002 we held our first HOS Conservation Conference at Peter Symonds' College, Winchester. The meeting brought together conservation professionals with HOS speakers to consider the various conservation activities currently underway in the county. Topics covered included pressures on our coastal habitats, the impact of agricultural changes on our river valleys and, more generally on our farmland birds, and the work that is being done to maintain our heathlands. The meeting was well attended and will, hopefully, be repeated at regular intervals in the future.

There are many other aspects of HOS activities in 2002 that I could mention. These included publication of the 2000 Bird Report, the Members' Day and AGM, the HOS trip to India and ongoing activities such as our Newsletter, *Kingfisher,* our e-mail discussion group, *hoslist,* and the excellent series of outdoor and indoor meetings. I want to take this opportunity to thank all those who have helped to make these things happen. I also want to urge any HOS members who would like to get involved in running the Society to get in touch with me or another committee member. We need all sorts of help to keep our Society moving ahead so if you can spare a little time and would like to get involved please don't be backward in coming forward!

John Eyre

OBITUARIES

Guy Reginald Mountfort - 1905-2003

Guy Mountfort, who died on 23 April 2003, was the first President of Hampshire Ornithological Society. He had lived in Hampshire as a boy and it was here that his interest in birds and wildlife took root. He moved back to the county, from Sussex to Lyndhurst, in June 1978 and became the Society's President on its formation in March 1979. He served until 1985 when James Hancock succeeded him. Guy was not only an outstanding ornithologist but a vigorous international campaigner for wildlife conservation. By associating his name and reputation with HOS he gave the Society substance and credibility in its critical early years.

The following is based on the obituary published in the Guardian, 30 April 2003.

Guy Mountfort, who was an advertising executive by profession, is perhaps best known to birdwatchers through his book *A Field Guide To The Birds Of Britain And Europe* (1954) which revolutionised UK bird-watching. On a business trip in 1949, he visited Pennsylvania's Hawk Mountain, to watch the migration of its famous birds of prey. There he met Roger Tory Peterson, the doyen of US ornithologists, whose field guides to the birds of America had set new standards in the field. The two of them agreed to produce a similar book covering Britain and Europe, with Peterson doing the illustrations, and with species geographical distribution expert Phil Hollom as the third co-author. It answered a longstanding need for a compact, comprehensive, easy-to-use, accurately illustrated book to help resolve identification dilemmas. As *Birds Of Britain And Europe*, it reached a fifth edition in 1994, and appeared in 13 foreign language editions. Mountfort's other books included *The Hawfinch* (1957), *Portrait Of A Wilderness* (1958), *The Vanishing Jungle* (1969), *Tiger* (1973), *So Small A World* (1974), *Back From The Brink* (1977), *Saving The Tiger* (1981), *Wild India* (1985), and *Rare Birds Of The World* (1988).

He also played a leading role in the founding, in 1961, of the World Wildlife Fund (the World Wide Fund for Nature from 1986 to 2000, but now known as WWF). The WWF emerged from a meeting that Mountfort had with other distinguished naturalists who were concerned about the unprecedented risk to the wildlife heritage: Julian Huxley, Peter Scott and Max Nicholson. He was its treasurer from the outset until 1978, when he became a vice president, and he headed its campaign to save tigers from extinction.

His four-year crusade to save the tiger began in 1968 with a meeting with India's prime minister, Indira Gandhi, who agreed that the country's national symbol had to be preserved. In 1930 there had been eight subspecies of tiger in Asia, with a total population of about 100,000. By the 1960s at least three of those forms were extinct, and the most numerous, the royal Bengal tiger, had plunged to fewer than 2,000 in India, with possibly 600 more in neighbouring states. The threat of extinction prompted the Indian government to respond with a plan to spend $5m (of which the WWF raised almost $2m) over five years. The result was 17 well-managed and fully protected reserves; within a decade, the tiger population more than doubled.

From 1952 to 1962, Mountfort was honorary secretary of the British Ornithologists' Union, and from 1970 to 1975 its president. As well as the WWF's Gold Medal in 1978 for Operation Tiger, in 1971 he received the OBE, and in 1980 he became a Commander of the (Dutch) Order of the Golden Ark.

By the time of his 95th birthday in 2000, Mountfort was philosophical about the numerous environmental changes that he never got round to addressing. As he told *Bird Watching magazine*, 'No one can personally take on all the world's problems. The main problem in this new century will be the demands of the increasing human population throughout the world. This will be the main factor determining the pressures on all forms of wildlife and their habitats. We must never let up on our commitment'

He is survived by his wife and two daughters.

June Irvine 1921-2003

June Irvine, an Honorary Life Member of Hampshire Ornithological Society, died on 21 June, 2003. She was well known, liked and respected by many HOS members. The following tributes are from some of her close friends:

'June was a remarkable woman who dedicated most of her life to helping people, birds, and the planet. She carried out this work with no fuss and was active until very near her death. As far as birds were concerned, she undertook a Common Bird Census in the New Forest for the BTO for many years in Rushpole Wood; studied plots in Broomy and Park Grounds Inclosures (*1977, Bird Study, 24, 105-11*); and recorded waders and wildfowl on the Sowley shore for what is now the WeBS. She also led walks on the coast and in the New Forest. In addition she found time to continue her learning by, for example, attending the HOS Conservation Conference in 2002. She was an active member of New Forest Friends of the Earth, and it was in this connection that I knew June best because we travelled to meetings together. She was a committed, kind, gentle woman, but because of her economic use of words, this was not always evident. Although she was involved in so many activities I suspect that watching birds, whether in this country or some exotic place abroad, was near the top of her list. She will be greatly missed.'

Jenni Tubbs

'All of us who have been involved in the preservation of the New Forest, its scenery and wildlife, will regret the passing of the altogether admirable June Irvine. For over forty years she played an important part in a series of campaigns to prevent the Forest being spoiled or damaged by assorted adversaries who included among others the Forestry Commission and Hampshire County Council.

'June was deeply involved in the campaign waged in the Verderers' Court and in the press to oppose illegal felling in the Ancient and Ornamental Woodlands, and to prevent the exploitation for commercial purposes of the native broad-leaved trees in the Statutory Inclosures. It was thanks to her and her friends and colleagues that this campaign was eventually won, a triumph enshrined in the Minister's Mandate of 1971, which remains in force to this day.

'June was for many years an active and effective member of the Council of the New Forest Association. It was therefore appropriate that she should give evidence on conservation issues at the Lyndhurst Bypass Outer Route Enquiry. Her evidence to the enquiry was cogent and authoritative and there is no question that the Inspector was greatly impressed by her deeply felt conviction and wide knowledge of the Forest. She remained undefeated in cross-examination; whereby the objectors' case was further strengthened.

'Those of us who were privileged to work alongside June all respected her excellent qualities. First among them were her intellectual honesty and moral courage. Not for June the cowardice of neutrality, the avoidance of getting involved. She was not afraid of getting her hands dirty in the cause of conservation: she did so as a matter of course. We shall miss deeply her strong presence, her wise counsel and her companionship. The Forest, its people and its wildlife are greatly in her debt.'

Timothy Dixon

'Together with Joan Bennett, also of HOS, we have enjoyed many holidays and birding days together. June was always very definite. A vague suggestion of some jaunt and she would be keen to join in so the three of us had some great holidays including Poland, USA, the Outer Hebrides and North Norfolk.

'She had infinite patience when needed. Having taken possession of two 'rescued' dogs, one of which must have had appalling treatment as it was absolutely terrified of all humans and just cowered in corners trembling, June spent hours on the floor for several days coaxing it to accept her presence. Eventually she was rewarded with a very happy and healthy little dog.'

Marion Campbell

'June was a pioneer in post-war Hants ornithology. She was a member of the Ornithological Section of the Field Club (the forerunner of HOS) and one of the first to join HOS, remaining active in the field of ornithology all her life. June was a keen and very formidable conservationist, formidable in the sense that she had strong opinions on the subject and was not afraid to say her piece when fighting developers etc. I had the pleasure of having her in one of the birding parties that I led abroad, to Greece, and had the opportunity of seeing her at work in the field. June was good company, a pleasant lady who seemed to get on with most people although she did not suffer fools or developers gladly. She will be missed by her many friends.'

John Taverner

EDITORIAL

First, thanks are due to the members of the society and other observers who contributed a record total of more than 35,000 observations to form the basis for this report. Nevertheless, it is clear from postings on the *HOSlist* web site and regional Pager services that not all records were submitted. Omissions in 2002 included a potential first for the Hampshire list, together with the under-reporting of species of conservation concern including several key areas of the county such as the New Forest. To achieve a more balanced and comprehensive report I would encourage those who didn't submit their records for 2002 to the County Recorder to do so in future. Observers are urged to submit records preferably at the end of each quarter, or as soon as possible after the end of the year and certainly no later than 31st January; any records received after this cannot be guaranteed inclusion in the next annual report.

The task of record assessment continues to be expertly managed by the County and Assistant Recorders, John Clark and Keith Betton, and a dedicated team responsible for entering records into the Cobra data management system: Jason Crook, Mark Edgeller and Matthew Shaft. The *HOS Records Panel* considered over 100 records of scarce species for the year. In most cases, the standard of submissions was very high but unfortunately a few records were not accepted because the notes provided lacked sufficient detail to convince the panel that the identification had been fully substantiated.

For the mammoth job of compiling the systematic list, the editorial team were fortunate in being able to call on no less than 25 authors, who were allocated their own species groups:

Russell Wynn	Divers, Grebes, Tubenoses & Gannet	**Graham Osborne**	Redshank to Phalaropes
Paul Norris	Swans & Geese	**Mark Edgeller**	Skuas & Gulls
Alan Cox	Shelduck to Mallard	**Martin Pitt**	Terns, Tits to Treecreeper, & Raven
Mike Wall	Pintail to Garganey		
Nick Montegriffo	Diving Ducks	**Dave Pearson**	Auks, Flycatchers & Shrikes
Trevor Carpenter	Cormorants, Herons [except Little Egret], Spoonbill	**Simon Woolley**	Pigeons to Cuckoo
		John Eyre	Owls to Larks
Peter Carr	Little Egret	**Keith Wills**	Hirundines to Accentors
John Clark	Raptors, Dartford Warbler	**Peter Hutchins**	Chats & Thrushes
Alan Abbott	Gamebirds	**John Collman**	Warblers [except Dartford Warbler]
Paul Winter	Rails		
John Shillitoe	Oystercatcher to Lapwing	**Steve Keen**	Corvids [except Raven]
Peter Raby	Knot to Ruff	**Keith Betton**	Starlings, Sparrows & Buntings
Paul Boswell	Snipe to Curlew	**Matthew Shaft**	Finches

With such a large group of writers, careful editorial control is required to ensure consistency across the entire document. To this end, Keith Betton, John Clark, Jason Crook, Keith Wills and Russell Wynn devoted considerable time to reviewing the systematic list suggesting various changes to the text; as such, some of the species accounts have been altered and edited, to provide a reasonable degree of uniformity and to allow comparison with previous years. In sincerely thanking the author and review teams for their superb efforts, I must also apologise if inadvertently these changes have caused offence to any author.

Some 247 species were recorded during 2002: of the rarities, the highlight was the addition of Stilt Sandpiper to the Hampshire list. The year also saw the first county breeding records of Goshawk and Avocet. On the debit side, the regular Avon valley wintering flock of European White-fronted Geese appears lost and Bewick's Swan numbers continue to fall. Better news is the continuing importance of county estuaries and river valley habitat to wintering birds; in particular waders where winter county peak totals for Grey Plover were at 7% and Black-tailed Godwit at 20% of recently estimated British populations. I am grateful to Russell Wynn, Trevor Carpenter, Wayne Percy *et al* and David Unsworth for their papers, which provide detail of these highlights.

Glynne Evans has summarised the rich diversity of bird study being undertaken in numerous surveys for BTO sponsored projects by society members. Next year we will be looking to report, in more detail, the findings of completed projects. Meanwhile, Gilbert Rowland's paper contrasts 24 years of change in bird numbers in one extended habitat – the Basingstoke Canal. Barry Duffin's paper on breeding Savi's Warbler at Titchfield Haven chronicle an even longer span of 33 years; sadly as elsewhere in Britain breeding has not been recorded in recent years. Once again, Duncan Bell has coordinated the Ringing Report, which highlights the considerable activity being undertaken in the county to further our understanding of bird movements.

Compiling the report has been a team effort: my fellow members of the editorial team are Martin Pitt, whose assistance in the task of compiling the systematic list has been invaluable, and Mike Wall, who has combined the task of Production Editor with the quest for photographic and art work. Last, and by no means least, we are indebted to Dan Powell, Rosemary Watts/Powell and David Thelwell for their excellent illustrations which ennervate the report, Steve Roberts for his study of a nesting Goshawk, and to the photographers who kindly contributed images for publication: Dennis Bright, Trevor Codlin, Jason Crook, John Levell, Dan Philpott and Mike Wall. Reflecting on my first year as Editor of the report, I would like to thank all those people who have guided and encouraged me; coordinating the report has been a somewhat daunting but rewarding task. John Clark must be singled out for praise in communicating his awesome knowledge of the county avifauna with humour, clarity and precision.

Alan Cox
November 2003

House Sparrows (David Thelwell)

REVIEW OF THE YEAR 2002

Alan Cox

January

The influence of a continental high-pressure ridge ensured a cold and frosty start to the month until 4th, thereafter milder weather prevailed. By the middle of the month active Atlantic depressions pushed their associated fronts across the country, bringing generally overcast and damp conditions with strong west winds at times. In the last week of the month acute Atlantic depressions moving rapidly north-eastwards brought south-westerly gales to the county's coastline and heavy rain on the 26th.

Predictably the early cold snap brought a small flock of Smew to Blashford Lakes, a male and five redheads and six Bitterns were reported across the county. Offshore the west Solent to Hurst Castle stretch held an exceptional concentration of 27 Red-throated, two Black-throated and four Great Northern Divers. A Red-necked Grebe was at Needs Ore Point on 14th, no longer a regular winter record. In Langstone Harbour ten Slavonian Grebes rivalled the regular flock of 12 Black-necked Grebes. A Snow Bunting stayed over from 2001 on Hurst Beach but was not seen after 6th as cloudy, milder conditions replaced the chilly surface air. A **Siberian Chiffchaff** *P.c.tristis* was at Eastleigh SF (2nd and 10th).

At coastal sites the Brent Goose population comprised of 17,000 Dark-bellied Brents *B.b.bernicla*, 17 Pale-bellied Brents *B.b.hrota* and five **Black Brants** *B.b.nigricans* (as accepted by *British Birds*). There were also a record number of 3660 Grey Plovers and a population of 1100 Black-tailed Godwits. Inland lower winter rainfall had reduced the Avon Valley Black-tailed Godwit total to three, compared to a record 2600 a year earlier. Rather more for concern was the absence from the Avon Valley of White-fronted Geese; it would appear that regular wintering of the species is now lost to Hampshire.

Dedicated raptor-watchers located 15 Hen Harriers at roosts across the county, the majority from the New Forest. Unusual gull sightings followed windier weather mid-month: in Langstone Harbour a second-winter **Ring-billed Gull** returned to join the now regular adult there; and there were two **Iceland Gulls**, a third-winter at Weston Shore and an adult off Hurst Castle. More exciting still was a claim of a **Ross's Gull** flying west off Hurst Castle on 25th. Unfortunately no record has been submitted to date of this potential county first but a well-watched adult Ross's Gull arrived three days later in Devon.

February

A deep complex low-pressure system centred between Iceland and Scotland brought very unsettled weather in the first week. The south-westerly gales heralded very wet and windy weather throughout the month with a brief respite mid-month when the wind backed to the north-west; despite the wind and rain the air temperatures were unseasonably high.

The gales at the end of January and into February produced auk and Kittiwake movements into The Solent but on a relatively small scale compared to neighbouring counties. Nevertheless at least 40 Guillemots and 20 Razorbills were present off Hurst Beach on 2nd/3rd, exceeding previous county records. A Shearwater species was at Stokes Bay on three dates between Jan 29th and Feb 5th, although Sooty Shearwater was suspected it was not confirmed. There were a **Leach's Petrel**, two Great Skuas and two **Little Auks** off Hill Head on 1st, and a second petrel, probably Storm, off Hurst on 2nd. A second-winter **Iceland Gull** was first seen at Hill Head on 7th and thereafter ranged as far west as Weston Shore on numerous dates. Raptor-watchers found three wintering Marsh Harriers and 15 Merlins, which included a first for the Alresford Pond raptor roost and four in the

Exton/West End Down area.

Jack Snipes were reported from both inland and coastal sites during February with 59 over the whole winter period. Over-wintering waders included 45 Green Sandpipers, 30 Greenshanks, twelve Spotted Redshanks, three Whimbrels, two Little Stints and, unusually, a Curlew Sandpiper. There were 69 Water Pipits reported with population estimates of 28 on the Lower Test Marshes and 15 at Titchfield Haven. Wintering Blackcaps are becoming more evident as garden birds with eight or more individuals noted in both Winchester and Stockbridge. The only recorded Great Grey Shrike of the early year was at Black Gutter Bottom, New Forest on 13th. A sufficiently well documented record of Mealy Redpoll was accepted for Lakeside CP, Itchen Valley 16/17th. Hawfinch numbers totalled 57, with reports from 11 sites during the winter period; 20 at Romsey in January exceeded the largest New Forest count of 15 on 24th.

March

A month of variable weather conditions, commencing with mainly overcast conditions as a series of weak fronts crossed the country. An intense low moving in from the east caused gales on 9th and heavy rain. Then chilly easterly winds for a few days originating from an anticyclone over Scandinavia. Falling pressure in the south-west approaches brought more rain in gale force north-easterlies on 14th/15th. A low-pressure system centred in mid-North Atlantic followed with mild southerly winds on 16th/17th but rain, heavy at times, spread in later. By 20th a period of mainly dry, sunny anticyclonic weather prevailed to the month's end, bringing higher air pressures and clear skies. When the temperature reached 18°C on 29th it felt like early summer.

Two Short-eared Owls were in Langstone Harbour throughout March and another at Dibden Bay on 19th. The second-winter **Iceland Gull** remained on Southampton Water until it was last seen on 15th. Brent Geese leaving the eastern harbours in the second week seemingly signalling the end of the winter period. First spring migrants were however a little earlier; a Chiffchaff and White Wagtail *M.a.alba* on 3rd at Farlington, and Red Kite at Keyhaven on 7th. The disturbed air on 9th brought the first trans-Saharan migrants, Sand Martins, into Farlington and Needs Ore.

Low air pressure blocked any significant early passage: nevertheless the first Wheatear was at Sinah Common on 10th; a singing Blackcap on 11th; a second Red Kite at Keyhaven (then Hayling Island) on 12th; and a Swallow struggled into Titchfield Haven on 15th with a Little Ringed Plover nearby at Hook-with-Warsash. Light southerly winds on 16th accelerated arrivals with a Ring Ouzel at Black Gutter Bottom and a Sandwich Tern at Needs Ore. The same day a Tree Pipit at Sway equalled the earliest ever arrival date, but a Hobby at Old Winchester Hill preceded by 13 days the earliest mark just set in 2001. On 17th an Osprey flew north over Lakeside CP and the first Willow Warbler arrived in the New Forest; two days later there was one of just two spring records of Black Redstart. Two adult and two first-winter Little Gulls were at Sinah GP 20th-24th and an adult **Glaucous Gull** was on Hurst Beach on 23rd. An Eider passage, together with wintering birds, produced a March total of 117 with 30 staying on throughout the summer. The Pied Wagtail roost at Basingstoke peaked at 494; on a more minor scale six Grey Wagtail roosted at Alresford Pond. A trickle of early migrants continued with Whitethroat (22nd), House Martins (23rd), Spoonbill (25th), male Garganey (28th/29th), Yellow Wagtail (29th) and Sedge Warbler (30th). Perhaps the arrival of the month was a **White-spotted Bluethroat** *L.s.cyanecula* seen briefly at Hook-with-Warsash on 30th.

April

Unbroken sunshine continued for the first three warm weeks of the month as a result of an anticyclone system moving south through Britain, with light winds initially north-easterly then veering to the south-west. Vigorous Atlantic depressions crossed northern Britain on 26th, bringing increasingly wet and windy conditions thereafter, with 90% of the month's rainfall in the last 5 days.

Early in the month from the east of the county were two well-documented Goshawk records. There were few new arrivals in the first half of the month as fine weather failed to stimulate any substantial passage as a result of the blocking north-easterly winds. At Farlington there was a trickle of White and Yellow Wagtails and a Spoonbill from 1st-4th, and a third summer **Ring-billed Gull** in Hayling Bay. The first **Rough-legged Buzzard** since 1998 was at Needs Ore on 5th. Sea watching was poorly rewarded with very light passage, but an early Pomarine Skua flew east on 7th off Hurst. New arrivals to coastal sites were Reed and Grasshopper Warblers (4th and 7th), Common Tern (6th), Whimbrel (9th) and Little Tern (10th). Titchfield Haven recorded more Red Kites on four dates up to 21st. Four Hoopoes were recorded between 7th and 22nd and a Wryneck was at Basingstoke on 13th.

As winds veered to the south-west so migration quickened: the first Cuckoo, Redstart and Lesser Whitethroat were seen on 16th; the following day there was a sizable passage of 157 Common and 15 Arctic Terns. Unusual species included a first summer **Purple Heron** at Farlington from 14th-17th and a pair of **Black-winged Stilts** spent just one day at Titchfield Haven on 17th. New coastal arrivals included Black Tern, Turtle Dove, Swift and Whinchat on 21st and Roseate Tern on 24th. Inland a Montagu's Harrier was at Martin Down on 24th. There were several sites with double-figure counts for Wheatear and the county day total was 52 on 25th. Departures noted were the last Water Pipit at Farlington (13th), Redwing (18th) and Fieldfare (21st). Even as late as 27th there was still a flock of 47 Corn Buntings gathered at Hoe Cross; their later dispersal contributed to some 55 county breeding territories. Stormy weather on 28th produced a Great Northern Diver, Great Skua and **Sooty Shearwater** off Hurst.

May

*Unsettled weather continued into **May**, but staying mostly dry until 12th with easterly drift conditions established by rising pressure over Scandinavia. On 13th an Atlantic low moved north-east over northern Britain and associated fronts brought heavy rain to the county with fresh mainly south-west winds. By 15th an anticyclone over Europe brought a spell of hot weather until 18th when a vigorous low-pressure system, over the near Atlantic, caused the weather to become very unsettled until 30th. An extended continental ridge brought warm, sunny dry weather to 31st.*

Observations of seven Montagu's Harriers, three males and four females, between 4th-11th came from several localities, mainly in the New Forest. An Osprey flew north over Needs Ore on 12th. The following day a Honey Buzzard flew in off the sea at Hurst followed by records from the New Forest on 11th, and four other sightings from 17th/18th. The first Quail was heard at Martin Down on 7th. On 9th seven Nightingales were at Ashlett Creek, Fawley; that evening the first Nightjar was recorded at Hazely Heath. The following evening there were further Nightjar sightings at Abbotts Wood and Longmoor Inclosures. Whimbrel spring passage peaked on 10th at Langstone Harbour with 42 grounded and 56 over flying east. On 12th a **Greenland Wheatear** *O.o.leucorhoa* was reported from the Lymington/Hurst area. The stormy wet weather on 13th produced the best passage movements of the spring with a first summer Little Gull at Farlington and 142 Common Tern; the latter total was eclipsed at Titchfield Haven where 640 passed east. On 13th expectations must have been running high at Stokes Bay with 51 Little Gulls passing east the previous day, indeed truly memorable sea-watching ensued: 1152 Common Terns, 231 Little Terns, 37 Gannets, 14 Fulmars, eight Black Terns, four Arctic Skuas, four Arctic Terns, four Roseate Terns and a Pomarine Skua to ice the cake. Invariably the last passerine summer visitor and seemingly getting later, the first Spotted Flycatcher was at Farlington on 14th, 16 days beyond the average arrival date.

Unusual sightings were a **Pectoral Sandpiper** at Farlington 16th and a **Black Stork** flying up the Test Valley the following day. The jewel of the sea-watcher's year, a **Long-tailed Skua,** was reported off Hill Head on 17th. A Spoonbill visited Needs Ore from 17th-21st and there were four at Farlington on 21st. Avocets successfully bred for the first time in Hampshire with young first seen on 23rd, as described later in this *Report*. A male Red-backed Shrike was observed for four hours at the private reserve of Eelmoor Marsh on 24th. This date also saw the latest ever record of Merlin for the county, a male at Beaulieu Road. There was an intriguing series of evening sightings of a Storm Petrel off Hurst beach between 26th and 29th; perhaps a non-breeder blown here on the winds from the Atlantic depression but also the sort of feeding excursion exhibited by breeding birds. The most numerous species noted on spring passage was Common Tern with a total of 5600 between Apr 6th and May 31st.

June

*The first days of **June** started well with unbroken sunshine and day temperatures above 22°C but it soon became wet with heavy rain overnight on 5th, producing unsettled weather thereafter, as a cool showery south-westerly air stream covered the region. High pressure on the near-continent improved the situation from mid-month and by 26th there was plenty of sunshine under the influence of a ridge of high pressure stretching from the Azores. At the end of the month low pressure over Scandinavia fed cool north-westerly winds but there were good sunny periods and dry weather for the most part.*

A **White Stork** was in the blue skies over Beaulieu on 1st; a Short-eared Owl lingered at Farlington and the same, or another, was at Keyhaven on 6th. Two late Arctic Skuas were off Hurst on 6th. Red Kites were prominent with 14 sightings from seven localities: one at Titchfield Haven on 1st; an astonishing seven seen from Portsdown Hill on 5th and the last at Stratfield Saye on 29th. Farlington Marshes had a sequence of unusual birds: a **Red-necked Phalarope** on 7th; a Spoonbill on 11th; and finally a **White Stork** flew west on 27th. Titchfield Haven competed with two late Little Stints on 5/6th, then four Roseate Terns 17th/18th, a **Temminck's Stint** on 20th and a female **Woodchat Shrike** on 24th. The Woodchat Shrike surprisingly was just the 4th record for Hampshire and the first since 1981. Elsewhere a Wryneck was located in the New Forest on 23rd.

The spring had seen consolidation of Mandarin and Gadwall as breeding birds and success for Goosander, with 11 juveniles in the Avon Valley, the third successive year in which breeding was either confirmed or suspected. A survey of the Itchen Valley helped establish a new county high for Little Grebe with 129 breeding pairs. Little Egret breeding pairs increased once more to at least 19.

Five pairs of Honey Buzzard were known to have bred successfully each rearing two young. One of the most exciting events of the year was the confirmation by Wayne Percy, Andy Page and Alan Lucas of the first breeding of Goshawk in Hampshire; six young were reared at two nesting sites as described later in this *Report*. Peregrine Falcon expansion continued with at least five young raised at three out of five eyries discovered, all on man-made structures.

There was breeding success for Lesser Black-backed Gulls for the second successive year in central Southampton and docks areas and, additionally, attempted at Eastleigh.

Doubtless with minds focussed on the football World Cup then taking place in South Korea and Japan, Southampton city centre office workers christened two nimble-footed juvenile Lesser Black-backed Gulls *Owen* and *Beckham*.

With virtually no suitable habitat available Rock Pipit is a scarce and unlikely county breeder; nevertheless seven/eight pairs bred in the west Solent area, some in crevices within the walls of Hurst Castle. Of passerines giving cause for concern there were 45, mainly New Forest territories, for the reasonably stable Wood Warbler; but just four confirmed breeding sites for Willow Tit. A county breeding survey revealed some 20 Bearded Tit territories at four locations with 19 juveniles seen at Farlington.

June saw the first returning birds with a Common Sandpiper at Hayling Oysterbeds on 21st and at Titchfield Haven three days later. A juvenile Sand Martin was noted at Farlington Marshes but there was no news of any westerly passage until 292 Swifts were seen early on 27th at Hook-near-Warsash. There were six Crossbills in Acres Down on 29th, the first evidence of an influx into the county. The north-easterly winds on 29th produced two Manx Shearwaters, a month's peak count of 28 Gannets and an Arctic Skua off Hurst Beach.

July

An unsettled and cool start to the month with sunny intervals and frequent outbreaks of rain as low-pressure systems and their associated fronts traversed the country. Early on it was a mixture of sunshine and showers with heavy overnight rain on 8/9th. A ridge of high pressure extending from the Azores from 13th brought three days of unbroken sunshine and very warm conditions; a small active low crossed central Britain on 19th/20th bringing humid but still hot conditions to Hampshire. The remaining days of the month were very hot with temperatures peaking at 29°C but on 31st there were local heavy showers across the county.

At least two Spoonbills were in The Solent for most of July and there were two Roseate Terns reliably to be found at Titchfield Haven. The roost of Little Egret peaked at 72 on Horsea Island, Portsmouth Harbour. Small numbers of Little Ringed Plover were at coastal sites but the maximum of seven was inland at Eversley GP on 7th. Two Montagu's Harriers were reported from the New Forest area on 13th (adult male) and 29th (ring-tail).

Rosy Starlings dispersed into western Europe in June in unprecedented numbers but missed Hampshire, but with 20 mid-July national records two adult **Rosy Starlings** were finally located, providing garden ticks for lucky residents in Petersfield and Eastleigh. The Petersfield resident is one of our *Report* writers but the recently retired editor of this *Report* went one better. Russell Wynn was carrying out his local patch survey on 21st around Pennington Marsh when he discovered a splendid **Stilt Sandpiper,** in almost wholly retained adult summer plumage. It was a new species for Hampshire and the first British record for five years, all the more remarkable with just one other Nearctic vagrant located in the country all month. The Stilt Sandpiper remained at Pennington until Aug 3rd and an account of the bird's finding/description is included in this *Report*.

Signs of returning passage and post-breeding dispersal gathering pace was most evident in Langstone Harbour: Great Crested Grebe numbers increased to 63; the first returning Grey Plover (22nd); 43 Greenshanks (24th); 27 Common Sandpipers at the Hayling Oysterbeds (26th) and on 30th four juvenile Garganey, ten Wigeon and the first Knot. Elsewhere 350 Sand Martins assembled at Needs Ore on 13th and 80 Gannets were at Sandy Point, Hayling on 23rd. A phenomenon, either of more discerning observation, or changes in gull distribution, has led to the identification of mid-summer Yellow-legged Gull *L.c. michahellis* roosts in Kent, Sussex and Hampshire. A key "loafing" area within the county is now identified as Redbridge Wharf, adjacent to the Lower Test Marshes, where some 50 Yellow-legged Gulls were noted on 21st. At the month's end a **Balearic Shearwater** was seen off Hurst Castle.

August

The weather was mainly sunny throughout but at times it was exceptionally humid. With weak low pressure over or near Britain, frequent showers threatened but often missed the county; an exception was 4th with heavy rainsqualls affecting coastal sites driven on easterly winds. Low pressure moved away by 12th allowing a weak ridge to extend from the Azores. It was mainly dry with good sunny periods and very hot thereafter until 20th when, with low-pressure moving over the North Sea, the pattern became unsettled and overcast at times. In the last week of the month an Azores high extended its influence over the region creating some strong west winds on 29th.

Ringing successes at Titchfield Haven provided an insight into the clandestine passage of some of the more skulking warblers through the county, with two **Aquatic Warblers** and 19 Grasshopper Warblers netted during August. Almost as difficult to see was a **Spotted Crake** with brief sightings also at Titchfield Haven on three dates 11th, 21st and 22nd. Waders provide perhaps the most evocative aspects of returning passage. In the eastern harbours there were peaks of: 800 Grey Plovers; over 1000 Dunlins and 620 Black-tailed Godwits, with a further 380 in The Solent refuges. The scarcer *Calidris* waders included a **Temminck's Stint** (Farlington Marshes, 4th) and a total of 34 Curlew Sandpipers. A few juvenile Knots graced Farlington in late August; no more than a few weeks old they had completed a trans-Atlantic crossing from Greenland or the Canadian Arctic. Greenshank records come from both inland and coastal sites totalling 130. There were good numbers of Green (63) and Common (50) Sandpipers but Wood Sandpipers (14) were rather scarce. The gull and tern roost in Langstone Harbour included 2000 Common Terns. There were Roseate Terns at Titchfield Haven all month with a juvenile and three adults seen on separate dates. Black Tern passage was light with the largest group being nine at Sandy Point on 31st.

With the high pressure ridge over Europe there had been many summer sightings of Bee-eaters in Britain, but Hampshire had to wait until 16th/17th for its first **European Bee-eater** at Longstock. A second bird provided an exotic garden tick at Ashley, New Milton on 26th. There were five reports of Wryneck between 19th and 29th; a juvenile Red-backed Shrike at Farlington on 22nd and a **Melodious Warbler** at Needs Ore on 24th.

Scarce raptors during the month included two Montagu's Harriers (Hook-with-Warsash and Old Basing) and a Honey Buzzard over Basingstoke on 25th. At the end of the month Yellow Wagtails were observed at five roosts totalling 300 birds; a considerable improvement on recent years. This presumably indicated breeding success in eastern counties, or the near continent, as Yellow Wagtail *M.f.flavissima* is now almost extinct as a breeding species in most southern counties, including Hampshire. Spotted Flycatchers were at their most numerous in the county with 148 seen in the second half of the month. Sporadic reports of Crossbill consolidated into a sizable influx with a cumulative 200 from several New Forest sites on 31st.

September

*Dry and rather warm overall with high pressure dominating **September** with periods of strong north to north-east winds. A depression from Biscay on 8th moved into southern Britain, leading to overcast conditions and heavy rain overnight; there were squally winds during 9th and heavy rainfall pm. From 10th the weather became dry and bright under the influence of a ridge of high-pressure stretching from an anticyclone over Scandinavia.*

The steady continental high-pressure systems produced good thermal conditions for the passage of larger species: several sightings of **White Stork** reported between 2nd and 11th possibly referred to the same individual and in addition there were nine Honey Buzzards between 2nd and 13th. Wryneck passage continued with six seen at intervals throughout the month. A juvenile **Bluethroat** was ringed at Titchfield Haven on 1st and a second juvenile Red-backed Shrike was at Farlington on the same date, with a third at Sandy Point from 13th-16th. A **Spotted Crake** frequented Woolmer Pond on 7th and one to two Bitterns returned to Titchfield Haven on 15th. A **White-rumped Sandpiper** was at Testwood Lakes on 15th but elusive.

Notable autumn passage in the first half of the month included Whinchat with 402 bird-days and a minimum of 63 bird-days for Curlew Sandpiper. Numbers of Yellow Wagtail on passage continued to be high with 1123 bird-days recorded. The roost at Titchfield Haven on 7th held 440 individuals with other roosts in the county totalling 230 over the same period; counts of unprecedented magnitude for the last 20 years. Surprising too were early autumn records on 21st of a Lapland Bunting, which flew over Barton-on-sea and a first-winter Red-necked Grebe at Milton, Portsmouth which remained until Oct 9th.

The build up of Yellow-legged Gulls *L.c.michahellis* continued with 88 reported during the month, 70 at Redbridge Wharf. At least one first-winter **Caspian Gull** *L.c.cachinnans,* was located at Keyhaven 25/27th and again in early October. The first-winter plumage of this taxon has only been described in recent years but is now regarded as one of the most distinctive of the large white-headed gull complex.

October

High pressure and dry, bright weather dominated until 11th; afterwards it was much more unsettled with Atlantic depressions crossing the country and significant amounts of rain recorded in the county on 12th, 13th, 15th and 21st. There were strong notherly winds on 14th and a severe storm with south-westerly winds 26-27th. A few overnight frosts towards the endof the month indicated the onset of the second winter period.

An early highlight was the discovery of a first-winter **Richard's Pipit** at Taddiford Gap on 5th - an unusually confiding bird that remained at least until 7th. Sea-watching was generally quiet with a few scattered auk records; storms on 15th produced a **Leach's Petrel** sighting at Milford on Sea followed by a **Sooty Shearwater** at Hayling Bay on 20th. However, the storm on 27th was unproductive although sadly an immature Great Skua was found dead on Hurst Beach.

Winter visitor numbers started to increase with 55 Red-breasted Mergansers in Langstone Harbour and eight more Black-necked Grebes added to the summering pair. At Keyhaven/Pennington there were 110 Golden Plovers. A **Grey Phalarope** was at the IBM Lake, Portsmouth 15/16th and an early Black-throated Diver was off Hill Head on 20th. There was a fair Ring Ouzel passage with 25 birds widely distributed over the first three weeks of the month. A **Yellow-browed Warbler** at Shedfield on 24th was the sole representative of northern breeding scarce or rare *Phylloscopus* warblers found in October.

On 26th the first Water Pipit was back in the Pennington area and a new county record was set for a Lesser Black-backed Gull count; appropriately it was the County Recorder who logged 5500 leaving a roost at Ibsley Water, Avon Valley.

November

November was one of the wettest months on record with the weather dominated by an Atlantic low and a series of secondary depressions sweeping along the south coast; a major depression 10th –14th brought strong south-west winds. Rainfall was extremely heavy, particularly 6th-13th and 22-24th, causing the first river valley floods of the year.

Dedicated sea-watchers had to brave some atrocious weather; the Atlantic depressions produced a Leach's Petrel from Hurst Beach on 8th, with a Little Auk off Hurst Castle on 12th and off Hill Head on 23rd. A first-winter Glaucous Gull was off Milford on Sea on 14th. Up to 40 Little Gulls and thirteen Velvet Scoters were recorded with four of the latter lingering off Needs Ore on 10th and six off Hill Head from 17th-24th. In addition there were small numbers of Grebe and Diver movements with Langstone Harbour holding 99 Great-crested, 30 Little, 17 Black-necked, two Slavonian, and one or more Red-necked Grebes during the month. A **Richard's Pipit** was again the month's star bird, albeit briefly at Pennington 9th. A **Siberian Chiffchaff** was present at Lower Test Marshes on 11th. A Ring Ouzel was at Farlington Marshes on 16th and a Snow Bunting there on 18th; three **Twites** were located on Hurst Beach on 22nd and at Keyhaven on 27th.

Late passage included 4750 Wood Pigeon, 30 Redpolls at Keyhaven/Pennington on 4th; and 19 Avocets Langstone Harbour on 27th. The Bearded Tit populations of the coastal reserves were unusually easily viewable with 20 at Farlington, eight at Needs Ore and visible inter-site movements during the month. A coordinated survey of known Great Grey Shrike wintering territories revealed seven in the New Forest. Crossbills were in evidence with a coastal passage noted at Keyhaven 17th and 48 in Alice Holt Forest on 24th.

December

Atlantic depressions provided a mild but wet start to the month with northerly winds veering westerly. Higher air-pressures over Scandinavia then led to drier weather and lower temperatures from 9-12th and again 18-20th as chill winds swung first easterly then south-west. The last ten days of the year were very mild but wet.

Unusual birds reflected mid-winter: a Siberian Chiffchaff near Langstone Harbour on 10th; a Lapland Bunting at Keyhaven on 13th; a flock of 17 Bewick's Swans flying east over Farlington on 16th; and a further sighting of three Twites feeding along Hurst Beach on 20th. Recording at Titchfield Haven produced 26 Cetti's Warblers, 17 Water Rails and up to three Bitterns during December. A group of eight Pale-bellied Brents associated with 4400 Dark-bellied Brents in Langstone Harbour, with another in the Keyhaven area.

The now flooded Avon Valley and associated Blashford Lakes provided feeding habitat for up to 8000 Wigeons and 2000 Black-tailed Godwits, the latter being double the number at all coastal sites combined. The year ended with the adult Ring-billed Gull returning to the Broadmarsh slipway, Langstone Harbour for its fifth winter in the last six years.

LIST OF OBSERVERS AND CONTRIBUTORS

The following are the many observers who have sent observations direct to the Recorder, or participated in BTO Surveys, without which this report would not be possible. We apologise for any errors or omissions.

Key to surveys:
BBS *Breeding Bird Survey (Summer 2002)*
BWWM *Breeding Waders of Wet Meadows/HOS River Valley Survey (Spring/Summer 2002)*
LGS *Lowland Grassland Survey (Summer 2002)*
PE *Peregrine Survey 2002*
WFBS *Winter Farmland Bird Survey (Winter 2002/03)*

Adams, M C
Allen, C
Allnutt, D
Andrews, J
Archer, B M
Arnold, J
Austin, M (BBS)

Ball, D
Barbagallo, M (BBS, WFBS)
Bates, CM (WFBS)
Beckett, P
Bell, D A
Bell, N M G
Bennett, G (BBS)
Bennett, M
Benson, C
Betton, K F
Bevan, P (BBS)
Bill, D I
Billett, D F
Billett, R A
Birdguides
Bishop, D
Blakeley, A F
Blunden, A C (BWWM)
Bonser, R
Boras, W
Boswell, L
Boswell, P
Boswell, S
Bowes, I R (WFBS)
Brickwood, M

Briggs, A
Briggs, K B (BBS)
Broadhurst, A (WFBS)
Broadley, D
Brown, I H
Brown, R I
Brunton, S
Bryant, M
Budd, P A
Bull, A
Burton, J F
Bushell, A
Butler, T
Butterworth, A M B (BBS)

Calderwood, G
Calderwood, I
Campbell, M R
Carpenter, R J
Carpenter, T F
Carr, P
Casson, J
Champion, R
Chapleo, C
Chapman, J
Chapman, R A (PE)
Chawner, J (BBS, BWWM)
Christie, D A
Clark, A
Clark, J M
Claxton, A J
Clay, G H
Cloyne, J M

Cockburn, C
Codlin, T D
Colenutt, S R (BWWM)
Coles, L
Collins, A R
Collins, C B
Collins, M
Collman, J R
Colvile, R
Compton, D K
Cook, R
Cooke, R E
Cooper, M
Cooper, M
Cooper, P F
Cox, A J (BBS, WFBS)
Cox, I N (BBS)
Cozens, B
Crisp, K
Crook, J
Cross, A
Crowley, P J
Cuthbert, C R

Darvill, B (BWWM)
Darvill, G (WFBS)
Davis, A
Dawson, A
Dawson, C
Day, J
de Potier, A
de Retuerto, M A (BWWM)
Dedman, J W (BBS)

Dicker, G
Dicks, D E J (BWWM)
Doherty, M E
Doran, T M J
Downey, B
Doyle, K (BWWM)
Duffin, B S
Durnell, P R
Dyason, S (BWWM)

Edgeller, M L
Edmunds, R D
Edwards, M S D (BWWM)
Ellicock, J H
Evans, D G (BBS)
Evans, G C (BBS,BWWM,LGS,WFBS)
Evans, S (BBS, BWWM, LGS, WFBS)
Eyre, J A (BBS, WFBS)

Faithfull, J
Farmer, S F G
Farwell, G
Fathers, J R (BWWM, WFBS)
Feare, C J (BBS)
Fellows, B J
Firth, K J
Ford, R E
Friend, B J
Friend, P

Gammage, P A
Gent, C R
Giddens, G
Gilbert, S
Gilchrist, W L R E (BBS)
Gillingham, M
Goater, B
Goddard, D J
Gooderham, G E
Goodspeed, J R
Gove, W (BWWM)
Gowen, J
Graham, A C
Graham, K D
Greaves, A N
Green, A E (BBS,BWWM,LGS,WFBS)
Green, D G

Gumn, D G (WFBS)
Gutteridge, A C

Hale, A P S
Hallier, R
Hampton, M
Hartill, S
Harvey, S C
Hay, M J W
Hayden, A (BWWM)
Hayward, R (BWWM)
Hedley, B
Heritage, J
Hilton, J I
Hobby, P
Hobern, D
Hobson, J A
Hockin, P
Hold, A J (BWWM, WFBS)
Holliday, P
Hollins, J R (BBS, WFBS)
Holt, D
Homer, A J (WFBS)
Horacek-Davis, G
Hoslist
Houghton, D
Howard, M J
Howell, R
Hughes, R
Hughes, R M
Hull, J (BWWM, LGS)
Hull, N (BWWM, LGS)
Hunt, N
Hunt, P R (WFBS)
Hutchins, P E
Huxley, G H

Ingram, S

Jacobs, R
James, D B L
James, R
James, R M R
Jennings, F
Jennings, T J
Jones, C
Jones, M

Keane, P S (BBS, BWWM)
Keen, S G
Kimber, R W
King, R A
King, S S (BWWM, PE)

Lachlan, C (BBS)
Langford, M (BWWM, WBBS)
Lankester, S R (BBS)
Lawes, M
Lawman, T A
Lawn, M R
Le Brocq, P F
Leaver, C
Legge, W G D
Levell, J E (BWWM, WFBS)
Levett, R K
Lewis, J
Linfoot, R
Lintott, E A
Lister, D
Litjens, M
Little, J A
Littleboy, N
Locke, A (BBS, WFBS)
Lord, P
Lord, R
Love, M
Lovegrove, K
Lowings, V
Lushington, R
Lymbery, P J (BBS)

Macleod, G J M (BWWM)
Macleod, S (BWWM)
MacPherson, I
Mallett, J B (WFBS)
Mansfield, S J (BWWM)
Marchant, R H (WFBS)
Marriott, B J (BWWM)
Marshall, L
Marston, P C
Martin, A
Martin, K P
Maton, O
Maundrell, A J (BBS, WFBS)
McCarthy, M G

Mead, J
Middlecote, B
Milner, K (WFBS)
Mitchell, D (BBS
Mitchell, M (BBS)
Montegriffo, N
Moody, A
Moody, M P (WFBS)
Moon, J
Moon, J
Morrison, P (BBS, BWWM)
Morrison, S M (BBS, BWWM)
Mortimore, J
Mortimore, K
Moseley, J C (BBS)
Mould-Ryan, R B
Munts, D

Napper, E
Nash, P
Needs Ore Log
New Forest Ornithologists' Club
Newman, M A H (BBS)
Newsham, E
Norris, A Y (BBS,BWWM,LGS,WFBS)

Offer, D C (BWWM)
Oram, M A
Oram, P
Orchard-Webb, M
Orchard-Webb, M
Orr, N W
Osborne, G
Osmond, R

Page, A G (BWWM)
Pain, J W C (PE)
Palmer, M J
Parfitt, A
Parkes, A S
Parminter, T
Parsons, A J
Peace, N D (BBS)
Pearce, A
Pearce, K
Pearson, D J
Percy, W

Peters, S P
Philpott, D J
Pibworth, I
Pinchen, B J
Pitt, M J (BBS)
Poile, K
Pointer, R G (BBS, WFBS)
Polley, A J
Porter, J
Portugal, S
Powell, D
Preston, R
Priest, S N (BBS, WFBS)
Pringle, C
Purkiss, A E
Pyke, L

Quested, R (LGS, WFBS)

Raby, P
Radden, D
Rafter, M
Ralphs, I L
Randall, G
Ransom, D
Raper, M
Rare Bird Alert
Raynor, E M
Raynor, P J
Reeves, D
Rhodes, A S
Rich, G
Richards, C
Rickwood, B
Rittman, M
Roberts, B J (BBS, BWWM, WFBS)
Roberts, E (BWWM)
Roberts, E T (BBS)
Robertson, D
Rogers, G
Rogers, L
Rolfe, M D
Ross, J G
Rowe, J
Rowland, G J S
Rowland, R J
RSPB

Sayer, K
Schmedlin, R
Scott, J G (BWWM)
Scott, M A
Scott, W J
Shaft, M (BBS, LGS, WFBS)
Sharkey, B (BBS, BWWM, WFBS)
Shaw, A
Sheldrake, P (BBS, WFBS)
Shergold, M J
Shillitoe, J R D (BBS, LGS, WFBS)
Ship, R
Short, D
Short, M
Short, V (BWWM)
Shrouder, J
Simcox, W F (WFBS)
Simms, J R
Simpson, A (PE)
Simpson, I
Small, R G
Smallbone, A C (BBS)
Smart, A
Smart, A D G
Smith, B E
Smith, C J (BBS)
Smith, L M (BWWM)
Smith, P
Smith, P J S
Smith, P M
Southam, M
Southworth, I (BWWM)
Sporne, S H
Stanley, T G (BBS)
Stephenson, G C
Stevens, L A
Stone, B
Stouse, K
Strangeman, P J (BBS)
Stride, L (BWWM)
Sutton, B
Switzer, J

Talbot, K
Taverner, J H
Taylor, A
Taylor, D H

21

Terry, M H
Thelwell, D A (BBS, BWWM, WFBS)
Thirlwell, I
Thompson, P G L (BBS,LGS,WFBS)
Thornton, G A (BBS)
Thurston, M H
Timlick, T
Tinning, P
Titchfield Haven web site
Toft, R
Treacher, D
Truckle, W H
Tubbs, J M
Tucker, J
Twine, P
Twyford, I

Unsworth, D J (BWWM)

Vokes, K

Waddington, J I
Walker, T H (BWWM, LGS, WFBS)
Waddell, T R

Wall, M J (BBS, BWWM)
Walmsley, W
Ward, M
Wardley, M
Waters, W E
Watson, R F (BBS)
Watts, I R
Wearing, M F
Webb, R
Welch, P
Wells, J N (BBS, WFBS)
West, R
Westerhoff, D V (BWWM)
Westerhoff, G B
Westmacott, J
Westmacott, R
Whale, B J
Whittles, F M (WFBS)
Williams, A (WFBS)
Williamson, I M (WFBS)
Williamson, M J
Willits, N
Wills, K B (WFBS)
Wilson, D C

Wines, J
Winspear, R J (BBS, LGS)
Winsper, J L (BBS)
Winter, P A
Winter, P D (BBS)
Wiseman, E J (BBS, BWWM, WFBS)
Wiseman, W J
Wood, J (BBS, BWWM, LGS, WFBS)
Wood, JKR (BBS,BWWM,LGS,WFBS)
Wood, S (BBS, WFBS)
Woodburn, W
Wooldridge, G
Woolfries, S
Woolley, S
Woolley, S K (BBS, WFBS)
Wright, A
Wright, S J
Wynde, A R (WFBS)
Wynn, R B

Yates, S R (BBS)
Yelland, D (BBS, WFBS)
Young, K
Young, L (BWWM)

SYSTEMATIC LIST OF SPECIES

Species sequence and taxonomy follows the third edition of the British Ornithologists' Union publication *The British List*, with the exception of Yellow-legged Gull *Larus cachinnans* (which see). Note that the BOU's newly introduced changes to species order will not be implemented before 2004 in HOS publications. These changes will involve the taxa Anseriformes and Galliformes being placed at the start of the British List. Also note that Hooded Crow (*C. c. cornix*) is treated as a separate species to Carrion Crow (*C. c. corone*).

Each species account begins with a brief statement of its status in the county. These use certain terms that have an approximate numerical range attached to them, as shown below:

	Breeding pairs	Winter/Passage
Very rare	Fewer than 5 records	Fewer than 10 records
Rare	Less than annual	Less than annual
Very scarce	1-10 per year	1-20 per year
Scarce	11-100	21-200
Moderately common	101-1000	201-2000
Common	1001-5000	2001-10,000
Numerous	5001-30,000	10,001-60,000
Abundant	30,000+	60,000+

For rare species, three numbers are given in brackets after the status statement. These refer to the numbers of individuals recorded (i) prior to 1951, (ii) between 1951 and 2001 and (iii) in 2002. Observers are reminded of the importance of producing notes of supporting evidence for all sightings of scarce species as detailed in Guidelines for Submission of Records in this *Report*. A number of claimed sightings appearing on Internet and Pager Services of scarce species have either not been submitted or adequately documented.

The species accounts for many wildfowl, waders and other waterfowl include tabulated monthly maxima for various localities. These are largely based on the monthly Wetland Bird Survey (WeBS) counts, which have kindly been provided by Keith Wills (inland sites), Dave Unsworth (coastal sites) and Anne de Potier (Chichester Harbour). In the tables, any site name that is indented is a sub-site of the site above. The most frequently used example of this is the complete counts for Chichester Harbour and the sub-totals for East Hayling and Warblington, which form the Hampshire sector. Comments and county totals given in the species accounts apply only to the Hampshire sector unless otherwise stated. Sites in tables and lists are usually arranged coastally from east to west and then inland from west to east, unless otherwise stated. Most tables give the approximate monthly county totals (**APPROX COUNTY TOTAL**) for all records including the normally smaller numbers from unlisted sites. Within the tables and accompanying text, the following symbols have been used:

figures in bold, e.g. 1279 = an internationally important concentration, i.e. greater than 1% of the north-western European winter or passage population of that species.

figures in italics, e.g. 743 = a nationally important concentration, i.e. greater than 1% of the British winter or passage population of that species.

figures followed by asterisks, e.g. 473* = a record count of that species at the locality concerned.

It should be noted that no data were received from the Breeding Bird Survey (BBS) in

2002 in time for this systematic list report. There are numerous references to the terms 'bird-days' and 'bird-months' in the systematic list. Bird-days is normally used to give the sum of the numbers of birds recorded at a well-watched site over a given period, e.g. totals of 3, 2, 1, 2, 4, 0, 2 recorded over a week would indicate 14 bird-days, although the number of different individuals involved could actually be anywhere between 4 and 14. Bird-months is normally used to indicate the sum of numbers of birds recorded in a given month over a period of several months or years, e.g. totals of 6, 3, 2 recorded in June, July and August would indicate 11 bird-months.

The following abbreviations have been used in the report:

BBS	=	Breeding Birds Survey (BTO)	m.o.	=	many observers
BoH	=	Birds of Hampshire[1]	NF	=	New Forest
CB	=	Cress Bed	NNR	=	National Nature Reserve
CP	=	Country Park	RT	=	Rubbish Tip
FMD	=	Foot and Mouth Disease	SF	=	Sewage Farm/Works
GC	=	Golf Course	SP	=	Sand Pit
GP	=	Gravel Pit(s)	WBS		Waterways Bird Survey

[1] *Birds of Hampshire, Edited by JM Clark & JA Eyre [published in 1993 by the Hampshire Ornithological Society]*

N, E, S and W = the points of the compass; these are combined with numbers to show the direction in which birds are moving, e.g. 17 W.

Red-throated Diver
Gavia stellata

A scarce winter visitor and passage migrant.

It was another good showing for this species with a maximum of 98 noted. However, as in 2001, the exact numbers were difficult to calculate, mostly due to the presence of long-staying birds in the Hurst area at both ends of the year.

The largest count in the first winter period was of 27 off Hurst on Jan 13th (RBW, MPM). This is a new county record and was on the same date as the peak count there in 2001. Inland birds were recorded at Testwood Lakes on Feb 16th and at Broadlands Lake on Mar 4th. Spring passage included a total of 18 moving east through The Solent between Mar 2nd and May 12th.

The first return was off Hurst on Oct 13th and numbers in the second winter period built up to a maximum of 17 in November and reduced to 11 in December. Inland records were of one at Testwood Lakes on Dec 22nd that left to the south and an oiled bird at Fleet Pond (Dec 26th-28th, when it was picked up dead).

All records are summarised below, followed by the approximate monthly totals:

Sandy Point/Hayling Bay: 2 E Apr 17th; 2E May 12th; 1, Nov 3rd.
Langstone Harbour: 1, Jan 28th; 1, Nov 26th and 30th.
Southsea: 1 W, Mar 14th.
Stokes Bay: 1W, Feb 3rd.
Hill Head/Brownwich: 1, Jan 12th/13th; 1, Feb 2nd; 1 E, Dec 6th.
Hook-with-Warsash: 1, Jan 2nd; 1, Nov 14th and 17th.
Weston Shore: 1, Jan 6th; 1,Feb 10th; 1, Nov 17th.
Eling: 1, Nov 28th.
Dibden Bay: 1, Feb 17th.
Lepe/Needs Ore: 3 W, Jan 12th; 1, Jan 28th (dead and oiled).
Hurst Beach/Milford on Sea: up to 27 in Jan; up to 5 in Feb; 14 E Mar 2nd-May 12th; 1, Oct 13th; up

to 9 in Nov; up to 6 in Dec.
Testwood/Broadlands Lakes: 1, Feb 16th; 1, Mar 4th; 1, Dec 22nd (left S).
Fleet Pond: 1, Dec 26th (oiled) - found dead on 28th.

J	F	M	A	M	J	J	A	S	O	N	D
38	8	4	8	10	0	0	0	0	2	17	11

Black-throated Diver   *Gavia arctica*

A very scarce winter visitor and passage migrant.

About 15 were reported during the year, although as with the previous species the presence of long-staying birds in the Hurst area makes it difficult to assess the true numbers involved. Records in the first winter period comprised at least one seen off Hurst on several dates between Jan 12th and Feb 18th, one flying east at Needs Ore on Jan 12th, one off Black Point, Hayling on Jan 29th, one flying west off Stokes Bay on Feb 1st (later seen flying west off Hurst) and one off Hill Head on Feb 26th. In spring one flew east off Hurst on May 9th and one was off Hill Head on May 12th.

The first return was one off Hill Head on Oct 20th. In the second winter period at least one was again seen off Hurst on several dates between Nov 12th and Dec 16th, two were off Hill Head on Nov 17th (seen flying up Southampton Water with a Great Northern Diver), two were in Langstone Harbour on Dec 12th before departing east, one was at Needs Ore on Dec 24th and one was off Black Point, Hayling on Dec 30th.

Great Northern Diver   *Gavia immer*

A scarce winter visitor and passage migrant.

It was a relatively poor year for this species compared to recent standards, with about 24 individuals recorded. Numbers were similar at both ends of the year, with maxima of eight in February and seven in December. A small passage in May included one flying east at Hill Head on 28th (MHT), which becomes the latest spring record for the county. The first autumn return was on Nov 3rd at Hurst Castle. The records are summarised below, followed by the approximate monthly totals:

Black Point/Hayling Bay: 1-2, Feb 5th-19th; 1 E, Mar 30th; 1 E May 12th; 1, Dec 30th.
Langstone Harbour: 1, Feb 8th-21st; 1, Nov 16th-Dec 6th.
Portsmouth Harbour: 1, Dec 7th-31st.
Stokes Bay: 2, Jan 29th.
Hill Head/Brownwich: at least one in Jan-Mar; 1, May 1st; 1 E, May 28th; 1, Nov 17th and 29th.
Hook-with-Warsash/Hamble Estuary: 1, Jan 13th-Feb 28th.
Calshot: 1, Mar 1st-3rd; 1, Dec 31st.
Lepe/Needs Ore/Park Shore: 1, Jan 11th; 1, Nov 23rd-Dec 8th.
Lymington-Hurst/Milford on Sea: at least 3 in Jan-Apr; 1 E, May 8th; at least 2 in Nov-Dec.

J	F	M	A	M	J	J	A	S	O	N	D
7	8	6	3	3	0	0	0	0	0	6	7

Diver sp.   *Gavia sp.*

Several reports of unidentified divers were received, mostly referring to birds seen flying distantly offshore. The monthly totals are tabulated below:

J	F	M	A	M	J	J	A	S	O	N	D
3	4	0	1	2	0	0	0	0	4	2	3

The annual totals 1993-2002 of bird-months for diver species are as follows:

Annual bird-months	1993	1994	1995	1996	1997	1998	1999	2000	2001	2002
Red-throated Diver	31	38	55	108	93	101	67	79	116	98
Black-throated Diver	5	16	11	17	12	14	16	14	9	15
Great Northern Diver	11	28	23	22	19	73	53	52	52	41

Little Grebe   *Tachybaptus ruficollis*

A moderately common resident, passage migrant and winter visitor.

Numbers at the main sites at both ends of the year were generally about average. However, the year was notable for the large number of breeding pairs reported, with a total of 129 pairs compared to just 73 pairs in 2001. This increase was largely due to a detailed survey of the R. Itchen above Winchester, which produced 48 territories. Monthly maxima at the main wintering sites are tabulated below:

	J	F	M	A	M	J	J	A	S	O	N	D
Chichester Harbour, E. Hayling	-	6	8	-	-	-	-	-	5	13	24	10
Langstone Harbour	38	50	60	4	6	6	6	11	29	50	53	58
Portsmouth Harbour	50	26	43	-	-	-	-	-	13	30	35	18
Needs Ore	3	9	11	4	6	-	3	7	11	3	3	5
Lymington/Hurst	14	25	13	2	-	1	-	-	11	26	21	31
Avon valley												
Sopley-Avon Causeway	16	6	32	-	-	-	-	-	12	25	30	35
Blashford Lakes	41	26	58	21	-	-	30	58	47	38	27	26
Ibsley-Bickton	37	-	-	-	-	-	-	-	24	30	10	15
above Fordingbridge	38	12	8	-	-	-	-	-	32	29	4	12
Stockbridge-Fullerton (R.Test)	31	-	36	-	-	-	-	-	-	-	47	45
Winchester SF	-	-	4	10	9	8	22	26	20	17	1	-
Woolmer Pond	-	1	22	30	20	26	26	32	14	7	2	-

Maxima at other sites with double-figure counts were as follows: 10, Curbridge, Jan 5th; 10, Arlebury Lakes, Dec 10th; 12, Northington, Jan 13th; 13, Winnall Moors, Dec 8th; 11, Basingstoke Canal, Dec 28th; 14, Fleet Pond, Nov 18th; 22, Eversley GP, Aug 24th; 14, Ashlett Creek, Oct 8th; 13, Calshot, Jan 13th; 10, Dibden Bay, Feb 10th; 18, Broadlands Lake, Jan 13th; 16, Romsey, Mar 12th; 17, Timsbury GP, July 24th.

A good total of 129 breeding pairs was recorded as follows: R. Itchen (above Winchester), 48; Blashford Lakes, 14; Woolmer Pond, ten; IBM Lake, Cosham, Timsbury GP, R. Test (Longstock), six each; R. Itchen (below Winchester), five; Eversley GP, R. Test (Romsey), four each; Broadlands Estate, Warsash, three each; Abbotts Ann, Milton Reclamation, Basingstoke Canal, two each; Foley Manor (Liphook), Keyhaven Marshes, Rudley Mill (Wickham), Coldrey Park; Selborne, Stratfield Saye Park, West Green, Bramshill Plantation, Sway, Brown Loaf NF, Southampton Common, Mottisfont, Testbourne, Overton Lagoons, one each.

Great Crested Grebe   *Podiceps cristatus*

A moderately common resident, passage migrant and winter visitor.

Wintering numbers at the main site, Langstone Harbour, remained at a high level at the start of the year and similar numbers were recorded there after the breeding season. Wintering numbers elsewhere were normal. In the breeding season a relatively poor total of 61 breeding pairs was recorded, compared with 78 pairs in 2001. Monthly maxima at the main localities are tabulated below:

	J	F	M	A	M	J	J	A	S	O	N	D
Langstone Harbour	114	95	78	47	42	44	64	100	112	110	99	80
Portsmouth Harbour	30	5	6	1	1	2	1	1	4	7	26	13
Hill Head/Brownwich	41	6	6	1	2	0	0	0	1	1	15	11
Southampton Water	26	16	19	6	8	5	10	13	19	2	16	27
Blashford Lakes	72	37	49	30+	12	-	51+	30+	61	48	44	52
Fleet Pond	11	23	30	22	21	10	16	10	20	22	22	9
Eversley GP	10	9	10	6	10	8	8	8	8	19	25	23
Yateley GP	9	6	7	6	6	6	-	-	6	19	25	23

Maxima at other sites with double-figure counts were as follows: 11, R. Avon (above Fordingbridge); 20, Lepe, Jan 11th; 11, Needs Ore, Nov 17th; 13, Hayling Bay, Jan 29th; 17, Lymington/Hurst, Nov 12th; 10, Sowley Pond, Dec 11th; 12, Wellington CP, Oct 6th; 16, Broadlands Lake, June 10th.

A total of 61 breeding pairs was recorded as follows: Blashford Lakes, 19; R. Avon, Somerley Park, 14; Yateley GP, ten; Fleet Pond, four; R.Avon, Woodgreen, Wellington CP, three each; Allington GP, Sowley Pond, two each; Camp Farm GP, Broadlands Lake, Mottisfont, Lower Test Marshes, one each.

Red-necked Grebe *Podiceps grisegena*
A very scarce but regular winter visitor and passage migrant.

Red-necked Grebe (Dan Powell)

A relatively poor year, with a minimum of nine reported. In the early year single birds were at Needs Ore on Jan 13th, Feb 9th and Mar 16th (DJU, MJWH, MR) and one was at Hill Head on Feb 15th and 16th (MR, THWS).

In the autumn, an early first-winter was at Milton Reclamation (Portsmouth) from Sep 21st - Oct 9th (IT *et al.*). Two were seen nearby off Farlington Marshes on Oct 9th(BD). What was probably one of the same birds was also seen nearby at Sinah GP on Oct 23rd (GHC) and in Langstone Harbour on Oct 28th and from Nov 7th-30th (JCr *et al.*). One was present off Hurst Castle from Nov 16th-29th (RBW, MPM, BG), with another off Hurst

Beach on Dec 30th (SGK). Finally, one located at Weston Shore on Dec 28th (ARC) remained into 2003.

Slavonian Grebe   *Podiceps auritus*
A scarce winter visitor and passage migrant.

Numbers in the early year built up to a maximum of 37 in February. Peak counts during that month included eight in Langstone Harbour and at Black Point and ten in the Lymington-Hurst area. The last spring bird was at Pennington Marsh on Apr 23rd.

The first return was also at Pennington Marsh on Oct 22nd and numbers in the county then built up to about 19 in December. Monthly maxima from the main sites are shown below, followed by individual records from other sites and the approximate monthly totals:

	J	F	M	A	M	J	J	A	S	O	N	D
Langstone Harbour	10	8	1	0	0	0	0	0	0	0	2	5
Needs Ore/Lepe	3	6	5	0	0	0	0	0	0	0	3	1
Lymington-Hurst	6	10	7	3	0	0	0	0	0	1	9	9

Black Point: Up to 8, Jan 29th-Feb 13th; 1, Nov 14th.
Hayling Bay: 1, Jan 13th and 29th; 3, Feb 13th; 1 W, Feb 28th; 1, Mar 2nd; 1-2, Dec 25th-30th.
Hill Head/Brownwich: 1-2, Jan 30th-Mar 17th.
Hook-with-Warsash: 1, Feb 2nd-9th; 1, Mar 20th.
Weston Shore/Dibden Bay: 1, Feb 8th and 15th; 2, Nov 30th; 1-2, Dec 14th and 15th.

J	F	M	A	M	J	J	A	S	O	N	D
22	37	17	3	0	0	0	0	0	1	17	19

Black-necked Grebe   *Podiceps nigricollis*
A scarce winter visitor and passage migrant; rare in summer but has bred.

Overall, numbers were almost identical to 2001, although fewer birds were seen during spring. In the early year, numbers at the main site, Langstone Harbour, peaked at 15 in February, with just eight seen elsewhere at the coast. The only spring migrants were two off Hill Head on Apr 17th. Two again summered in Langstone Harbour and for the third year running a single bird was present at an inland site during May and June.

Returning migrants built up in Langstone Harbour from late August onwards, peaking at 18 in November. Monthly maxima at the main sites are tabulated below, followed by other individual records and approximate monthly totals:

	J	F	M	A	M	J	J	A	S	O	N	D
Langstone Harbour	12	15	15	2	2	2	2	4	8	11	18	15
Lepe/Needs Ore/Park Shore	4	4	2	0	0	0	0	0	0	0	4	5

Black Point, Hayling: *2, Mar 17th.*
Hill Head: *2, Apr 17th; 1, Dec 11th.*
Eling: *1, Dec 22nd.*
Lymington-Hurst: *2, Jan 9th; 1, Dec 30th and 31st.*

J	F	M	A	M	J	J	A	S	O	N	D
18	19	19	4	3	3	2	4	8	11	22	23

The annual totals 1993-2002 of bird-months for the scarcer grebes are as follows:

Annual bird-months	1993	1994	1995	1996	1997	1998	1999	2000	2001	2002
Red-necked	12	6	23	37	24	15	12	8	11	9
Slavonian	75	85	100	168	156	113	87	89	120	116
Black-necked	139	136	187	195	91	106	112	106	137	136

Fulmar   *Fulmarus glacialis*

A scarce passage migrant, most frequent in spring and early autumn.

It was an average year by recent standards. Small numbers in the first winter period included one found dead at Hurst Castle on Feb 1st. Spring passage was apparently heaviest in the east of the county, with peaks of 16 west in Hayling Bay on Apr 30th and 27 mostly moving east off Sandy Point on May 13th.

Very few were seen during the summer and autumn and the only late year record was of one found dead at Pennington Marsh on Dec 27th. The approximate monthly totals are shown below:

J	F	M	A	M	J	J	A	S	O	N	D
3	8	2	54	48	3	0	7	1	0	0	1

Sooty Shearwater   *Puffinus griseus*

A rare vagrant (0,6,2).

One was seen at long range off Hurst at 1735 hrs on the unusual date of Apr 28th (MPM, TP, MC) and another single was seen close inshore in Hayling Bay at 1330 hrs on the more typical date of Oct 20th (TAL). These are the seventh and eighth records for Hampshire and the former is the first for April.

Manx Shearwater   *Puffinus puffinus*

A scarce, but in some years increasing to moderately common, passage migrant.

Another good year, with about 300 reported. As usual nearly all reports came from Hurst, with the first being two flying west on Jan 23rd. The next were not seen until Apr 30th, when five flew east and after that small numbers were noted on several evenings in May and June. As in 2001 there was a very large movement in settled conditions and light winds on one evening in June. The movement was of 255 seen heading south or south-west through Christchurch Bay between 2000 and 2115 hrs on June 28th (MPM, RGS). The condensed nature of this passage can be shown by the fact that just two were noted moving east the following evening.

Elsewhere, the only record was of one flying west off Stokes Bay on Sep 7th. All records from Hurst are summarised below, followed by the approximate monthly totals:

Hurst/Milford on Sea: 2 W, Jan 23rd; 5 E, Apr 30th; 24 E in May; 264 in June including 255 S/SW on 28th; 4, July 2nd; 3 S, July 20th; 3, Aug 9th; 1 E, Oct 24th; 1 E, Oct 27th.

J	F	M	A	M	J	J	A	S	O	N	D
2	0	0	5	24	264	7	3	1	2	0	0

The annual totals 1993-2002 of bird-months are as follows:

Annual bird-months	1993	1994	1995	1996	1997	1998	1999	2000	2001	2002
Manx Shearwater	1	24	7	50	34	13	68	125	646	308

Balearic Shearwater
Puffinus yelkouan

A very scarce but increasing passage migrant, mostly late summer/autumn (0,52,1).

After the record numbers of 2001, it was disappointing that the only record was of one off Hurst Castle at 1148 hrs on July 31st (MPM, SB). This brings the Hampshire total to 53.

Shearwater sp.
Puffinus sp.

There were several records of unidentified shearwaters corresponding to about 16 birds. Notable records included one off Hurst on Jan 23rd that was probably Sooty (*cf* Manx Shearwater), one off Stokes Bay on Jan 29th, Feb 1st and 5th (which may also have been Sooty), two off Hordle on July 9th and seven off Hurst on May 6th.

Storm Petrel
Hydrobates pelagicus

A very scarce visitor, usually after autumn gales (1,147,1).

One was seen off Hurst Beach on the evenings of May 26th, 28th and 29th (MPM, AL). Assuming only one bird was involved, this brings the Hampshire total to 148 (since 1951).

Leach's Petrel
Oceanodroma leucorba

A very scarce autumn and winter visitor, usually appearing after gales (11,136,3).

In the early year one was seen off Hill Head in stormy weather at 0800 hrs and again at 1335 hrs on Feb 2nd (BSD, MJH, SM). In the late year single birds associated with autumn storms were seen being blown north over Hurst Beach on Oct 15th (MPM, AL) and moving west off there on Nov 8th (MPM, MC). These records bring the Hampshire total to 139 since 1951.

Petrel sp.
Oceanodroma/Hydrobates sp.

One seen feeding off Hurst Castle (MR, DJU, RBW) from 1115-1315 hrs on Feb 2nd departed to the west and was later seen off Milford on Sea, but unfortunately remained unidentified.

Gannet
Sula bassana

A moderately common passage migrant and non-breeding summer visitor; scarce but increasing in winter.

Smaller numbers were seen compared to 2001, with no large counts reported after late July. The year started with small numbers seen off Hurst and Hayling Bay in January, but only two were recorded in February and none in March. A small spring passage in April and May peaked on May 13th, with 21 off Sandy Point, 20 off Hurst and 11 inside The Solent at Stokes Bay. The usual summer gathering off Hurst peaked at 340 on July 27th; other high counts at this time included 80 off Sandy Point on July 23rd, 32 off Lepe on July 26th and 34 off Warsash on July 31st.

A record of 60 on the sea off Pennington Marsh on July 29th that flew west out of The Solent may have related to roosting birds.

Numbers dropped sharply in early August and there were no significant counts in the late year. Monthly maxima at the main localities are tabulated below followed by the 1993-2002 annual county totals:

	J	F	M	A	M	J	J	A	S	O	N	D
Sandy Point/Hayling Bay	1	0	0	4	21	2	80	14	0	0	0	0
Hurst/Milford on Sea	7	1	0	36	30	89	340	34	6	4	5	0

Annual total	1993	1994	1995	1996	1997	1998	1999	2000	2001	2002
Gannet	414	746	540	583	534	501	835	997	3336	875

Cormorant   *Phalacrocorax carbo*

A moderately common non-breeding resident, passage migrant and winter visitor.

About 560 records were received, slightly more than in 2001. The largest count was 164 in the Avon valley at the Sabines Farm roost on Dec 22nd while in the beginning of the year there were 111 at Langdown/Hythe on Jan 19th. These figures are well down on the maximum counts of 2001 when 200+ were recorded at both ends of the year.

The largest recorded movement was 77 north at Broadlands on Nov 17th. Monthly maxima at the main sites are tabulated below:

	J	F	M	A	M	J	J	A	S	O	N	D
Langstone Harbour	65[1]	22	29	26	24	45	60	70	97	106	32	32[1]
Portsmouth Harbour	23	31	-	-	-	-	-	-	30	67	59	35
Titchfield Haven[1]	22	28	16	7	-	-	13	12	-	30	14	30
Eling/Lower Test Marshes	53	27	34	7	7	4	14	23	17	14	40	30
Langdown/Hythe[1]	111	110	72	15	-	5	34	51	91	96	124	133
Needs Ore	4	-	-	3	4	-	2	5	4	22	14	7
Lymington-Hurst	5	4	7	4	4	5	6	5	13	22	13	16
Blashford Lakes	40	25	27	2	-	-	-	-	17	48	21	54
Avon valley: Sabines Farm[1]	-	110	-	-	-	-	-	-	-	47	40	164
Broadlands Estate (R.Test)[1]	22	16	36	11	1	-	-	-	15	23	77	47
Alresford Pond	38	36	20	10	4	7	4	4	6	9	28	35
Fleet Pond[1]	70	73	45	14	4	0	4	17	25	49	58	63
Yateley GP	42[1]	26	18	-	1	-	-	7[1]	2	6	26	42[1]

([1] =*night roost*)

In addition to the tabulated counts a night roost was discovered at Hucklesbrook Lakes (Avon valley), which held 31 on July 14th and 24 on Dec 22nd (*cf* Sabines Farm).

Shag   *Phalacrocorax aristotelis*

A scarce but increasing winter visitor and passage migrant.

The number of records was down by more than 20% on 2001 but the total number of birds was very similar. The highest count was at Hurst Castle where 13 flew east into The Solent on Oct 16th.

Monthly maxima for the main sites are tabulated below:

	J	F	M	A	M	J	J	A	S	O	N	D
Langstone Harbour/Eastney	1	9	3	-	3	1	4	4	3	4	3	-
Southsea Castle	1	2	1	-	-	-	-	-	-	3	-	1
Lymington-Hurst/Milford	3	5	1	2	2	-	-	-	2	13	2	-

There were no inland records. All other records are listed below, followed by the approximate monthly totals:

Cracknore Hard: 1, Feb 2nd.
Needs Ore: 1, Feb 23rd.
Sandy Point: 2 E, Apr 3rd.
Taddiford Gap: 5, Oct 7th.
Hordle: 2 W, Nov 1st.
Hill Head: 1, Nov 18th.
Portsmouth Harbour: 1, Dec 14th.

J	F	M	A	M	J	J	A	S	O	N	D
5	17	5	4	5	1	4	4	5	25	8	2

Bittern   *Botaurus stellaris*

A very scarce but regular winter visitor.

There were confirmed sightings of two at Fleet Pond on several dates in the first winter period and of three at Titchfield Haven throughout December. Elsewhere there were 21 records from 13 sites involving 19 bird-days; a huge increase compared to the six records submitted in 2001. Sightings at Blashford Lakes, Testwood Lakes and Alresford Pond occurred in both winter periods.

At Fleet Pond, two were present in the early year between Jan 1st until Mar 3rd thereafter one until Mar 12th (compared to Mar 11th in 2001 and Mar 10th in 2000). In the late year the only records were of one on Nov 12th and again from Dec 25th-29th.

At Titchfield Haven, in the beginning of the year, only one or possibly two were present with the last sighting on Mar 31st. There was a single summer record of one on July 12th. Two were seen on Sep 15th and then at least one until Dec 1st when up to three were seen regularly through to the end of the year. In 2001, a Sep 12th sighting had been noted as unseasonal but the continuous sighting of birds in 2002, from September through to the end of the year, suggests that September may be a normal arrival time.

Away from the two main sites it is difficult to assess the number of birds involved, as it must be assumed that some records refer to the same birds moving between geographically close sites. It is, however, likely that between six and seven birds were present in the county in both winter periods. All other records were of singles and are summarised below:

River Itchen: Abbots Worthy, Jan 1st and also *Easton*, Jan 1st and 6th.
Blashford Lakes complex: *Snails Lake*, Jan 6th and *Ivy Lake*, Jan 20th and Dec 10th.
Overton Lagoons: Jan 11th.
Itchen Valley CP: report Feb 3rd and nearby at *Lakeside CP* Dec 31st.
Lower Avon valley: A bird visited the garden of the New Queen public house at Avon on Feb 4th and 20th.
Alresford Pond: Feb 14th and Dec 22nd.

Testwood Lakes: Feb 17th and Dec 29th and nearby at *Lower Test Marshes:* Feb 23rd.
Beaulieu Estuary: Feb 20th.
Stockbridge/Fullerton: Mar 2nd.
Farlington Marshes : Dec 16th.

Little Egret   *Egretta garzetta*

A moderately common passage migrant and winter visitor; the scarce breeding population continues to increase.

Over 770 records were submitted. Whilst the coastal roosts never quite reached the 2001 totals they remained healthy. An interesting change of distribution pattern was the increased use of the major river valleys as wintering areas in comparison to previous years. The Itchen Valley saw a dramatic increase in its winter usage producing its highest daytime recorded totals ever for January, February and December. The nocturnal roost at Alresford Pond set a new site record of 56 on Jan 17th (CMC).

In line with the rest of the country breeding continues to increase in the county with the largest number of active nests ever recorded. The colony at the guarded site of Fort Elson increased to over 15 pairs; elsewhere in the county at least four pairs bred.

Monthly maxima at nocturnal roosts and the main daytime feeding/loafing areas are tabulated below:

	J	F	M	A	M	J	J	A	S	O	N	D
Thorney Island roosts (W Sussex)	15	43	47	37	14	58	118	189	-	41	65	37
East Hayling/Warblington	22	61	51	8	-	1	28	6	49	67	78	25
Langstone Harbour	10	5	27	16	22	41	47	55	87	88	27	14
Farlington Marshes	7	5	18	16	14	27	25	41	45	36	22	5
Portsmouth Harbour (daytime)	7	16	22	-	-	-	2	-	31	33	31	21
Horsea Island roost	-	-	8	-	-	-	72	110	92	-	-	-
Gilkicker to Titchfield Haven	1	3	8	6	3	7	2	3	5	4	2	1
Hamble Estuary/Warsash	5	13	5	3	5	1	21	7	26	13	10	12
Lower Test/Eling/Bury Marshes	6	6	8	7	8	9	15	13	6	8	6	6
Dibden Bay to Calshot	4	2	12	1	5	-	1	21	-	26	15	1
Fawley Refinery roost	-	-	-	-	-	-	-	-	-	8	10	-
Needs Ore/Lepe	2	4	4	4	2	2	13	23	42	18	13	12
Sowley Pond roost	6	-	-	-	-	-	35	42	-	-	-	39
Lymington-Hurst	8	17	13	14	8	3	14	25	31	26	16	7
Avon valley (above F'bridge)	33	44	25	-	4	-	-	-	7	5	19	49
Avon valley (below F'bridge)	19	10	10	13	5	6	1	-	3	5	-	6
Test valley	7	2	4	6	-	-	-	-	-	1	3	9
Itchen Valley (daytime)	83	26	16	22	8	-	1	-	-	7	21	51
Alresford Pond roost	56	32	32	7	6	-	-	-	2	20	1	6
Meon Valley	6	18	15	1	-	-	-	4	-	2	12	4
APPROX COUNTY TOTAL	**280**	**260**	**280**	**110**	**80**	**70**	**180**	**210**	**350**	**310**	**260**	**260**

[1]*Excludes Thorney Island Roost, West Sussex where many birds from Hampshire roost*

Grey Heron   *Ardea cinerea*

A moderately common resident, passage migrant and winter visitor. It is widely observed but a local, colonial breeder.

Grey Heron (David Thelwell)

A total of 381 records was received, a significant increase on the 2001 total. In addition data were received from the *BTO Census of Heronries*. The list below includes all sites where breeding has taken place in 2001 and 2002. Sites with no data shown were unable to be surveyed either because of the unavailability of the observer or in 2001 because of FMD restrictions. The data are tabulated below with the 2001 totals in brackets:

	2002	2001		2002	2001
Tournerbury, Hayling Island	10	(-)	Fleet Pond	1	(0)
Fort Elson, Gosport	65	(59)	Ramridge Copse, Weyhill	2	(-)
Trotts Wood, Marchwood	11	(9)	Arlebury Park	15	(-)
Fawley Refinery	-	(21)	Elvetham	26	(28)
Sowley Pond	16	(-)	near Fordingbridge, Avon valley	(3+)	(10+)
Somerley Park	12	(30)	Southington, Test valley	-	(0-1)
Holt Pound Inclosure	12	(17)	Efford	7	(8)
Kettlesbrook, Steep	2	(0)			

Monthly maxima at selected feeding localities/daytime roosts are tabulated below:

	J	F	M	A	M	J	J	A	S	O	N	D
Langstone Harbour	13	6	6	8	5	6	13	17	16	25	6	10
Portsmouth Harbour	9	9	8	-	-	-	-	-	5	10	7	10
Titchfield Haven	8	-	12	-	-	-	-	-	-	16	-	-
Lymington/Hurst Area	11	3	2	2	2	7	6	2	13	5	4	3
Blashford Lakes	7	6	-	-	-	-	25	19	40	14	5	13
Bury Marshes	5	4	6	1	3	3	3	7	5	3	3	2
Eling/Redbridge	1	-	-	2	2	8	9	7	8	4	1	2
Timsbury GP	2	11	1	-	-	-	-	-	5	-	-	-
Eversley GPs	6	3	2	2	1	-	8	6	4	4	3	2
Yateley GPs	8	2	3	2	2	2	-	-	4	7	1	5

The highest count was an unexceptional 40 at Blashford Lakes on Sep 29th. Movement records of interest included 12 south-west out to sea from Hurst on Sep 12th and five east together at Hook-with-Warsash on Sep 16th.

Purple Heron
Ardea purpurea

A very scarce visitor (1,30,1).

The only record was a first-summer, first seen at Farlington Marshes on Apr 14th (JCr, RAC) and again on 17th (RW). This record is the 32nd for Hampshire.

Black Stork
Ciconia nigra

A rare vagrant (0,8,1).

One flew east over Whitchurch at 1700 hrs on May 17th (JS). This record has been accepted by *British Birds* and is the ninth for Hampshire and the first since an adult at Tadley Common on Apr 15th 1995.

White Stork
Ciconia ciconia

A rare vagrant (5,22,4).

One flew east over Beaulieu on June 1st (EJW) and another flew west over Langstone Harbour at 1245 hrs on June 27th (RAC). One was feeding in a hay meadow at Somerley Park on July 14th (*per* JL). Single birds seen in the Sopley/Winkton area on Sep 3rd/4th (KP, BG), at Lepe on Sep 8th (JGR) and in flight over Oliver's Battery on Sep 11th (NH) presumably relate to the same individual. These records bring the Hampshire total since 1951 to 26.

Spoonbill
Platalea leucorodia

A scarce but increasing visitor, most frequent in spring and autumn but recorded in every month (20+,88,18).

Birds were recorded in each month from March to December. There were 68 records submitted, an increase on last year's 56. The total number of bird-days was 89 but the number of birds involved was probably 18, considerably less than last year's record estimate of 29. The first of the year was one seen flying down the river at Titchfield Haven on Mar 25th. An adult was at Farlington Marshes from Apr 4th-11th and four were there on the evening of May 21st. At least two, reported as an adult and first-summer, were seen at Titchfield Haven on numerous dates between July and early August. Inland a bird was seen in the lower Avon valley on August 30th. A long staying first-winter was in the Emsworth area from Nov 13th until Dec 25th. Details of sightings and the estimated annual county totals for the last ten years are as follows:

Titchfield Haven: 1, Mar 25th; 1, May 17th; 1-2, July 12th-Aug 9th.
Farlington Marshes /Langstone Harbour: 1, Apr 4th-11th; 4, May 21st; 1 first-summer, June 11th; 1 first-winter E, Oct 31st; 1 first-winter, Nov 24th (the Chichester Harbour bird).
Needs Ore/ Beaulieu Estuary: 1 immature, Apr 6th; 1, Apr 16th; 1 adult, May 17th-21st; 1 adult, Sep 3rd/4th; 2 juveniles, Sep 5th-10th and 1 remaining to Sep 21st.
Lymington/Hurst: 1 adult, May 17th (possibly the Titchfield Haven bird); 1 immature, June 15th.
Avon Causeway: 1, Aug 30th.
Bedhampton Creek: 1 first-winter E, Oct 31st.
Emsworth Harbour/Chichester Harbour: one first-winter, Nov 13th-Dec 25th, which roosted at *Great Thorney Deep, West Sussex* Dec 25th.

Annual total	1993	1994	1995	1996	1997	1998	1999	2000	2001	2002
Spoonbill	1	6	5	21	3	7	4	9	29	18

Mute Swan
Cygnus olor

A moderately common resident.

Numbers of Mute Swan in the county have remained reasonably constant for a number of years now. Reports in the breeding season referred to 90 pairs attempting to breed in 33 locations. In all 15 pairs were reported to have failed, but the remainder raised approximately 150 young including one brood of nine at Breamore. The number of pairs and the number of young raised were comparable to 2001 when 109 pairs raised 144 young.

Monthly maxima at sites where more than 20 are regularly recorded are as shown in the table below, with approximate monthly totals for the county as a whole:

	J	F	M	A	M	J	J	A	S	O	N	D
Chichester Harbour	85	60	29	37	49	-	131	99	139	98	94	105
Emsworth Mill Pond	73	56	89	97	82	108	-	114	85	68	45	48
Langstone Harbour	18	13	10	21	27	50	32	28	39	21	17	10
Canoe Lake, Southsea	51	67	53	29	30	12	13	18	44	46	45	57
Portsmouth Harbour	90	71	76	-	-	-	-	-	86	82	101	97
Lower Test/Eling Marshes	6	9	10	19	28	57	68	40	17	7	8	5
Lymington-Hurst	40	32	32	27	3	-	10	-	18	48	42	52
Sopley/Avon Causeway, R. Avon	83	22	87	-	-	-	-	-	81	51	81	81
Avon C'way/Ringwood, R. Avon	52	94	122	-	-	-	-	-	101	62	48	25
Ringwood/Bickton, R. Avon	176	217	203	132	-	-	-	-	34	49	118	126
Blashford Lakes	47	15	11	-	-	-	30	43	55	69	82	31
Avon above Fordingbridge	136	139	99	-	-	-	-	-	125	126	108	82
Broadlands Estate	61	145	73	-	-	-	-	-	52	25	61	102
Woodmill, R. Itchen	-	-	-	-	-	-	-	45	63	58	43	-
Stockbridge/Fullerton	38	16	-	-	-	-	-	-	-	-	16	24
Alresford Pond	25	13	7	12	42	79	81	66	52	43	13	2
Wellington CP	20	19	30	-	4	-	4	6	22	41	44	-
Tundry Pond	6	12	13	14	-	20	29	25	39	37	48	49
Yateley GP	23	10	8	23	32	-	-	10	11	12	25	25
Eversley GP	30	11	7	3	4	1	-	-	28	20	30	31
APPROX COUNTY TOTAL	**965**	**950**	**915**	**375**	**250**	**305**	**240**	**395**	**950**	**850**	**975**	**845**

Other notable counts were reported from the following sites: Ashe Park Lake (26, Jan 16th); Itchen Stoke (20, Mar 9th); Petersfield Heath Pond (18*, Mar 12th); Easton (21, Apr 5th); Chessel Bay (24, Oct 28th).

Bewick's Swan
Cygnus columbianus

A scarce and declining winter visitor and passage migrant, most frequent in the Avon valley.

As usual most reports related to birds wintering in the Ibsley area of the Avon valley but the continuing population decline there saw the lowest December numbers since 1964. At the start of the year just 30 were present, of which eight were first-winter. The table below illustrates this decline over the last ten years:

Avon valley	92/93	93/94	94/95	95/96	96/97	97/98	98/99	99/00	00/01	01/02
Bewick's Swan	170	97	96	139	88	93	35	45	37	30

The numbers in the Avon valley gradually dropped through January and February (27, Jan 18th; 22, Jan 19th; 21, Feb 17th; 17, Feb 22nd). The last at Ibsley were nine (including five first-winters) on Mar 6th but later were two first-winters at Bisterne on Apr 14th.

The first returning birds were four at Ibsley on Nov 17th. Numbers then increased slowly up to 15, including a first-winter, on Dec 14th. Elsewhere the only other report was an impressive flock of 17 which flew low east over Farlington Marshes , then east over North Hayling on Dec 16th (JCr, DB) and was later reported high over Thorney Island, West Sussex. This movement coincided with several days of very cold weather over north-western Europe.

White-fronted Goose   *Anser albifrons*

A scarce winter visitor and passage migrant which has declined in recent years.

During 2002 there were no reports from traditional wintering sites in the Avon valley at either end of the year. Following just two reports (maximum of eight) in November 2001 the winter of 2001/2002 was the worst for numbers in the Avon valley since regular recording began in the 1950s. The table below illustrates this decline:

Avon valley	92/93	93/94	94/95	95/96	96/97	97/98	98/99	99/00	00/01	01/02
White-fronted Goose	84	97	87	66	37	16	18	47	13	8

Up to 34 were seen elsewhere in the county, which represented a good return. The flock of 22 present at Tundry Pond from December 2001 departed to the south-west at 1520 hrs on Jan 1st (MAS). Also remaining from 2001 were two well-watched birds, normally associating with Brent Geese, at Keyhaven. These remained in the area until Mar 17th. Six were with Greylags at Horsebridge on Jan 12th. After a gaggle of five was seen at Park Farm on Feb 10th, presumably the same group was discovered at Needs Ore from Mar 2nd-5th with one remaining until Mar 17th. Other records, possibly referring to feral or escaped birds, included one at Charlton Lakes until Feb 10th and then from Sep 8th to the end of the year and one seen between Stockbridge and Fullerton on Jan 27th.

Greylag Goose   *Anser anser*

A moderately common and increasing resident, passage migrant and winter visitor.

The feral population in Hampshire seems to be reasonably stable. Monthly maxima at localities with counts exceeding 50 are tabulated below:

	J	F	M	A	M	J	J	A	S	O	N	D
Needs Ore/Beaulieu Estuary	251	351	236	153	151	-	48	16	182	113	148	69
Avon valley	182	256	271	44	-	140	214	400*	427*	322	326	308

Maxima recorded at other sites were as follows: Fleet Pond (47, Oct 9th); Tundry Pond (45, Aug 12th); Marwell Zoo (33, Jan 27th & Feb 17th); 26 at Lower Test Marshes (Feb 5th) and presumably the same Dibden Bay (Feb 10th); and Lakeside CP (23, Jan 13th). Meanwhile a group of four south-east over Black Dam NR was the first known record at that site. Successful breeding was noted in just four areas, 11 broods totalling 38 young being reported at Blashford Lakes (7), Ewhurst Park (2), and Hawley Lake.. Additionally, young were seen at The Vyne in July, although no breeding attempt was made at the site itself. At Itchen Abbas one was found paired with a Canada Goose.

Movements possibly involving genuine wild birds included four past Hurst Beach with Brent Geese on Mar 27th and two past Stokes Bay on Apr 7th.

Grey Goose sp.   *Anser sp.*

A flock of 20+ unidentified grey geese flew west over Titchfield Haven on Jan 9th.

Snow Goose   *Anser caerulsecens*
A scarce feral resident.

The bulk of the feral population remained in the Eversley area. Up to 17 (slightly down on 2001) were seen at Eversley GP between January and March of which one was a first winter bird and one was the individual that prefers the company of the resident Barnacle Geese. During the breeding season two pairs were noted at the usual Stratfield Saye breeding site on June 6th, but there were no reports of actual breeding. Later in the year the highest count at Eversley GP was 15 adults on Dec 9th. Other records in the north-east included 12 at Bramshill Police College on Sep 8th and two over Tweseldown on Dec 28th.

In the Avon valley two were present throughout the year. Elsewhere one visited Alresford Pond and Western Court on Apr 27th and one visited Baffins Pond sporadically between Jan 7th and Oct 7th; it often associated with a group of feral Barnacles and also visited Titchfield Haven.

Canada Goose   *Branta canadensis*
A common resident and partial migrant.

Monthly maxima at sites where 100 are regularly recorded are tabulated below:

	J	F	M	A	M	J	J	A	S	O	N	D
Chichester Harbour	44	65	25	14	12	-	17	157	152	50	71	114
Baffins Pond, Portsmouth	26	32	36	36	21	169	198	-	-	15	11	10
Farlington Marshes	188	110	25	33	56	112	82	109	53	247	261	163
Portsmouth Harbour/IBM Lake	3	27	61	-	68	195	159	230	460	233	30	35
Titchfield Haven area	2	72	44	-	-	-	-	-	-	118	-	336
Beaulieu Estuary	3	603	233	121	116	-	18	3	164	-	-	-
Lymington-Hurst	180	141	21	34	17	110	162	10	110	300	320	266
Avon valley	200	437	361	-	-	-	345	-	365	332	429	535
Testwood Lakes	98	56	-	10	18	23	29	111	2	5	100	40
Lower Test/Eling Marshes	17	105	40	13	18	200	250	327	583	83	103	160
Overton area/Lower Ashe Fm	120	112	56	44	31	1	-	-	-	17	89	26
St Mary Bourne	-	9	68	-	-	-	-	-	133	-	33	-
Arlebury Lakes/Alresford Pond	110	-	86	-	2	-	-	-	13	-	2	-
King's Pond, Alton	1	30	53	7	-	-	-	-	3	85	115	31
Wellington CP	30	-	13	-	14	-	19	-	313	419	-	-
Tundry Pond	305	200	146	-	9	18	58	322	646	70	315	345
Fleet Pond	151	49	8	-	3	12	4	465	607	110	11	-
Eversley GP	93	118	72	50	44	26	20	275	475	604	100	2
Woolmer Pond	-	2	12	8	-	-	-	285	243	2	-	-
The Vyne	-	-	-	-	-	-	-	189	224	285	236	24

Maxima from selected other sites were as follows: Petersfield Heath Pond (88, Oct 5th); Shepherds Spring (79, Sep 8th); Timsbury GP (76, Sep 10th); Broadlands Lake (60, July 15th); Dibden Bay (43, Jan 13th).

Barnacle Goose
Branta leucopsis

A scarce resident (feral population) and rare winter visitor (wild populations).

As in recent years the majority of the population was centred on the Eversley area with a small, apparently declining, presence at Baffins Pond. After the record count of 270 at Eversley in September 2001, numbers fell back slightly in 2002. Monthly maxima for the two main feral flocks are tabulated below:

	J	F	M	A	M	J	J	A	S	O	N	D
Eversley GP	219	22	212	2	56	-	41	1	185	158	200	197
Baffins Pond	10	10	10	10	5	7	11	-	-	11	-	-

At the usual breeding site of Stratfield Saye Park on June 6th, there were 7 broods totalling 20 young and a further pair nesting. A total of 138 was counted at this site on July 27th.

Records of small groups came from: Easton (16, Jan 26th-Mar 9th); Needs Ore (7, Apr 1st/2nd; 3 Apr 20th) and Hook-with-Warsash (1, Mar 3rd-14th; 6, June 11th). Two birds were noted in the Avon valley (Mar 30th; and 1-3 between Oct 26th and Dec 24th), at The Vyne on May 5th and Lower Test Marshes on Sep 7th. Single bird reports in the early year were from Farlington Marshes , Eling/Redbridge, Calshot, Horsebridge, Chilling and Ashe; then between Sep 30th and Nov 30th at Northington, Wellington CP and Tundry Pond.

Brent Goose
Branta bernicla

Dark-bellied Brent Goose *(B.b.bernicla)*

A numerous winter visitor; small numbers summer.

As usual, internationally important numbers frequented Chichester and Langstone Harbours in both winter periods with some evidence of a decline in numbers in the three eastern harbours. Monthly maxima at localities with counts exceeding 100 and the approximate monthly totals for the county are tabulated below:

	J	F	M	A	M	J	J	A	S	O	N	D
Chichester Harbour	7470	6111	5288	20	5	-	5	6	6	1093	3960	5886
East Hayling	2428	2899	1644	-	-	-	-	-	-	634	1094	1975
Langstone Harbour	5019	4725	4506	170	6	4	7	6	1536	1340	4230	4408
Farlington Marshes	3000	-	3000	9	1	1	1	-	-	450	1700	1880
Portsmouth Harbour	1570	1540	1626	-	-	-	-	-	19	397	1853	2185
Hill Head/Brownwich	102	-	300	5	-	2	-	-	37	500	-	-
Hamble Estuary	1200	1000	715	-	-	-	-	-	1	142	903	947
Calshot	125	30	250	-	-	-	-	-	9	-	-	-
Beaulieu Estuary	2015	782	1000	675	156	2	-	-	4	400	679	1441
Lymington-Hurst	2000	1800	1100	29	2	3	1	1	2	447	1440	1212
APPROX COUNTY TOTAL	17460	12880	14140	890	165	12	9	7	1600	4300	12280	14040

The first evidence of spring departure came from Stokes Bay where 90 were observed flying east on Feb 26th. Further visible migration in March was observed from Stokes Bay (83 E, Mar 31st); Hayling Bridge (200 E, Mar 16th); Langstone Harbour (200 SE, Mar 15th; 455 E at dusk, Mar 21st); Hurst (60 E, Mar 17th; 67 E, Mar 22nd; 50 E Mar 31st). By April most birds had departed with just a few stragglers still leaving mid month: Sandy Point (10 NE and 13 E, Apr 14th); Langstone Harbour (25 SE, Apr 14th).

In the summer months small numbers, as usual, were noted at many sites along the coast. The first arrival of the autumn occurred on Sep 14th when 15 returned to Langstone Harbour. Arrivals at Langstone Harbour continued through September with numbers rising to 109 on Sep 18th, 495 on Sep 23rd and 1536 on Sep 29th. In the Lymington/Hurst area a flock of 485 on Nov 11th was noted to contain 69 first-winters (14%).

Away from coastal sites, ten north over Crookhorn, Waterlooville on Jan 2nd, six at Stratfield Saye Park on Sep 26th, seven south-west over Beaulieu Road, NF on Oct 31st and a single bird at Lakeside CP on Nov 29th were the only records.

Pale-bellied Brent Goose (*B. b. hrota*)

A very scarce winter visitor and passage migrant.

Numbers continue to increase with 16 individuals noted in early 2002 and a minimum of 13 recorded later in the year. Early year records were as follows:

Cams Bay GC: 1, Jan 1st.
Park Shore/Needs Ore: 2, from Jan 2nd-Feb 16th; then 1 until Apr 27th.
Pennington Marsh: 1, Jan 2nd.
Farlington Marshes : 6, from Jan 4th-Feb 5th; a further individual from Feb 5th with a maximum of 7 on Feb 14th; 5, Mar 1st; 4, Mar 3rd; 3, Mar 10th; 1-2 thereafter until last Apr 9th.
Keyhaven Harbour: 5, Apr 17th may have been birds on migration.

The Farlington Marshes group contained a pair of which one was thought to be a *hrota* x *bernicla* hybrid that has been excluded from the counts above. Wandering birds from Farlington were also recorded at nearby Hayling Oysterbeds and at the north shore of Langstone Harbour between early January and Apr 13th. Other records of single birds from grassland sites around Langstone Harbour presumably involved the Farlington birds, as follows: St. John's College Playing Fields (Jan 8th); Southsea Cricket Pitch (Jan 12th-16th); and Portsmouth Outdoor Centre (Feb 20th). An individual reported at Port Solent on Jan 28th and Feb 25th was presumably the same in Portsmouth Harbour on Feb 9th and at Portchester on Feb 23rd.

In the second winter period the first arrival flew over Hurst Castle towards the IoW on Oct 16th. It was probably this bird with Dark-bellied Brents in the Sturt Pond area from Oct 19th-Nov 18th, then at Keyhaven from Nov 19th-27th and latterly with Dark-bellied Brents on Eling Great Marsh from Nov 28th-Dec 7th. At Farlington one returned on Nov 7th, joined by another and a pair (one being the probable hybrid) on Dec 1st. At least one was then present in the Farlington area on and off until the end of the year. An additional group of nine (including at least one first-winter) was briefly between the Langstone Harbour Islands on Nov 11th.

Black Brant (*B. b. nigricans*)

A rare winter visitor (0, 9, 2).

Following the record influx into southern and eastern England at the end of 2001, the four individuals (excluding one intergrade with *bernicla* described below) located in Hampshire stayed on into 2002. *British Birds* accepted all four records as follows:

Portsmouth Harbour (Cams Bay/Frater): 1, Jan 1st -Mar 7th (TFC, IC).
Needs Ore/Park Shore: 1, Jan 1st-Mar 16th (MJWH, BG, NFOC, PDW).
Lymington/Hurst area: 2 (a male and female with separate flocks of Brents) from Jan 1st, the male until Mar 24th and the female until Mar 29th (RBW, MPM *et al*).

This brings the Hampshire total to nine to the end of 2001. A further three individuals with the characters of *nigricans* were discovered in February. One of these has been accepted by *British Birds* as follows:

Weston Shore: 1, Feb 25th (RB, NM).

A further bird was reported from the Hook-with-Warsash/Chilling area from Feb 10th-Mar 23rd (SM, RM *et al*). This was not accepted by *British Birds* since the description submitted did not exclude the possibility of an intergrade with *bernicla*. The apparent *nigricans* x *bernicla* intergrade which was first recorded in Langstone Harbour in 1998 was present in the Oysterbeds/South Moors area until Mar 25th and was also noted on Farlington Marshes for the first time ever on Feb 1st (JCr et al). However, an adult on West Lane fields, Hayling Island on Feb 15th was considered to be a pure *nigricans* (JCr).

In the second winter period four to five birds were located. The first was an adult at Shut Lake, Langstone Harbour on Oct 1st, which was not seen again (JCr). This may be the individual located at Sturt Pond, Milford on Sea on Oct 7th (MPM) and accepted by *British Birds*. A different adult to that present in the Hook-with-Warsash area in the early year was present from Nov 10th until Dec 10th at least (DH *et al)*. The intergrade with *bernicla* returned to the South Moors area of Langstone Harbour on Nov 29th and a further adult was discovered on a playing field at Portsmouth Outdoor Centre on Dec 15th and was then seen on various playing fields and on Farlington Marshes up to Dec 31st (CC, RAC, JCr *et al*).

The acceptances of the Weston Shore and Milford on Sea records brings the official Hampshire total to eleven, with a further four still under consideration.

2001 addition: One was in Portsmouth Harbour from Dec 11th-31st (IC, TFC, SM).

Egyptian Goose   *Alopochen aegyptiacus*

A very scarce feral resident.

Although there was no confirmed breeding numbers continue to increase with nine present in the north-east at the end of August.

The first record of the year was one at Petersfield Heath Pond, which was present from Mar 3rd to May 6th. There were two at Eversley GP on Mar 17th rising to four on Mar 30th/Apr 1st and again two in mid May. In the Avon valley one pair was at Bisterne on Apr 14th, two pairs at Oakford Coppice on Apr 21st and a pair at Blashford Lakes on June 20th, with both individuals seen there until July 14th.

Post breeding season there were four in the Avon valley at Somerley Lakes on Sep 30th and Sabines Farm on Oct 26th with one seen there until Nov 24th. Other records in the latter half of the year were confined to the north-east of the county. Up to three were recorded at Wellington CP (3, July 23rd: 1, Aug 28th; 2, Oct 6th and 23rd). Birds roosted at Eversley GP in the early autumn with seven to nine birds seen coming in at dusk from Aug 27th until Sep 15th. The maximum of nine on Aug 29th included two pale-headed birds. The last report from Eversley GP was of two on Nov 10th. The final report of the year concerned two at Yateley GP on Dec 9th.

Shelduck   *Tadorna tadorna*

A scarce breeder and common but declining winter visitor.

There were 353 records from 55 sites. The largest concentrations were at coastal sites but the maximum count, 700, from Langstone Harbour was well down on previous years. The peak county monthly total in February at 1670 was the lowest since 1999. Inland the highest total was 47 in the Avon valley on Dec 22nd and 25 at Testwood Lakes on May 11th. Monthly maxima at the main localities and the approximate monthly totals for the county are tabulated below:

	J	F	M	A	M	J	J	A	S	O	N	D
Chichester Harbour	885	574	493	298	96	-	54	46	39	62	218	366
East Hayling	326	307	39	34	6	-	4	-	-	20	76	129
Langstone Harbour	700	685	409	232	140	103	12	11	12	52	215	445
Portsmouth Harbour	149	72	62	-	-	-	3	-	-	-	39	39
Titchfield Haven	12	22	11	-	13	3	-	-	-	-	-	10
Hamble Estuary	39	38	36	9	8	2	-	-	-	-	6	13
Lower Test-Bury Marshes[1]	5	18	20	39	27	28	4	2	-	-	6	9
Fawley/Calshot	72	123	28	39	16	-	9	19	14	-	-	48
Needs Ore/Beaulieu Estuary	83	142	105	114	133	-	30	14	-	2	26	44
Pylewell/Tanners Lane	27	36	39	43	2	-	-	-	-	-	5	44
Lymington-Hurst	166	173	107	82	104	4	8	10	12	9	52	163
Avon valley	2	23	17	35	0	6	0	0	2	0	9	47
Alresford Pond	5	12	11	11	18	10	3	0	0	0	2	6
APPROX COUNTY TOTAL	**1600**	**1670**	**910**	**700**	**520**	**190**	**80**	**60**	**40**	**90**	**440**	**1030**

[1] includes Redbridge and Eling Marshes

Breeding was attempted at 16 sites and was confirmed at eight of these. In and around Langstone Harbour there were at least eight territories/breeding pairs with seven juveniles at Hayling Oysterbeds on Aug 29th and ten noted at Farlington Marshes on Sep 12th. Other coastal sites were Sinah GP (two pairs Apr 24th), Portsmouth Harbour (pair with juvenile July 13th), Lower Test/Eling (six territories/breeding pairs and at least eight young) and a pair with five young on the Beaulieu Estuary on July 27th. Inland there were seven pairs noted in the Avon valley with six young seen on June 21st. In the Test valley there were five pairs but no confirmed breeding. At least six pairs attempted breeding in the Itchen Valley with a single juvenile noted on Alresford Pond on July 21st. Elsewhere a pair bred successfully at Sparsholt College, with 6 young noted on June 1st and breeding was also suspected in Roydon Woods, NF.

Mandarin   *Aix galericulata*

A scarce or moderately common and increasing resident.

The county population appears stable with 255 records received from 58 sites. The Wey Valley in the east and Wealden Heaths to the south form the county stronghold, with further significant populations around the New Forest and in the north-east.

Regularly surveyed sites with five or more birds are tabulated below, and reflects the difficulty in observation and recording when birds disperse during the breeding season. The only double-figure counts away from the main sites in the early part of the year were Straits Inclosure (Alice Holt Forest) with 12 on Feb 17th and Roydon Woods, NF with ten on Mar 2nd. In the breeding season broods were reported from six sites and pairs noted at a further five sites, with juveniles also reported at Emer Bog, North Baddesley on Sep 2nd.

The first breeding noted was a female seen with 13 young on May 27th on the Broadlands Estate. There were two June records; a pair with six young at Petersfield Heath Pond and six juveniles present with 11 adults at Foley Manor Liphook. Confirmed breeding also came from Lepe, Lakeside CP (Eastleigh) and Steep in July and early August.

	J	F	M	A	M	J	J	A	S	O	N	D
Eyeworth Pond	-	10	10	7	10	-	-	-	-	-	6	17
Blashford Lakes	0	0	0	0	0	0	0	6	0	12	0	0
Clamp Kiln Farm	4	5	6	-	-	2	1	-	3	7	4	6
Liss Forest	-	2	3	-	4	1	2	2	41	60*	50	10
Headley Mill Pond	70	44	-	4	-	-	-	-	17	-	-	10
Passfield Pond	1	4	14	2	-	-	-	-	67*	15	23	17
Fleet Pond	5	12	3	3	0	0	0	0	4	0	0	1
TOTAL REPORTED	132	86	74	30	33	21	29	60	153	145	182	111

[1] *excludes young*

Post-breeding dispersal maxima away from the tabulated sites included 28 at Beaulieu on Aug 31st, ten at Woolmer Pond on Sep 9th and 21 at Curbridge on Oct 19th. At the year's end there were 15 at Bramshill Police College on Dec 29th.

Wigeon   *Anas penelope*

A common winter visitor and passage migrant; a few summer each year.

In the first winter period numbers were lower than in previous winters particularly in the Avon valley with a January count of 2650 compared to 6450 in 2001. The cold start to the year saw the estuaries holding the highest concentrations, with the peak being 2061 on the lower Test. Most birds had left their winter quarters by late March/early April with the last at Farlington Marshes being recorded on Apr 23rd. A female remained on the Broadlands Estate until the end of May and there were two records for June from coastal sites.

The first observation of returning birds was ten flying into Farlington Marshes on July 30th. Heavy rainfall in mid-September and then again in October and November created suitably wet feeding habitat. In consequence the county population exceeded 4000 by late September, 7000 in October-November and 13,000 in December; with the increased Avon valley population at 6900 accounting for the difference between the first and second winter periods. The autumn flocks at Farlington Marshes were the highest since the 1980s. Monthly maxima at regularly watched localities peaking at 80 or more and the approximate monthly totals for the county are tabulated below:

	J	F	M	A	M	J	J	A	S	O	N	D
Chichester Harbour	1462	831	637	6	0	0	0	1	173	1978	897	1434
East Hayling	323	157	57	0	0	0	0	0	4	27	92	192
Langstone Harbour	1520	661	808	24	1	2	10	97	1612	1575	501	850
Portsmouth Hbr/Cams Bay	291	167	85	0	0	0	0	31	274	340	163	89
Titchfield Haven	584	850	350	8	2	1	0	30	220	270	0	680
Hamble Estuary	191	162	250	5	0	0	0	5	150	141	97	177
Lower Test/Eling/Bury M'rshes	2061	2256	1337	13	0	0	0	0	256	512	977	1529
Dibden Bay-Fawley	744	922	327	0	0	0	0	0	8	58	388	266
Needs Ore/Beaulieu Estuary	1297	768	1652	8	3	0	1	13	202	1490	961	1135
Pylewell/Sowley Pond	210	60	43	0	0	0	1	0	1	654	596	250
Lymington-Hurst	370	232	177	0	0	0	2	12	330	304	264	400

table continued overleaf

(continued)	J	F	M	A	M	J	J	A	S	O	N	D
Avon valley												
Sopley-Avon Causeway	260	-	500	0	0	0	0	0	2	25	495	1345
Avon C'way-Wattons Ford	543	1450	593	0	0	0	0	0	11	256	1607	3262
Blashford Lakes	1465	659	445	0	0	0	0	4	788	1118	791	2223
Ellington-Bickton	250	-	180	0	0	0	0	0	0	0	135	75
Broadlands Estate	98	114	4	1	0	0	0	0	9	5	25	340
Allington GP	72	35	37	0	0	0	0	0	13	50	66	95
The Vyne	80*	14	8	0	0	0	0	0	5	23	38	58
Tundry Pond	21	32	46	0	0	0	0	1	22	25	87	201*
Eversley GP	207	469	218	0	0	0	0	5	77	146	303	396
APPROX COUNTY TOTAL	10860	9090	6960	34	5	3	15	200	4040	7180	7240	13740

Away from these areas notable counts were: 64 at Sherfield-on-Loddon on Jan 19th; 115* at Longwater Bridge (Fareham) on Feb 3rd; 35 at Fleet Pond on Sep 12th; 95* at Yateley GP on Oct 23rd; 55 at Wellington CP on Nov 2nd; 110* at Testwood Lakes on Nov 10th; and 76 at Dogmersfield Lake on Dec 17th.

Gadwall   *Anas strepera*

A moderately common winter visitor and scarce breeder.

Records were received from 84 locations. The approximate county total exceeded 2000 for the first time in both January and December; this despite the numbers recorded at Blashford Lakes being well down on 2001. In addition the number of adult birds seen in the breeding season has doubled in the last two years. The use of deep-water gravel pits shows the continuing adaptation of the species through feeding association with diving species such as Coot. The peaks at both ends of the year appear short-lived and probably reflect cold weather movements as low temperatures were recorded in January and December.

Monthly maxima at localities peaking at 70 or more and the approximate monthly totals for the county are tabulated below:

	J	F	M	A	M	J	J	A	S	O	N	D
Needs Ore/Beaulieu Estuary	-	16	6	29	8	-	2	8	69	33	4	18
Sowley Pond/Pitts Deep	80	4	-	-	-	-	-	-	6	-	4	45
Lymington/Hurst	13	24	1	4	2	-	-	-	2	-	-	70
Ibsley-Hucklesbrook Lakes	42	121	30	30	-	-	22	-	-	-	-	64
Blashford Lakes	557	232	80	33	17	-	46	91	148	199	346	713
Overton Lagoons	110	77	36	79	76	32	-	6	-	22	35	77
Ashe Park	102	34	32	44	15	-	-	-	-	3	2	5
Allington GP	180	29	2	-	-	-	-	10	37	100	98	120
Winchester SF	32	76	110	94	83	52	5	22	4	-	5	8
Alresford Pond	37	58	30	49	32	148	75	25	117	94	49	17
Dogmersfield Lake	60	18	38	0	0	0	0	0	0	0	88	103*
Stratfield Saye Park	81	135	10	-	-	61	37	54	83	15	5	126
Yateley GP	241*	140	38	0	0	0	0	12	7	162	185	152
Eversley GP	271*	39	32	7	9	7	1	25	24	182	115	108
Wellington CP	62	99	89	-	4	-	2	10	14	60	82	50
APPROX COUNTY TOTAL	2280	1400	800	530	320	420	230	300	560	1040	1260	2040

Peak counts at other sites with 30 or more recorded were as follows: Farlington Marshes (40, Jan 27th); Fawley Refinery (56, Nov 29th); Avon valley (36, Mar 3rd; 45

Dec 22nd); in the Itchen Valley at Avington Lake (52, June 10th), Northington (66, Oct 6th) and Arlebury Lakes (49, Nov 18th); in the north-east at The Vyne (30, Apr 19th), Bramshill Plantation (87, Dec 7th including 32 normally resident at Wellington CP) and Tundry Pond (44, Dec 18th).

During the breeding season there were reports from 23 sites and 32 broods noted at 12. In the Itchen Valley there were 13 broods with four at Avington Lake, two at both Winchester SF and Alresford Pond and singles at Arlebury Lakes, Easton, Itchen Stoke, Winchester College Meadows and Ovington. There were ten broods or more (including 65+ juvs) at Stratfield Saye Park. Elsewhere there were four broods at Overton Lagoons, three at Blashford on North Somerley Lakes and two on Woolmer Pond. In addition 21 pairs were noted in the Avon valley although breeding details were not reported.

Teal   *Anas crecca*

A scarce resident and common winter visitor.

Monthly maxima at the main localities with a peak count of more than 100 and the approximate monthly totals for the county are tabulated below:

	J	F	M	A	M	J	J	A	S	O	N	D
Chichester Harbour	2426	956	587	68	2	-	9	28	263	756	801	1013
East Hayling	481	492	166	-	-	-	-	-	183	263	136	276
Langstone Harbour	538	417	303	169	2	11	12	200	440	646	215	308
Portsmouth Harbour	159	137	98	-	-	-	-	-	23	8	53	56
Titchfield Haven	331	-	428	51	0	15	13	78	118	113	175	212
Hamble Est./Hook-with-Warsash	398	86	157	4	-	-	-	48	176	219	281	146
Lower Test/Eling/Bury Marshes	325	653	298	26	-	4	1	5	106	115	303	965
Dibden Bay-Calshot	458	259	64	-	-	-	-	-	-	-	1150	328
Lepe/Beaulieu Estuary	415	419	327	32	2	-	6	29	118	405	1063	318
Sowley Pond/Pitts Deep	310	40	-	-	-	-	-	-	33	-	25	54
Lymington-Hurst	669	150	215	48	-	-	8	104	450	490	590	210
Avon valley												
Sopley-Avon Causeway	18	4	175	-	-	-	-	-	2	2	52	500
Avon C'seway-Wattons Ford	233	680	58	6	0	0	0	0	200	600	675	2865
Blashford Lakes	445	182	292	3	2	0	0	40	95	148	127	1531
Broadlands Estate	180	175	81	-	-	-	-	-	6	25	100	144
Alresford Pond	-	-	12	17	1	4	1	4	128	156	27	63
Avington Lake	154	12	11	6	-	-	-	-	7	36	50	125
Stratfield Saye Park	158	20	-	-	-	-	-	47	91	92	82	96
APPROX COUNTY TOTAL	**5820**	**4190**	**3060**	**440**	**11**	**37**	**70**	**690**	**2640**	**3620**	**5370**	**8200**

Away from these sites notable flocks were at Wade Court, Havant (195, Jan 31st; 155, Feb 6th), Woolmer Pond (80, Sep 1st) and The Vyne (79, Sep 15th; 76, Nov 21st; 77, Dec 21st). Additionally, 72 flew west over Odiham on Oct 10th.

The very high rainfall and flooding attracted large flocks totalling 4500 into the Avon valley during the second winter period. The weather dependency of the county population is reflected in the rapid build-up into November and then another surge into December. By contrast numbers during the breeding season were extremely low with disappointingly no proven breeding, although birds were present at four or five potential breeding sites.

Mallard
Anas platyrhynchos

A common resident and winter visitor.

Records were received from 97 sites. The estimated January total of 5320 appears to be the highest recorded since the 1970s; the maximum site count was 420 at Titchfield Haven. The highest concentration was in September with 1000 on the River Test below Romsey, including 504 on the Broadlands Estate. Breeding reports were sparse: 65 territories at Lower Test Marshes NR on June 1st; 42 juveniles on Overton Lagoons on May 2nd; 12 pairs and 39 young at Fleet Pond in early June; 11 pairs with broods on the Basingstoke Canal in June. The only other reports were from Sway (two pairs raised five young) and Hook Links (four pairs with broods). A brood of seven juveniles was seen at King's Pond, Alton on the very late date of Nov 30th.

There were constant month-by-month estimates of the county population in the autumn and second winter period at around 4400. This suggests that national dispersal or continental influx into the county occurred in late August or early September, perhaps indicated by transitory increase in numbers at coastal localities. At Foley Manor, Liphook 312 individuals were counted on Aug 21st resulting from the release of hand-reared birds as wildfowler's quarry. Monthly maxima at the main localities where numbers peaked at 150 or more and approximate monthly totals for the county are tabulated below:

	J	F	M	A	M	J	J	A	S	O	N	D
Langstone Harbour	118	98	116	84	145	128	78	169	119	167	166	93
Portsmouth Harbour	222	102	84	-	-	-	-	-	120	68	168	172
Titchfield Haven	420	400	328	-	-	-	-	-	-	302	284	356
Lower Test Marshes	330	193	114	55	73	186	256	262	353	125	159	206
Sowley Pond	290	40	-	4	-	-	-	-	40	11	-	40
Lymington-Hurst	207	115	60	119	150	12	49	225	245	251	124	104
Blashford Lakes	290	57	108	-	-	-	88	-	142	404	113	318
Broadlands Estate	247	190	130	47	29	35	19	20	504	340	260	224
Test valley –Saddlers Mill	118	72	79	-	-	-	-	-	152	70	123	135
Itchen Valley – Woodmill	-	-	-	-	-	-	-	203	209	158	129	-
Itchen Valley - Winnall Moors	187	167	186	-	-	-	-	-	-	171	153	150
Itchen Valley –Northington	20	61	65	-	-	-	-	-	182	125	142	-
The Vyne	116	9	40	-	-	26	30	50	15	-	189	122
Stratfield Saye Park	-	20	-	-	-	28	24	403	55	316	130	119
Fleet Pond	70	90	-	-	-	12	100	125	160	70	75	34
Petersfield Heath Pond	194	111	86	44	54	57	93	74	101	96	116	125
APPROX COUNTY TOTAL	**5320**	**3330**	**2430**	**730**	**760**	**760**	**1320**	**2270**	**4350**	**4400**	**4400**	**4390**

The maxima at other localities with peak three-figure counts were as follows: East Hayling (140, Sep 7th); Emsworth Mill Pond (134, Jan 7th); Baffins Pond (119, Jan 7th); Cams Bay (100, Sep 5th); Needs Ore/Beaulieu Estuary (148, Sep 8th); Shepherds Spring Lakes (100, Jan 13th); St Mary Bourne (100, Feb 10th); Alresford Pond (124, Jan 24th); Sherfield-on-Loddon (108 Jan 3rd); King's Pond, Alton (111, Jan 4th); Headley Mill Pond (114, Jan 6th) and Yateley GP (103 Dec 12th).

Pintail
Anas acuta

A moderately common winter visitor and passage migrant; occasional in summer.

Numbers in the first winter period were up on the previous December, but nowhere near the record numbers of the corresponding period in 2001, primarily due to the lack of flooding in the Avon valley. The maximum count in this area was a count of c.280 on Feb 10th at Avon Causeway. Langstone Harbour and the Lymington-Hurst area consistently held three figure totals throughout January and February, after which numbers dropped away rapidly through March and April.

The only summering record was of a single drake in Langstone Harbour on June 3rd; first returns were also there with three at Farlington Marshes on Aug 26th, followed by 11 at Keyhaven the next day. Renewed flooding in the Avon valley led to numbers between Sopley and Wattons Ford building up to 325 by Nov 24th, rising to a maximum of *950* by the end of the year – not quite the record numbers of 2001, but still the second highest county total. Other notable records were two large flocks settling on the sea or moving east off Hurst Beach, with 259 on Dec 17th and 281 on Dec 27th. It is likely that these movements originated from shooting disturbance in the Avon valley. Three figure counts at Farlington meant that by the close of the year the overall county total was not far short of the record numbers from January and February 2001.

Monthly maxima at the main localities and approximate monthly totals for the county are tabulated below:

	J	F	M	A	M	J	J	A	S	O	N	D
Langstone Harbour	215	127	103	11	-	1	-	5	89	105	41	170
Fawley	24	64	-	-	-	-	-	-	-	2	16	27
Needs Ore/Beaulieu Estuary	75	6	14	2	-	-	-	-	4	64	50	2
Lymington-Hurst	184	166	57	4	-	-	-	11	77	90	201	345
Sopley-Avon C'way, R.Avon	-	-	-	-	-	-	-	-	-	-	-	200
Avon Causeway-Wattons Ford	-	280	15+	-	-	-	-	-	-	3	325	750
Blashford Lakes	20	10	25	0	0	0	0	0	0	0	0	20
APPROX COUNTY TOTAL	**730**	**670**	**330**	**20**	**0**	**1**	**0**	**16**	**200**	**300**	**960**	**1650**

Inland, records were received from ten sites, mainly one to three birds, but 32 were at Broadlands Lake, Romsey on Mar 3rd. Other double-figure counts were 10 at Fishlake Meadows, Romsey (Dec 9th) and 15 south over Testwood Lakes (Dec 22nd).

Garganey   *Anas querquedula*

A scarce passage migrant and summer visitor. Occasionally breeds.

A very good year with a minimum of 50 seen between Mar 27th and Sep 12th; this was the best year since 1992. In spring a minimum of 31 individuals was seen. On the first date, a male was at Titchfield Haven with another at Pennington Marsh. Subsequently one or two were reported at 12 sites until the end of May, with spring passage peaking in early April, when nine (five males, four females) were recorded east off Hurst Beach. A well-watched pair at Woolmer Pond on Mar 29th was two of the first to arrive in the county and surprisingly stayed throughout April. Often elusive, any hopes that they might stay to breed were dashed when they weren't seen after May 1st. The only bird seen during June was a male at Farlington Marshes on 2nd/3rd.

Male Garganey, Titchfield Haven, May 2002 (Trevor Codlin)

An estimated 19 individuals were seen in autumn from July 30th, with three to five juveniles being present at Farlington Marshes from this date until Aug 20th; at least one remaining until Sep 7th. The last birds were a female and immature at Keyhaven reedbeds, departing on Sep 12th. Records by site followed by the approximate monthly totals are tabulated below:

Budds Farm SF/Farlington Marshes : 1 male, Mar 28th; 1 male, 19th Apr; 1 male between May 12th-16th; 1 male, June 2nd-3rd; 5 juvs. max., July 30th-Aug 20th with up to 2 until 30th and 1 until Sep 7th with a sixth bird Sep 4th.

Newlands Farm, Fareham: 1 female, May 28th.

Titchfield Haven: 1-2 males, Mar 27th-31st; 1 male, May 15th; 1 male Aug 4th; 1 female Aug 18th; 1, Aug 31st.

Hook-with-Warsash: 2 pairs, Apr 8th; 1, Aug 19th.

Lower Test Marshes: 1, July 30th-Aug 7th.

Park Shore/Needs Ore: 1, Apr 7th; 1 pair, May 11th.

Lymington/Hurst: 1 male, 9 dates between 27th Mar-Apr 11th; 9 E (4 males, 5 females), Apr 6th; 1 pair, Apr 8th; 2 males, May 9th-12th joined by third on 11th with 1 to 20th; 3, Aug 27th with 1 to Sep 7th; 1 female with 1 juv., Sep 10-12th.

Blashford Lakes: 1 male, Apr 21st; 1 male, May 5th.

Fleet Pond: 1 male Aug 20th; 1 male Aug 31st-Sep12th with juv./female on 4th.

Tundry Pond: 1 female/juv., Aug 31st-5th Sep.

Eversley GP: 1, Apr 16th.

Woolmer Pond: 1 pair, Mar 29th-Apr 9th also Apr 11th and presumably same pair May 1st; 1 juv., Sep 9th.

The Vyne: 1 male, Aug 29th.

Mar	Apr	May	June	July	Aug	Sep
5	23	12	1	5	18	8

2001 correction: delete record of one at The Vyne, Aug 28th 2001.

48

Shoveler
Anas clypeata

A moderately common winter visitor and passage migrant; formerly a few pairs bred annually.

In the early year, counts were substantially down on the corresponding period in the previous year, mainly due to a lack of flooding in the Avon valley. The highest counts were recorded in Langstone Harbour in February and March with main concentrations centred on Farlington Marshes and Budds Farm SF.

Again, there was no indication of breeding, with the usual scattering of mainly coastal summering records, although five juveniles were seen at Farlington on July 14th.

Reports of coastal passage in spring amounted to only 32, all moving E along Hurst Beach between Mar 29th and May 7th.

In the late year floods in the Avon valley brought exceptional numbers to the Blashford Lakes complex (*197*, Dec 28th) and between Sopley and Wattons Ford (*131*, Dec 22nd).

Monthly maxima at major sites and approximate monthly totals for the county are tabulated below:

	J	F	M	A	M	J	J	A	S	O	N	D
Langstone Harbour	83	*106*	*135*	31	3	2	9	59	103	96	50	65
Titchfield Haven	30	70	56	24	3	3	0	10	27	20	28	70
Hamble Estuary	9	8	40	1	-	-	-	2	7	15	10	22
Needs Ore/Beaulieu Estuary	8	50	58	44	7	-	8	10	20	1	45	9
Lymington-Hurst	73	93	80	33	1	-	10	8	3	24	60	56
Avon valley												
Blashford Lakes	98	52	73	2	0	0	0	13	39	68	61	197
Avon Causeway-Wattons Ford	-	44	32	3	0	0	0	0	0	0	36	131
Winchester SF	20	9	18	2	-	-	3	6	25	2	-	11
Alresford Pond	24	13	-	2	-	-	-	-	18	39	11	12
Eversley GPs	40	54	28	2	0	3	2	3	8	14	18	18
Yateley GP	39*	15	0	0	0	0	0	0	0	10	6	12
Petersfield Heath Pond	28	29	32*	2	0	0	0	0	0	0	0	4
APPROX COUNTY TOTAL	**780**	**760**	**960**	**150**	**17**	**8**	**34**	**160**	**270**	**440**	**480**	**805**

Other sites with maxima over 20 were as follows: Portsmouth Harbour (31, Jan 12th); Baffins Pond, Portsmouth (22, Jan 14th); Dibden Bay (55, Mar 24th); Fawley (max 46, Dec 23rd); Sopley-Avon Causeway (60, Nov 24th); Allington GP (max 30, Jan 1st) and Fleet Pond (max 23, Oct 12th).

Red-crested Pochard
Netta rufina

A very scarce feral resident, rare passage migrant and winter visitor, or escape.

A male was on Allington GP from Apr 6th-15th (DJU, CA). In the north-east of the county a male was at Wyck Pond on May 17th (PJS) and single females were at Fleet Pond on Sep 1st (WGDL) and Wellington CP on Oct 23rd and 27th (JMCk, KBW).

An increasingly large feral population of these ducks now breeds at Cotswold Water Park, near Swindon, Wiltshire, which may be the origin of some or most of the birds appearing in Hampshire.

Pochard   *Aythya ferina*

A scarce breeder and moderately common winter visitor.

As was the case in 2001, confirmed breeding was limited to Alresford Pond, where two pairs bred with single young being seen on May 18th and June 26th. The wintering population appears to be holding up with Blashford Lakes once again the stronghold of the species in the county.

The following table, limited to those localities with counts exceeding 50, shows the main wintering sites for the county and monthly totals.

	J	F	M	A	M	J	J	A	S	O	N	D
Titchfield Haven	97	105	93	1	0	1	0	0	0	8	71	102
Blashford Lakes	217	163	111	2	0	0	4	0	10	40	371	375
Testwood Lakes	4	81	2	0	0	0	0	0	0	0	8	2
Eversley GP	68	68	30	1	4	0	1	2	9	21	39	79
Yateley GP	36	38	47	0	0	0	0	0	0	18	47	85
Dogmersfield Lake	52	24	17	0	0	0	0	0	0	0	71	94
Fleet Pond	19	5	8	0	0	0	0	0	0	3	32	70
Tundry Pond	16	-	10	0	0	0	0	0	0	3	60	72
APPROX COUNTY TOTAL	**840**	**670**	**460**	**20**	**11**	**6**	**10**	**4**	**35**	**160**	**840**	**1075**

Other sites with counts exceeding 20 were as follows: in Langstone Harbour at Budds Farm SF (21, Dec 16th) and Sinah GP (33, Nov 2nd); at Sowley Pond (44, Jan 2nd; 23, Dec 9th; 30, Dec 11th); inland at Southampton Common (21, Feb 12th), Fishlake Meadows (30, Nov 23rd) and Timsbury GP (35, Jan 22nd), Allington GP (22, Dec 31st) and Northington (65, Mar 3rd); and in the north-east at Stratfield Saye Park (39, Jan 3rd) and Wellington CP (30, Jan 3rd; 20, Oct 23rd).

Tufted Duck   *Aythya fuligula*

A moderately common breeding species whose numbers increase considerably in winter.

The following table, limited to those localities with counts exceeding 50, shows the principal sites for the county and monthly totals.

	J	F	M	A	M	J	J	A	S	O	N	D
Langstone Harbour	7	52	56	38	43	4	30	2	13	41	22	17
Baffins Pond, Portsmouth	74	38	54	54	31	18	4	-	-	7	20	44
Blashford Lakes	315	293	279	39	-	-	68	42	116	142	280	360
Avon valley (Ibsley to Bickton)	130	-	115	-	-	-	-	-	-	-	6	2
Alresford Pond	62	20	13	32	45	14	17	3	3	6	27	2
Timsbury GP	55	28	32	22	-	-	4	-	10	12	20	77
Stratfield Saye Park	65	29	16	-	-	1	4	3	3	-	-	45
Arlebury Lakes	95	69	45	28	12	8	3	-	1	11	12	21
Fishlake Meadows	-	-	-	-	-	-	-	-	-	-	50	70
Testwood Lakes	35	64	32	4	5	8	9	33	20	4	36	25
Overton Lagoons	29	44	49	74	-	48	8	1	-	11	2	19
Yateley GP	160	192	140	74	4	-	-	15	38	108	190	227
Eversley GP	151	118	142	54	48	32	48	52	35	67	111	157
APPROX COUNTY TOTAL	**1640**	**1410**	**1560**	**661**	**360**	**180**	**280**	**260**	**440**	**700**	**820**	**1590**

Breeding records were received for 78 pairs with 27 pairs raising a total of 114 young. Without doubt, the most important area for breeding in the county was upstream of Kings

Worthy on the River Itchen, where there were 24 pairs, plus an additional 26 unpaired birds.

The list below shows the number of breeding pairs and, where known, the number of young (in brackets) from each pairing.

	Pairs (Young)		Pairs (Young)
Langstone Harbour		**Test valley**	
Farlington Marshes	1 (7)	Timsbury GP	2
Islands	1	Mottisfont	2
Avon valley		Testbourne	8
Harbridge	1	Overton Lagoons	1 (2)
Ibsley Water	2 (6,6)	Southington Lane	1
Ellingham Lake	2 (4,?)	**Itchen Valley**	
Mockbeggar Lake	3 (5, 5, 4)	Headbourne Worthy	1 (5)
North Somerley Lakes	4 (6, 5, 4, 8)	Arlebury Lakes	1 (1)
North-west		Kings Worthy	24
East Wellow	1	**North-east**	
Lockerley	2	Liss Forest	1
Romsey		Woolmer Pond	1 (7)
Broadlands Lake	2	The Vyne	3 (7, 1, ?)
Saddlers Mill	2	Stubbs Farm Ponds	1 (6)
Water Meadows	2	Stratfield Saye Park	3 (1, 2, 1)
		Coldrey Park	1 (3)
		Eversley GP	5 (4,4,4,3,3)

The wintering population continues to remain steady at about 1600.

Scaup   *Aythya marila*

A very scarce winter visitor and passage migrant.

A much better year than 2001, with a total of 18, recorded mainly in the Lymington/Hurst area and in Langstone Harbour.

In the Lymington/Hurst area, four were reported in the first half of the year: one at Normandy on Jan 1st; two at Keyhaven on Feb 7th and another there on Feb 28th. In the late year seven were reported: at Keyhaven two males and one female on Dec 17th, two first-winter females and one first-winter male on Dec 28th; and one first-winter male at Pennington Marsh from Dec 22nd to 31st.

In Langstone Harbour, four were reported. An adult female was off Hayling Oysterbeds on Jan 20th and in the second winter period a long-staying adult female, initially on Budds Farm SF, was seen from Oct 24th to the end of the year. In addition, two first-winters were in Broom Channel from Dec 17th-28th.

Elsewhere, single females/first-winters were on Snails Lake, Blashford from the start of the year until Mar 3rd (possibly a hybrid, see *HBR2001*), at Headbourne Worthy Jan 5th, on IBM Lake on Jan 6th, at Bury Marshes on Jan 26th and at Camp Farm GP from Dec 29th-31st.

The only passage bird noted was one east off Hurst Beach on Oct 15th.

Aythya hybrids

The drake "Ferruginous Duck" type *aythya* hybrid was present on Budds Farm SF from the start of the year until Feb 26th and again from Oct 17th-Dec 19th. This bird was first recorded on Nov 23rd 1999 and has now over-wintered for the last four years. It shows characteristics of a Ferruginous Duck / Pochard hybrid.

At Timsbury GP a Tufted Duck and Pochard pairing resulted in four hybrid young. Tufted Duck / Pochard hybrids were on Ewhurst Lake on Dec 30th and Brownwich Pond on Dec 28th.

Eider *Somateria mollissima*

A scarce winter visitor and passage migrant; small numbers usually summer.

The number of resident birds continues to increase, favoured sites being in The Solent off Hill Head (max. 55 on Mar 5th), the Beaulieu Estuary (max. 27 on Nov 5th) and Pennington Marsh (max. 70 on Dec 27th). There was an early year peak in March and a distinct passage through April and May. About thirty birds remained throughout the summer. The county population peaked in December when about 150 were present.

The monthly maxima of birds at the principal sites are tabulated below, followed by the county totals:

	J	F	M	A	M	J	J	A	S	O	N	D
East Hayling/Hayling Bay	10	9	3	2	8	0	3	3	1	0	1	3
Titchfield Haven / Hill Head	8	3	21	20	20	0	0	0	1	14	12	70
Beaulieu Estuary/Lepe	5	5	23	3	0	0	1	1	0	2	27	11
Lymington/Hurst	17	26	55	18	38	30	21	33	27	12	30	35
Other sites	44	13	1	9	2	0	5	9	12	39	11	30
APPROX COUNTY TOTAL	86	47	117	62	62	30	30	46	41	65	68	147

Passage was rather erratic with the following counts of five or more in spring and no sizeable movement thereafter until Nov 2nd:

Hayling Bay: 8 E, May12th.
Hill Head: 5 E, Mar 13th; 14 E, May 4th; 5 W, May 17th; 16 E, Nov 2nd.
Needs Ore/Lepe: 14 E, Mar 23rd; 9 E, Apr18th; 7 W, 20th; 13 E 27th; 8 W, May 5th; 11 W, 12th.
Hurst Beach/Milford on Sea: 10 W, Apr 21st; 24 W, May 12th.

Long-tailed Duck *Clangula hyemalis*

A very scarce winter visitor and passage migrant.

A total of six was observed with three past Hurst/Milford on Sea and three also in Langstone Harbour.

Off Hurst Beach/Milford on Sea an adult male flew east on May 26th (MPM); following several days of gales in the late year an adult male flew west on Nov 8th (MPM) and a first-winter flew east on Nov 12th (MPM). In Langstone Harbour, a first-winter was at Farlington Marshes from Nov 23rd-25th (JCr, RAC, TJJ) and two (an immature male and a female) lingered in Langstone Channel between Dec 16th and 27th (JCr).

Common Scoter
Melanitta nigra

A moderately common passage migrant; small numbers usually summer.

The majority of records in Hampshire of Common Scoter are coastal and refer to migrating and resting birds. Migrating birds, which are primarily recorded in spring, mostly pass to the south of the Isle of Wight and not through The Solent and are therefore only potentially visible from the extreme west and east ends of the county. The records in 2002 reflected this.

Significant easterly passage included: 72 past Stokes Bay on Mar 30th; 187 past Milford on Sea on Apr 6th; 99 past Hurst Castle and 101 past Sandy Point on Apr 17th.

One or two birds were recorded in Langstone Harbour in most months of the year, with a peak count of four on Sep 25th. Several summered off Hill Head, with the count peaking at 21 in August.

Inland, a pair was on Ellingham Lake, Blashford on the evening of July 14th for at least one hour.

The monthly totals for passage and resting birds are tabulated below, followed by the county totals:

	J	F	M	A	M	J	J	A	S	O	N	D
Passage												
Hayling Island	0	0	4	125	69	12	30	6	0	0	0	0
Stokes Bay	4	2	73	21	7	0	0	0	17	0	0	0
Hook-with-Warsash	8	0	0	1	0	0	11	20	0	2	1	0
Lymington/Hurst	10	7	5	403	186	53	77	5	0	39	67	21
Resting Birds												
Hill Head	4	8	20	2	12	19	15	21	4	15	14	10
Needs Ore	10	3	0	1	0	0	0	15	12	1	0	0
APPROX COUNTY TOTAL	**36**	**20**	**100**	**550**	**270**	**84**	**135**	**67**	**33**	**57**	**82**	**31**

Velvet Scoter
Melanitta fusca

A scarce passage migrant and winter visitor.

A much better year than in 2001 with approximately 35 past Hurst Beach some of which rested on the sea for a few days, peak counts were nine on Mar 31st and six on Nov 21st. Six also lingered off Hill Head in mid-November.

The county total is difficult to ascertain but probably exceeded 40. Records were as follows:

Stokes Bay: 3 E, Mar 30th.
Hill Head: 6, Nov 17th-24th.
Park Shore/Needs Ore: 4 W, Nov 10th.
Hurst Beach: 1, Jan 1st; 6, Mar 30th; 9, Mar 31st; 2E, Apr 6th; 3W, Apr 9th; 2 E, May 7th; 1, May 12th; 1, May 16th; 2, Oct 22nd; 4 W, Nov 10th; 2 W, Nov 12th; 6, Nov 21st; 1, Nov 23rd; 1, Nov 27th; 1 E Dec 28th.

Goldeneye
Bucephala clangula

A moderately common winter visitor.

The eastern harbours of Chichester, Langstone and Portsmouth held the majority of wintering birds. Very few birds remained into April and most returned from November onwards. The monthly totals for principal locations are tabulated below, followed by the county totals:

	J	F	M	A	M	J	J	A	S	O	N	D
Chichester Harbour	27	51	28	0	0	0	0	0	0	0	38	48
Langstone Harbour	41	47	32	1	0	0	0	0	0	6	24	50
Portsmouth Harbour	42	19	20	0	0	0	0	0	0	0	19	44
Dibden Bay	6	9	4	0	0	0	0	0	0	0	0	3
Lymington/Hurst	12	12	4	0	0	0	0	0	0	0	3	19
Blashford Lakes	16	16	11	0	0	0	0	0	0	0	6	13
Lower Test Marshes/Eling	6	11	0	0	0	0	0	0	0	0	0	7
APPROX COUNTY TOTAL	**157**	**167**	**100**	**2**	**0**	**0**	**0**	**0**	**0**	**7**	**93**	**187**

Away from these sites, very few birds were recorded. Inland single birds were at Alresford Pond on Jan 24th, Broadlands Lake on Mar 3rd, Fleet Pond on Apr 24th, Wellington CP on Oct 23rd, Woolmer Pond from Nov 10th-13th, Dogmersfield Lake on Nov 17th, The Vyne on Nov 27th and Yateley GP on Dec 9th.

Smew   *Mergus albellus*

A very scarce winter visitor.

It was a better year than 2001 with a total of eight, two males and six redheads. Seven were in the in the Avon valley in the first winter period with one in the second.

All but one record was from the Blashford Lakes complex. A male and two redheads were reported on Spinnaker Lake on Jan 3rd; these and a further three redheads were reported 4th-6th. Thereafter numbers declined as birds left Spinnaker Lake for Mockbeggar and Linbrook Lakes. One to three, the male and two redheads, where seen between Feb 6th and 26th and one to two redheads between Mar 10th and 13th. A male returned to Linbrook Lake on Dec 30th/31st.

Elsewhere, a redhead was at Sopley on Jan 15th/16th.

Red-breasted Merganser   *Mergus serrator*

A moderately common winter visitor and passage migrant; rare inland.

The eastern harbours of Chichester, Langstone and Portsmouth held the majority of wintering birds. Very few birds remained into May and they generally returned through October and November.

Monthly maxima at the principal localities and the estimated monthly totals across the county are tabulated below.

	J	F	M	A	M	J	J	A	S	O	N	D
Chichester Harbour	144	156	159	23	1	0	0	0	0	3	134	180
Langstone Harbour	92	71	198	68		0	0	0	2	55	90	107
Portsmouth Harbour	73	36	125	0	0	0	0	1	0	0	79	126
Weston Shore/Dibden Bay	24	10	20	0	0	0	0	0	0	0	0	0
Hamble Estuary	3	7	2	0	0	0	0	0	0	4	0	11
Beaulieu Estuary	7	10	27	15	0	0	0	0	0	4	3	7
Lymington/Hurst	50	54	16	5	0	0	0	2	1	10	92	70
Titchfield Haven / Hill Head	11	7	15	4	1	0	0	0	0	1	2	3
APPROX COUNTY TOTAL	**410**	**360**	**565**	**125**	**1**	**0**	**0**	**3**	**3**	**77**	**410**	**520**

Away from the principal sites, up to eight were in The Solent off Pitts Deep on Apr 14th and six were recorded in Emsworth Mill Pond on Dec 2nd.

On the coast, there was some evidence of movements with peak counts of 13 east on Apr 17th and 35 west on Nov 11th. Passage birds were noted as follows:

Hayling Island: 2 E, Feb 28th; 2 W, Apr 3rd; 13 E, Apr 17th.
Stokes Bay: 1 E, Apr 20th; 2 E, Apr 21st; 2 E, Dec 6th.
Needs Ore: 3 W, Oct 5th; 4 W, Oct 19th.
Hurst Beach: 35 W, Nov 11th.

Goosander   *Mergus merganser*

A scarce winter visitor and recently established very scarce breeder.

There are two main concentrations in the county, centred on roosts in the Avon and Blackwater valleys. Birds feeding on the River Avon during the day return at dusk to the Blashford Lakes complex to roost, which perhaps also attracts birds from further afield including Dorset. The peak count was 30 at Mockbeggar Lake on Feb 23rd including nine males. Birds from several sites in the north-east of the county roost at Eversley GP, where they are joined by birds from Berkshire. The peak count of 45 at Eversley GP was on Jan 3rd and included 26 adult males.

In the Avon valley, breeding was confirmed at Bickerley Common where a female was seen with ten young on June 11th. Five were still present on August 11th (as pictured on left).

Breeding was confirmed for the second year running in the Avon Valley (John Levell)

Passage was noted as follows:

Hurst Beach: 1 W, Jan 27th; 1 E, Feb 10th;
Pennington Marsh: 1 juvenile, E July 22nd.
Tipner Lake: 3 redheads E, Dec 10th.

Monthly maxima at the principal localities and the monthly totals for the county are tabulated below. Birds seen in the vicinity of one of the roosts are assumed to be included in the count for that roost. Note that these totals include records for all sites, not just those shown in the table.

	J	F	M	A	M	J	J	A	S	O	N	D
Blashford Lakes (roost)	19	30	13	1	0	0	0	0	0	0	2	23
Broadlands Lake	-	7	-	-	-	-	-	-	-	-	-	2
Eversley GP (roost)	45	16	9	-	-	-	-	-	-	-	24	34
Tundry Pond	12	7	5	0	0	0	0	0	0	0	9	15
Bramshill Police College	5	18	6	0	0	0	0	0	0	0	0	12
Bramshill Plantation	6	2	3	0	0	0	0	0	0	0	1	8
Yateley GP	17	7	0	0	0	0	0	0	0	0	4	4
APPROX COUNTY TOTAL	**69**	**53**	**28**	**4**	**3**	**12**	**1**	**5**	**0**	**3**	**32**	**62**

The 15 reported from Tundry Pond on Dec 13th including seven males. Winter peak county totals for the ten year period 1992/93-2001/2 are as follows:

Winter peak	92/93	93/94	94/95	95/96	96/97	97/98	98/99	99/00	00/01	01/02
Goosander	33	79	41	132	210	85	79	73	47	55

Inland, there was a first record for Black Dam NR, Basingstoke with a male south-west on Jan 6th.

Ruddy Duck
Oxyura jamaicensis

A scarce resident and winter visitor.

The only sites with significant numbers of birds were, once again, Alresford Pond and Blashford Lakes.

The monthly maxima of birds at the principal sites are tabulated below, followed by the countywide totals:

	J	F	M	A	M	J	J	A	S	O	N	D
Blashford Lakes	2	5	6	3	4	0	0	0	1	1	0	2
Alresford Pond	1	-	6	10	10	8	7	2	0	0	0	0
APPROX COUNTY TOTAL	5	5	21	19	20	8	8	4	4	4	2	2

During the breeding season three pairs were present at Alresford Pond and two at Timsbury GP.

Elsewhere two males and a female were seen at Zion's Hill Pond between Mar17th and May 5th, there was a pair at Wellington CP on May 11th, three at Fleet Pond on Sep 4th and three first-winters at Lakeside CP on Sep 13th. Records of single birds came from ten other sites.

Honey Buzzard
Pernis apivorus

A very scarce summer visitor and passage migrant.

In May, the first arrival noted was one moving north over Keyhaven on 8th. Further presumed migrants moved north-east over Fleet Pond on 12th, east over Barton on Sea and north over Awbridge on 17th and north over Stokes Bay the next day.

During the breeding season seven to eight pairs were located, with five known to have bred successfully each rearing two young. Birds were at breeding sites between May 15th and Sep 5th. Additionally, single birds were seen over Winklebury, Basingstoke on June 17th, at Bickton on June 21st and in the Test valley on Aug 25th.

A total of 11 presumed migrants was recorded in autumn. The first was one circling over Milford on Sea on Aug 27th. One moved SSE over Dibden Purlieu and another landed in poplars at Daw Lane, Hayling Island on Sep 2nd. A juvenile moved south-east over Petersfield on Sep 5th, one south over Lower Test Marshes on 7th and another south-east over Ower (Romsey) on 8th. One drifted south over Keyhaven at 0710 hrs on Sep 9th and was then joined by two more. A pale phase juvenile flew north-east over Langstone Harbour on Sep 12th and one moved east over Needs Ore on 13th.

Red Kite
Milvus milvus

A scarce visitor, but becoming more frequent due to the presence of released birds in southern England, and has bred in the county at least once in recent years.

As shown in the table below, records were received for all months with a clear peak between March and June. However, there was no suggestion of breeding at any locality:

J	F	M	A	M	J	J	A	S	O	N	D
1	5	15	17	8	17	2	1	3	1	3	2

Records of possible migrants at coastal sites came from Keyhaven on Mar 7th, 12th and 25th, Hayling Island on Mar 12th, Titchfield Haven on Apr 1st, 7th, 10th, 21st and June 1st and Farlington Marshes on Apr 21st. One or two were present in the Cheesefoot Head area between Feb 23rd and Apr 17th and from Oct 9th into 2003. An incredible seven moved west over Sheepwash Farm, west of Waterlooville, on June 5th. Other records, all of single birds on one date only unless otherwise stated, came from: Alresford, Beacon Hill, Bisterne, Bramley, Bricksbury Hill (1, Feb 18th; 2, Feb 27th), Bullington Cross, Calthorpe Park (Fleet), Carpenters Down Wood, East Meon, Eversley GP, Faccombe, Hannington (2, June 7th), Hale, Itchen Stoke, Itchen Valley CP (May 17th and June 5th), Kingsclere, lower Test valley (five sightings between Feb 21st and June 2nd), Medstead, Minley, the New Forest (nine sightings between Mar 17th and June 5th, including one of two together on May 27th; three sightings between Sep 25th and Dec 19th), Old Winchester Hill (1, Jan 11th-21st and Apr 23rd), Preston Candover, Rownhams, Shedfield Common, Somerley Park (Mar 7th and June 5th), Steep, Stratfield Saye Park, Tidbury Common, Whitchurch and Wickham Common.

1995 addition: One pair apparently bred and raised two young.

1996 addition: One pair bred and raised three young, all of which were wing-tagged by English Nature. This was the first confirmed breeding in Hampshire since 1864. Unfortunately, the birds did not nest in the following year and in fact there has been no further evidence of successful nesting since in the county.

Marsh Harrier
Circus aeruginosus

A scarce visitor, most frequent in spring and autumn but occasional in mid winter; has bred once, in 1957.

The records received probably referred to around 25 individuals, the lowest total since 1998. However, the recent trend of wintering in the county was maintained with a male present at Titchfield Haven at both ends of the year.

The second-winter male present at Titchfield Haven in late 2001 remained until Apr 10th. Other early year records of males at Park Shore on Jan 22nd, Hook-with-Warsash on Feb 20th, Lepe on Feb 26th and Keyhaven on Mar 5th possibly referred to the Titchfield individual.

Presumed spring migrants were a female at Titchfield Haven on Mar 23rd, 29th and Apr 10th, a male at Needs Ore on Apr 5th and 9th, one north-west over Timsbury on Apr 28th, an immature male north over Pig Bush on May 1st, a female over Lyndhurst on May 2nd, a female/immature ENE over Farlington Marshes on May 12th, an adult male east over Hurst Beach on May 16th, a male at Itchen Valley CP on May 23rd and one seen moving north-east from Hurst Beach on June 12th.

What was presumably the previous winter's male returned to Titchfield Haven on July 16th and remained until the year's end. Other sightings from there were of female/immatures on July 18th, Aug 1st and 9th. Further reports of autumn migrants were of a female south-west over Tweseldown (Fleet) on July 31st, another south-west over Hook-with-Warsash on the same day, a juvenile hunting over saltmarsh at the north end of Portsmouth Harbour on Aug 4th, female/juveniles at Langstone Harbour on Aug 6th, 17th, 18th, 24th, 28th and Oct 7th, female/juveniles at Keyhaven on Aug 15th, Sep 1st, 5th and 11th, single birds at Lower Test Marshes on Aug 24th, Sep 10th and 28th and one flying east over Stokes Bay on Sep 9th.

Away from Titchfield Haven, the only sightings after Oct 7th were of a single bird at Needs Ore on Nov 7th, Dec 3rd and 10th (reported as a female on the final date) and a male at Bisterne on Dec 10th.

The minimum monthly totals are tabulated below:

J	F	M	A	M	J	J	A	S	O	N	D
1	1	2	4	3	1	3	5	4	2	2	2

Hen Harrier   *Circus cyaneus*

A scarce winter visitor and passage migrant.

In January and February, there were regular reports from three areas, with up to five males and three ringtails roosting in the New Forest, one ringtail roosting at a site in the east of the county and two ringtails roosting at Alresford Pond. The only other records at this time involved a male and a ringtail at Martin Down, a male at Danebury and a ringtail at Needs Ore, all on single January dates. There was evidence of passage in spring, with a male in the Pennington/Keyhaven Marsh area from Mar 1st-Apr 9th and single birds on one date only between Mar 2nd and Apr 21st at Kings Somborne, Needs Ore, Ashley Warren, Preston Candover, Martin Down, Whitsbury Down, Cheesefoot Head, Hurst Beach and Long Valley. Possibly three males were still present in the New Forest in the first week of April with the latest at Yew Tree Heath on 21st, while at Alresford Pond the last was on Apr 27th.

An adult male flew in off the sea at Hurst Beach and moved off high to the north-east on June 2nd (MPM). This is only the third ever in that month.

Three were seen in September: a ringtail moving north over Horndean on 16th, a male at Bishop's Dyke on 21st and a ringtail at Pennington Marsh on 26th/27th. Further returns were evident from mid October, with at least one male and one ringtail in the north-west of the New Forest from 12th and a ringtail at Woolmer Pond the next day.

In November and December, records indicate that up to five males and four ringtails were roosting in the New Forest. The only other records were of a ringtail at Woolmer Pond on Nov 7th, one at Hazeley Heath on Nov 29th and a male roosting at Alresford Pond from Dec 15th into 2003.

The approximate monthly totals are tabulated below:

J	F	M	A	M	J	J	A	S	O	N	D
15	8	17	9	0	1	0	0	3	3	11	8

The map below shows the distribution of all Hen Harrier records in 1992-2002:

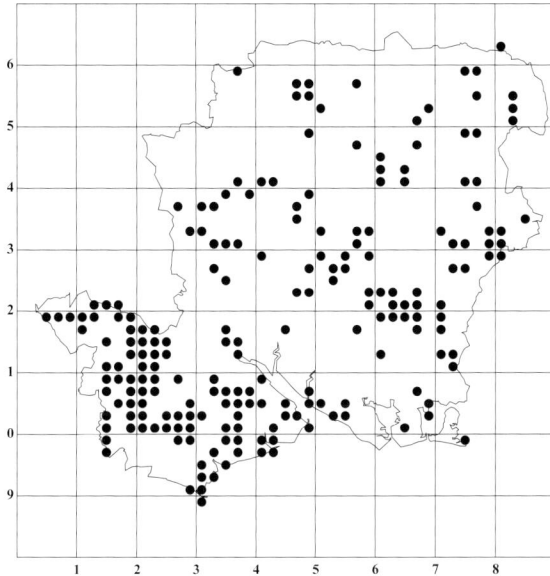

Hen Harrier records in Hampshire 1992-2002

Montagu's Harrier   *Circus pygargus*

A very scarce passage migrant and summer visitor.

It was a good year, with at least six reported in spring between Apr 24th and May 21st, at least two during the breeding season and four in autumn between July 31st and Aug 26th. However, there were no reports of breeding being attempted in the county.

The first was a female at Martin Down on Apr 24th. A series of records in May comprised a first-summer male at Black Gutter Bottom and Ocknell Plain on 4th, a male at Martin on 5th, a female there on 8th, another female in the Beaulieu Road area on 8th/9th, a male moving high to the south over Ocknell Plain on 11th, a male at Ibsley on 15th and a female at Keyhaven on 21st.

During the summer adult males were at Martin Down from June 14th-18th, at Hampton Ridge on June 28th and Broomy Bottom on July 13th. A female was at Southwick on June 27th.

In autumn, a ringtail was at Sway on July 29th, a juvenile was at Hook-with-Warsash on Aug 17th and an adult male flew high to the south over Longcross Plain on Aug 26th.

The HOS *Records Panel* would appreciate observers continuing to submit brief notes to support sightings of this species and also to remind them that the possibility of Pallid Harrier should not be forgotten!

Goshawk   *Accipiter gentilis*

A very scarce resident.

Goshawk (Steve Roberts)

Two pairs bred successfully in the New Forest, raising a total of at least six young (WP, AP, AL). After many years of rumour and counter-rumour about this species breeding in Hampshire, this exciting development has been fully documented in a paper at the end of this Report.

The only records away from the breeding area with adequate supporting notes involved single birds at three separate sites in the south of the county on Apr 2nd, 4th and Aug 12th.

Sparrowhawk   *Accipiter nisus*

A common resident, passage migrant and probable winter visitor.

In the New Forest study area, the survey was conducted along the same lines as in previous years and aimed to check all known breeding sites. Coverage was deemed at least comparable with previous years yet only 22 nests were located compared with a mean of 30 during 1997-2001. Of the 22 nests, only one failed late into incubation and the rest successfully reared young. A minimum of 83 young and 11 unhatched eggs was recorded. Of 73 young that were ringed, 43 were males and 30 were females. Despite the low total of nests located, their productivity was exceptionally good, averaging at least 4.0 chicks per successful nest and 3.8 for all nests found (AP *et al*). Elsewhere, evidence of breeding was obtained for 11 pairs, with five known to have raised young.

One arriving off the sea at Hayling Bay on Apr 14th was the only indication of possible migration.

Buzzard
Buteo buteo

A moderately common and increasing resident, passage migrant and possible winter visitor.

In the New Forest study area, 41 territories were occupied with 16 nests producing at least 25 young. The apparent reduction compared with 2001, when 55 territories were located, is partly attributed to many pairs moving to new sites and their nests not being located (JMT *et al*). In addition, six pairs raised eight young at Roydon Woods. In the Avon valley, there were eight pairs on the Bisterne Estate and 12 at Somerley Park. Records of displaying birds in February-April in other areas of the county totalled around 270 at 52 sites/areas, including 27 over Broadlands Estate and surrounding woodlands on Feb 10th, 27 between Morestead and Longwood Warren on Mar 16th and 14 seen from Casbrook Common on Mar 29th.

With the spread of Buzzards to virtually all parts of Hampshire, it is increasingly difficult to obtain evidence for genuine movements into or out the county. Perhaps the most significant sightings came from the Langstone Harbour/Hayling Island area, where 13 were seen in spring between Mar 23rd and May 11th including birds arriving off the sea on Mar 23rd, Apr 23rd and 25th and 13 in autumn between Sep 2nd and Oct 24th including seven soaring over West Hayling Shore on Sep 2nd, three of which moved off high to the west. The only other sighting in this area was of one on Dec 5th.

Rough-legged Buzzard
Buteo lagopus

A rare winter visitor and passage migrant (11,43,1)

One flew south-west over Blackwater, Needs Ore between 1155 and 1200 hrs on Apr 5th (MJWH, BJP). This is the first since 1998.

Osprey
Pandion haliaetus

A scarce passage migrant.

The recent increase was maintained, with a total of 130 records submitted compared with 120 in 2001. Spring records, which are generally assumed to refer to birds moving quickly through the county, referred to around 25 individuals between Mar 17th and June 18th, while autumn records involved a minimum of 25 individuals between July 20th and Oct 5th. In contrast to spring, autumn birds often linger for several days or even weeks and thus birds noted at the same or adjacent locations over a long period are assumed to be the same.

The first early record was of a bird moving north-east over Lakeside CP, Eastleigh on Mar 17th. A small influx was apparent between Mar 29th and 31st, with reports from five sites during this period. Subsequent spring records were evenly spread through till May 17th, to be followed by a flurry of sightings at five sites between June 4th and 18th, with the latest at East Aston Common near Longparish.

The first returns were on July 20th, when single birds were noted at Harbridge and Keyhaven. However, the next was not until Aug 14th, when a juvenile was seen in Langstone Harbour. There were then virtually daily sightings until Oct 5th, with most coming from the Langstone Harbour area including three juveniles on Aug 29th and Sep 3rd, one adult and two juveniles on Sep 5th and 8th and three juveniles on Sep 12th. The last of the year was at Keyhaven and Hurst Castle on Oct 5th.

Individual records are listed below, followed by the approximate monthly totals:

Coast
Lymington/Hurst area: 1 NE, Mar 29th; 1, Apr 12th; 1 N, Apr 15th; juv N, July 20th; 1 S, Aug 21st; 1 SW, Aug 28th; juv, Sep 11th-17th; adult, Oct 2nd-5th.

Titchfield Haven: 1, Mar 29th left E; 1, May 3rd, left E; 1, Aug 21st/22nd; 2, Sep 12th; 1, Sep 21st; 1, Oct 3rd.

Stokes Bay: 1, Mar 30th.

Beaulieu Estuary/Lepe: 1, Apr 3rd; 1 N, May 14th; 1, Aug 17th-Sep 3rd with 2, Aug 26th; 1, Sep 19th.

Langstone Harbour: 1, May 8th, 10th and 12th; 1 SE, June 4th; up to one adult and 3 juvs, Aug 14th-Sep 27th.

Pylewell: 1 SE, May 17th.

Hook-with-Warsash: 1 SW to Fawley, Aug 22nd (presumably the Upper Hamble Estuary bird).

Upper Hamble Estuary: juv, Aug 24th-31st; 1, Sep 21st.

Lower Test Marshes: 1, Aug 27th; 1, Sep 20th (assumed to be Upper Hamble Estuary birds).

Cams Bay, Portsmouth Harbour: 1 SW, Sep 5th.

Sowley Pond: 1, Sep 17th (assumed to be the Lymington/Hurst bird).

Chichester Harbour: adult, Sep 18th (assumed to be a Langstone Harbour bird).

Inland
Lakeside CP, Eastleigh: 1 NE, Mar 17th; 1, May 17th left S.

Beaulieu Road area: 1 NE, Mar 30th; first-summer, June 8th; 1 W, Aug 29th.

Alresford Pond: 1, Mar 31st left N; 1 N, Apr 28th; 1, May 1st.

Old Winchester Hill: 1, Apr 3rd; 1, June 10th.

Setley Plain, NF: 1 N, Apr 25th.

Beaulieu Heath East: 1, Apr 27th.

Testwood Lakes: 1 N, May 12th.

Stratfield Saye Park: 1, June 6th.

East Aston Common: 1, June 18th.

Ibsley area: 1, July 20th; 1, Aug 30th-Sep 8th.

Pipers Waite/Longcross Plain, NF: 1 S, Aug 22nd; 1 S, Sep 1st.

Mockbeggar NF: 1, Sep 7th (assumed to be the Ibsley bird).

Milkham Inclosure, NF: 1, Sep 8th (assumed to be the Ibsley bird).

Bisterne, R. Avon: juv, Sep 22nd and 29th.

Southampton Common: 1 S, Oct 3rd.

J	F	M	A	M	J	J	A	S	O	N	D
0	0	6	7	7	5	2	12	14	3	0	0

Kestrel   *Falco tinnunculus*
A common resident, passage migrant and winter visitor.

Evidence of breeding was obtained for 21 pairs, but only five of these were reported to have bred successfully, raising a total of 13 young. This clearly represents only a small proportion of the pairs in the county.

Merlin   *Falco columbarius*
A scarce winter visitor and passage migrant.

Another excellent year, with 220 records submitted compared with 215 in 2001. Around 90 sightings for the period up to May 24th involved at least 32 individuals and 120 for the period from Aug 22nd involved a minimum of 26 individuals.

In the early year, there were regular reports from Langstone Harbour, the Beaulieu Estuary, the Lymington-Hurst area and the New Forest involving a minimum of 15 individuals. Also of note were records of one roosting at Alresford Pond on Feb 11th and 14th and up to two males and two female/immatures in the Exton/West End Down area between Feb 2nd and Mar 3rd. The remaining sightings referred to single birds on one or two dates only at Ashley Warren, Cheesefoot Head, Dibden Bay, Eversley GP, Faccombe, Fawley, Fleet Pond, Great Litchfield Down, Marchwood, Old Winchester Hill and Winchfield. The last were at Farlington Marshes on Apr 18th and Needs Ore on Apr 27th apart from a late male at Beaulieu Road on May 24th.

The first return was a juvenile at Langstone Harbour on Aug 22nd; a second bird on Sep 13th joined this but the next elsewhere was at Titchfield Haven on Sep 22nd. Subsequent records from the New Forest and the three main coastal sites involved a minimum of 14 individuals including three at Needs Ore on Oct 8th. Single birds were at Titchfield Haven on Sep 22nd/23rd, Nov 15th and Dec 31st and at Testwood Lakes on Dec 1st, 15th and 22nd. The remaining sightings referred to single birds on one date only at Barton on Sea, Cheesefoot Head, Hook-with-Warsash, Martin Down, Pitts Deep, Taddiford Gap and Warblington.

The approximate monthly totals are tabulated below:

J	F	M	A	M	J	J	A	S	O	N	D
14	12	11	6	1	0	0	1	5	12	13	11

The maps below show the distribution of all Merlin records in 2002, and for all records on the county database:

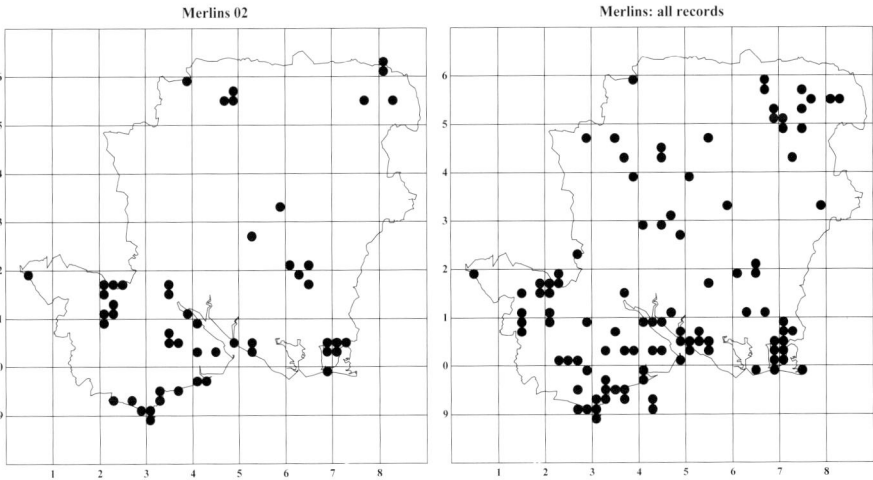

Merlin: distribution of records (left) for 2002 (right) all county records

Hobby
Falco subbuteo

A moderately common summer visitor and passage migrant.

Following last year's earliest ever observation of one arriving off the sea at Hurst on Mar 29th, two were at Old Winchester Hill on Mar 16th and then one or two were there on four dates up to Mar 30th (DKC). The next were at St Cross, Winchester on Apr 8th and Dibden Purlieu on Apr 14th, with daily sightings from Apr 20th. Only three were noted arriving off the sea and reported pre-breeding concentrations were also smaller than in recent years, with a maximum of seven at Bishop's Dyke on May 27th.

Breeding season records came from around 60 locations. Of these, breeding was confirmed at only six sites (with six pairs raising at least 10 young), pairs were noted at 28 sites and single birds at 25 sites.

Sightings continued throughout September but there was evidently a rapid departure in early October, with the last four at a breeding site on 3rd and one at Titchfield Haven on 4th apart from a late bird at Woolmer Pond on Oct 11th, 13th and 23rd.

Peregrine
Falco peregrinus

A scarce but increasing resident; numbers are augmented throughout the year by visitors from neighbouring counties. Probably also a passage migrant and winter visitor from further afield.

Records for January to March indicate that around 40 were present in the county. Away from known nesting areas, these included three at Stratfield Saye/Sherfield-on-Loddon on Jan 3rd and three at Ashley Warren on Jan 16th. Other inland areas with frequent sightings included Basingstoke Town Centre, with one on seven dates between Jan 12th and Mar 31st and Old Winchester Hill, with one on seven dates between Jan 18th and Mar 24th.

The *BTO Peregrine Breeding Survey* confirmed the presence of pairs on Fawley power station chimney (2 young raised), Sway Tower (two breeding attempts both failed) and on pylons at Marchwood (at least one young raised) and Ower (two young raised). A further pair occupied a suitable pylon at Applemore from March until early May but apparently did not breed. Most coastal sightings probably involved birds from these pairs or visitors from the Isle of Wight, although yet again frequent records of up to four different birds at Langstone Harbour in May and June suggest a local pair, possibly on a building in the Portsmouth Dockyard area. It would be appreciated if any observer could establish the whereabouts of this nest! Regular sightings in the New Forest and the Avon valley presumably originate from known nests in Hampshire or adjoining counties. Elsewhere inland, there were reports from several sites in or adjacent to the Test, Itchen and Meon Valleys which might indicate pairs nesting on pylons or other suitable structures.

Records for October to December indicate that around 35 were present in the county including three at Pennington/Keyhaven Marsh on Oct 14th, three at Needs Ore on Nov 17th and three at Lower Test Marshes on Nov 26th. Inland areas with frequent sightings included Old Winchester Hill, with one on eight dates between Oct 5th and Dec 30th and the upper Itchen Valley/Cheesefoot Head area, with at least two from Oct 9th until the year's end.

2001 correction: The record of breeding at Southampton Civic Centre should be deleted.

The map below shows the distribution of all Peregrine records in 2002.

Peregrines 2002

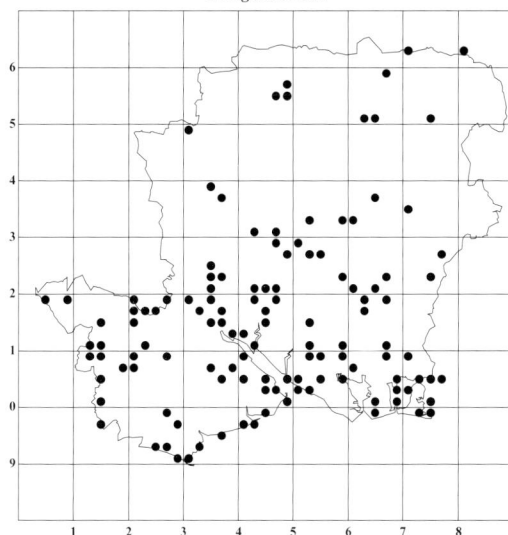

	1993	1994	1995	1996	1997	1998	1999	2000	2001	2002
Honey Buzzard	6	2	7	6	3	14	8	124	11	16
Red Kite	13	20	38	50	26	37	83	48	59	73
Marsh Harrier	28	42	42	32	34	27	34	55	62	30
Hen Harrier	89	83	88	97	102	113	112	89	54	75
Montagu's Harrier	4	8	6	9	5	5	6	7	3	16
Osprey	42	36	25	35	36	36	74	50	55	56
Merlin	86	90	70	83	64	70	69	83	94	86

Selected raptors 1993-2002(annual totals of bird-months excluding any breeding birds)

Red-legged Partridge   *Alectoris rufa*

A common resident; numbers are supplemented by releases.

A total of 40 records was received. In the early part of the year the only large covey reported was of 20 at Gander Down on Feb 3rd.

Autumn reports in excess of 30 were 76 at Blackfield on Sep 14th, 100 at Old Winchester Hill on Sep 19th, 200 at Coombe on Oct 13th, 36 at Cheesefoot Head on Oct 29th, 50 at Kingsclere on Nov 7th, 40 at Old Winchester Hill on Nov 29th, 60 at Ashley Warren on Dec 29th and 45 at Chilcomb on Dec 28th. (Most of these large concentrations are assumed to be birds released for shooting purposes).

Grey Partridge   *Perdix perdix*

A common or moderately common, but declining, resident.

There were 61 records from 35 sites with principal sites around Odiham, the Itchen Valley,

Winchester and at Martin Down. In the early year, the largest covey reported was 12 at Ashley Warren on Jan 8th (14 in total there). There were also of 11 at Hillside, Odiham on Jan 6th and 21st, Fobdown, Alresford on Jan 8th, Beacon Hill, Warnford on Jan 11th and Ewhurst Park on Jan 13th.

During the breeding season, a total of 20 pairs was reported as follows: seven at Martin Down; two each at Cheesefoot Head, East Meon, Long Down and Odiham Airfield and singles at Arlebury Water Meadows, Exton, Gander Down, Itchen Stoke and Long Sutton.

The largest gatherings subsequently were of 21 at Newfound, near Basingstoke on Sep 15th, 25 at Cheesefoot Head on Oct 12th, 12 at Hillside, Odiham on Oct 19th, 10 at Hillside, Odiham on Dec 9th, 14 at Four Lanes End on Dec 16th and 17 at Leckford on Dec 28th.

Quail   *Coturnix coturnix*
A very scarce and erratic summer visitor.

A poor year with just seven reported. The first was one at Martin Down on May 7th (LS). Through June and July there were the following reports of single birds calling: Bourley South/Bricksbury Hill on June 2nd (JAE), Martin Down on June 14th (LS), Sinah Common on June 23rd (TAL) and Farley Mount on July 28th (AW). Single birds were seen in Sep, one at Droxford on Sep 7th (DM) and the other at Abbotswood, Romsey on Sep 17th (DAT) where it was flushed twice in scrubby grassland with reasonable views obtained.

Pheasant   *Phasianus colchicus*
An abundant resident, the wild population being supplemented by releases.

Only 32 records were received and half of these were from the Langstone Harbour area, where records were previously unusual, and included a female on North Binness Island in June and November and seven on Farlington Marshes in October. Garden records were noted in Winchester and Chandlers Ford. Data on breeding territories was limited to two sites (Longstock, 7 and Longmoor Inclosure, 13).

Golden Pheasant   *Chrysolophus pictus*
A very scarce introduced resident.

This species appears to be virtually extinct in the county. There was one report of a single male at Lyeways Farm, Ropley on Aug 31st/Sep 1st (GHH).

Water Rail   *Rallus aquaticus*
A scarce resident, moderately common passage migrant and winter visitor.

Around 231 records were submitted from 61 localities and compares with 120 from 38 localities as recently as 1998.

The species was again under-recorded in the breeding season. There were eight territories at Titchfield Haven, one at Hook Lake, a singing male on five dates at Farlington Marshes (and a juvenile on Aug 10th), a recently fledged juvenile at St Cross, Winchester on June 25th and a pair with five young at Avon Water, Keyhaven on June 18th. Up to three were heard on four dates at Alresford Pond and breeding was strongly suspected at Stratfield Saye Park for the first time. Elsewhere during the breeding season single birds were recorded at 14 locations on one or two dates only. In addition, a juvenile was noted at Springhead, Greywell on Aug 31st.

Outside the breeding season, the only significant counts were 12 at Fleet Pond on Oct 25th, seven at Itchen Valley CP on Nov 9th and 17 at Titchfield Haven on Dec 16th.

Spotted Crake   *Porzana porzana*

A very scarce passage migrant (most frequent in autumn) and winter visitor; has bred (?,120,3).

A below average year with just three reported in the autumn. Single birds were at Woolmer Pond on Sep 7th (PT) and at Titchfield Haven on Aug 11th (P&SM, BSD) and Aug 20th-22nd (BSD).

Moorhen   *Gallinula chloropus*

A numerous resident and winter visitor.

Totals from *WeBS* counts gave early and late year peaks of 772 at 47 sites in January and 601 at 46 sites in December. The highest count of the year was of 61 in Portsmouth Harbour on Dec 7th. Counts in excess of 35 were made at ten sites as listed below:

Farlington Marshes : 58 (partial count), Oct 10th.
Portsmouth Harbour: 47, Jan 12th; 61, Dec 7th.
Titchfield Haven: 51, Mar 5th; 36, Dec 16th.
Avon valley, Sopley-Avon Causeway: 47, Jan 13th; 40, Mar 3rd.
Avon valley, above Fordingbridge: 47, Feb 10th; 52, Sep 29th.
Lower Test Marshes: 48, Oct 5th; 36, Dec 7th.
River Test, Stockbridge-Fullerton: 48, Jan 27th; 47, Mar 2nd; 39, Mar 31st.
Polhampton: 47, Mar 15th.
Ashe (source of R. Test): 37, Feb 10th.
Winnall Moors: 39, Jan 14th; 41, Dec 8th.

During the breeding season the only significant reports were of 20 pairs along the Basingstoke Canal, 20 territories at Lower Test Marshes and 28 at Titchfield Haven.

Coot   *Fulica atra*

A common resident and winter visitor.

Coot winter numbers have increased lately, matching national trends, to peaks of 3334 in 2000/2001 and 3545 in 2001/2002.

Away from Blashford Lakes, which again held a nationally important concentration, only 12 sites held in excess of 100 at any time. Monthly maxima at the main localities are tabulated overleaf.

	J	F	M	A	M	J	J	A	S	O	N	D
Sowley Pond	120	-	-	-	-	-	-	-	-	-	-	-
Blashford Lakes	1420	161	140	82	-	218	322	540	1086	1318	1243	1137
Ringwood-Fordingbridge, R. Avon	-	-	143	-	-	-	-	-	-	-	-	-
Ibsley-Bickton, R. Avon	32	140	-	-	-	-	-	-	2	6	24	92
Broadlands Estate	34	106	84	-	-	-	-	-	21	27	7	33
Stockbridge-Fullerton, R. Test	109	-	105	-	-	-	-	-	-	-	58	74
Ashe (source of R. Test)	89	146	130	94	-	-	-	-	-	-	6	-
Allington GP	80	24	28	-	-	-	-	-	41	85	117	75
Alresford Pond	12	5	16	-	34	118	156	205	172	211	16	4
Wellington CP	50	96	84	-	19	-	65	83	149	213	218	110
Dogmersfield Lake	20	45	26	-	-	-	28	32	57	65	121	71
Eversley GP	378	49	26	25	26	15	-	-	146	182	234	228
Yateley GP	119	72	67	51	41	30	-	45	60	138	119	129

Counts in excess of 50 were made at 14 sites as listed below:

Chichester Harbour (Hants Sector): 73, Jan 12th.
Langstone Harbour: 76, Jan 12th.
Portsmouth Harbour: 55, Jan 12th; 57, Nov 16th; 82, Dec 7th.
Needs Ore: 51, Mar 3rd; 65, Sep 15th.
Avon valley, Sopley-Avon Causeway: 86, Jan 13th; 90, Mar 3rd.
Avon valley, above Fordingbridge: 54, Feb 10th.
Charlton Lakes: 59, Feb 10th; 60, Mar 3rd; 64, Nov 17th; 69, Dec 8th.
Shepherds Spring/Anton Lakes: 56, Nov 10th.
Rookesbury Mill: 60, Sep 8th; 52, Oct 6th; 54, Nov 16th.
Overton Lagoons: 54, July 31st; 72, Oct 4th; 61, Nov 17th.
Winchester SF: 67, Feb 18th; 63, Mar 2nd; 58, May 27th; 63, June 28th; 71, July 28th; 73 Aug 1st.
River Itchen, north of Winchester: 52, June 1st.
Northington: 64, Oct 6th.
Black Dam NR, Basingstoke: 52, Jan 7th; 56, May 12th; 56, June 27th; 55, July 3rd; 58, Aug 9th; 55, Sep 18th; 56, Oct 24th; 55, Nov (undated).

Double-figure counts of breeding pairs were made at Yateley GP, 30; Titchfield Haven, 17; Wellington CP, 16; Eversley GP, 15; Blashford Lakes, 14; Lower Test Marshes, 10; Stratfield Saye Park, 10.

Oystercatcher   *Haematopus ostralegus*

A moderately common breeding resident, common passage migrant and winter visitor.

Numbers in 2002 were broadly comparable to those in 2001. The breeding population declined further, but numbers in autumn rapidly built up to normal levels and remained remarkably stable to the end of the year.

A total of 91 breeding pairs/territories was recorded (down from 119 last year). Records were distributed as follows: 49 at Langstone Harbour, five at Paulsgrove Reclamation, four at Titchfield Haven, five at Hook-with-Warsash, 14 between Lymington and Hurst, 15 at Ibsley Water and singles at Fawley Refinery, Pitts Deep/Lymington River, and North Somerley Lakes.

Monthly maxima at the main localities and approximate monthly totals for the county are tabulated below:

	J	F	M	A	M	J	J	A	S	O	N	D
Chichester Harbour	718	464	788	527	287	-	519	1106	1199	1140	950	1398
East Hayling	120	140	68	43	13	-	10	7	40	78	104	201
Langstone Harbour	1970	1365	1201	325	470	405	641	1764	1748	2532	1576	1409
Portsmouth Harbour	433	305	132	-	-	-	4	-	169	83	371	408
Titchfield Haven	124	148	70	96	88	133	127	115	159	174	60	85
Hamble Estuary	144	145	41	60	55	6	47	206	300	200	190	186
Weston Shore	2	38	68	-	32	-	-	-	-	60	50	55
Lower Test/Eling/Bury Marshes	88	77	64	26	22	7	4	5	7	104	73	87
Dibden Bay	193	111	95	-	-	-	-	-	-	-	137	124
Langdown/Fawley/Calshot	264	313	82	70	106	2	112	386	528	325	391	317
Lepe	-	140	114	-	65	65	64	91	175	-	-	-
Needs Ore/Beaulieu Estuary	294	357	309	461	228	-	199	135	198	2	137	222
Sowley/Lymington	33	15	12	31	40	-	20	6	103	35	-	-
Lymington-Hurst	24	233	200	127	91	32	95	237	90	80	284	170
APPROX COUNTY TOTAL	3689	3387	2456	1239	1210	650	1323	2952	3517	3673	3373	3264

Inland, records came from: St Cross, Winchester (2, Jan 28th), Bisterne (2, Mar 24th; 2, Apr 6th and 14th), Hucklesbrook Lakes (2, Mar 25th), Overton Lagoons, (1, Apr 19th), Ashe (1, Apr 20th; 1 E, Apr 25th), Beaulieu (1, Apr 28th), Ibsley (2, May 3rd), Itchen Valley CP (1 S, June 3rd), Testwood Lakes (1, June 8th), Long Down (3 S, July 27th).

Black winged Stilt   *Himantopus himantopus*

A rare vagrant (5,13,2).

A pair was located on the south scrape at Titchfield Haven at 0600 hrs on April 19th, where they stayed all day (PR, BSD *et al*). They were not seen subsequently. The record has been accepted by *British Birds* and brings the county total to 20. The last was at Normandy Lagoon Apr 29th and then Farlington Marshes Apr 30th 2000.

Black-winged Stilts, Titchfield Haven (Dan Powell)

Avocet

Recurvirostra avosetta

A scarce passage migrant, winter visitor and very rare breeding bird.

It was a remarkable year, with approximately 141 recorded and the first record of breeding in Hampshire. Although the year total includes some possible duplication, this is easily a new county record. The only other year with a three-figure total was 1958, which was boosted by three large flocks in the late year.

The early year was quiet. There were about 26 birds noted during the spring passage, which included an inland record, from Lakeside CP (Eastleigh) on Mar 15th.

On Mar 27th a pair appeared in the east Solent, to be joined by a second pair on Apr 5th. They subsequently nested and each hatched four young. All young of one pair disappeared soon after hatching, along with two of the other pair. On June 25th, the remaining two young and their parents were found in the harbour at Hill Head, having apparently walked there from their nest site. The two young were moved onto the reserve at Titchfield Haven where the parents joined them and successfully reared them. The young birds were ringed. Two ringed juvenile birds were subsequently seen for several days in August at Keyhaven, which were possibly the Titchfield birds.

Between ten and twenty birds were present in the west of the county during September and about 16 further birds seen during the autumn passage. A flock of 19 was recorded in Langstone Harbour in late November.

The records are listed below, followed by the approximate bird-monthly totals:

Farlington Marshes /Langstone Harbour: 1, Jan 6th-Feb 19th; 1/2, Apr 1st-5th; 3, Apr 13th; 1, May 8th and 12th-14th; 2, Aug 13th; 2, Sep 4th; 1, Sep 16th; 4, Oct 7th; 5, Oct 31st; 1-3, Nov 3rd-Dec 27th with 19, Nov 27th and 5, Dec 18th-22nd; 3, Dec 23rd; 1, Dec 24th and 26th/27th.

Titchfield Haven: 1 W, May 13th, 1 W, May 18th; 2, July 17th and 18th, 1, July 20th (the July birds are in addition to the breeding birds and young); 8, Aug 25th; 1, Nov 2nd, 7th and 9th; 2, Nov 16th.

Hook-with-Warsash: 2 E, May 4th

Lakeside CP: 1, Mar 15th.

Needs Ore/Park Shore/Sowley Marsh: 1, Jan 4th-19th and Feb 16th; 1 E, Mar 23rd; 1, July 16th; 5, Sep 4th; 1/2, Nov 17th-Dec 18th.

Pennington/Keyhaven Marsh: 1, Mar 31st-Apr 10th (with 2, Apr 3rd); 2, Apr 26th; 2, May 18th/19th; 2 ringed juvs, Aug 12th, 14th and 27th; 3 juvs (2 ringed), Aug 28th; 5, Sep 7th; 10, Sep 22nd; 1, Dec 16th and 22nd (probably the Needs Ore bird).

Hurst Castle: 4 E, Mar 4th; 1 E, Apr 17th.

Milford on Sea: 8 E, Aug 25th (probably same birds as Titchfield Haven); 7 W, Nov 10th; 2, Dec 4th.

J	F	M	A	M	J	J	A	S	O	N	D
2	2	9	15	12	4	6	13	23	9	34	12

In the ten year period 1993-2002 the numbers passing through and present in the county have fluctuated widely, but appear to be showing an increasing trend over the last few years, annual totals of bird-months are as follows:

Bird-months	1993	1994	1995	1996	1997	1998	1999	2000	2001	2002
Avocet	33	58	25	42	14	41	87	41	52	141

Stone Curlew
Burhinus oedicnemus

A scarce summer visitor.

The first were a pair at Martin Down on Mar 26th. RSPB survey work recorded 29 pairs, of which 24 attempted to breed, some pairs more than once to total 27 known breeding attempts. Seven young were reared from monitored nests and a further three were located. The number of pairs was higher than in any of the previous five years (average 21 pairs), but fledging success was lower (average 14 fledged young).

The only coastal record received was of a single bird at Farlington Marshes on July 22nd. Inland an autumn gathering at one site reached a maximum of 50 on Sep 10th.

2001 addition: Autumn gatherings totalling 54 birds were recorded at four sites.

Little Ringed Plover
Charadrius dubius

A scarce summer visitor and passage migrant.

The first record came from Hook-with-Warsash on Mar 15th, with inland records on the next two days. Inland passage was more widespread than in recent years. In the Avon valley spring passage birds were seen between Mar 30th and May 10th, with a maximum of ten at Ibsley Water on May 10th.

Approximately 17 breeding pairs were located, however young were successfully raised at only one of these. This was a very poor season compared to 2001, when 21 pairs raised at least 24 young.

Occasional passage birds were seen at coastal sites during June, but the peak period was during July and the first half of August, with the last being seen on Sep 19th.

Breeding records
Coastal sites: Pairs at 2 sites, 1 possibly laid eggs, but otherwise no signs of successful breeding.
Avon valley: 3 pairs, one laid three eggs.
Ringwood Forest: a territorial pair.
Test valley: 2 pairs, no evidence of breeding.
Itchen Valley: Possibly 2 pairs, no evidence of breeding.
Meon Valley: A pair, raised 3 young.
North East: 6 pairs, but no evidence of breeding success.

Spring passage records, away from known breeding sites are detailed below:

Passage records – coastal sites
Farlington Marshes /Langstone Harbour: 1, Apr 13th-14th (left high N); 1, May 2nd; 1, June 22nd; 1-2, July 5th-11th; 3 adults July 13th; 1 adult and up to 5 juvs July 17th-31st; 1 adult, Aug 8th; 1 W, Aug 22nd.
Titchfield Haven: 1, on 6 dates Apr 5th-May 5th; 3, Apr 14th; 2, May 17th and June 16th; 1-4 juvs, July 9th-24th; 1, July 26th-Aug 2nd; 1, Sep 15th-19th.
Hook-with-Warsash: 2, Mar 15th; 3, Mar 22nd.
Lower Test Marshes: 1, Apr 11th/12th; 2, Apr 20th; 1-2, June 8th-July 9th.
Needs Ore: 1, Apr 7th; 1 Apr 9th; 1, July 16th; 2, Aug 17th.
Keyhaven/Pennington Marshes: 1-5 24th Mar-19th May; 3, July 15th; 4, July 17th; 1 juv, July 28th; 4, July 29th; 3-6 juvs, July 31st-Aug 30th with 1 until Sep 17th.
Barton on Sea: 1E, Aug 13th.

Passage records – inland sites
Ibsley Water: 1, July 14th.
Sway ,NF: 3, May 12th, 1 bird until July 3rd.
East Wellow: 1, May 26th.

Testwood Lakes: 2-7, Mar 29th-May 11th with max. 7, Apr 3rd; 5, July 2nd; 1, July 9th.
Sparsholt College: 1, Apr 24th.
Lakeside CP: 1 NW, Apr 1st; 1, Apr 7th.
White Hill, Overton: 4, Apr 10th, 2, Apr 11th; 2, Apr 19th-22nd.
Overton Lagoons: 1-2, Mar 17th-28th; 3, Mar 31st; 3, Apr 21st; 4, Apr 23rd.
Ashe Park Lake: 1, July 14th.
New Alresford: 1, Apr 7th.
The Vyne: 1, Apr 7th; 1, Apr 13th; 4, Apr 19th.
Woolmer Pond: 1, Mar 23rd; 1 Apr 20th.
Eversley GP: 1 adult, July 4th; 5-7 inc. 1 juv, July 7th-13th; 1 adult and 1 juv, July 21st-Aug 12th.
Fleet Pond: 2, Apr 14th (arrived from NW and left ENE).
Farnborough Airfield: 2, Apr 4th; 3, Apr 15th.

Ringed Plover   *Charadrius hiaticula*

A moderately common breeder, common passage migrant and winter visitor.

Numbers in the first half of the year were similar to 2001, but were higher in the autumn and second winter periods. The number of breeding birds/territories was down on 2001.

Spring coastal passage was recorded at Hurst, where 16 flew east between Apr 6th and May 12th (max. 9 E, May 8th) and Hayling, where single birds flew east on May 13th and May 17th. Inland records came from the Avon valley with two at Harbridge Water on Mar 10th and 13th and single birds at Somerley Park on Apr 15th and Ibsley Water and Bisterne on Apr 21st. Autumn passage included six east at Hurst on Aug 9th, whilst inland single birds were at Fleet Pond on Sep 12th/13th and at Eversley GP on Sep 15th.

About 37 breeding pairs/territories were reported as follows: 18 at Browndown, 11-12 between Lymington-Hurst and single pairs at Langstone Harbour Islands, Hook Spit, Black Gutter Bottom, NF (raised two young), Southampton Old Docks, Marchwood, Hamer Warren (raised 3 young) and Eversley GP.

Records of monthly maxima at the main localities and the approximate monthly totals for the county are tabulated below:

	J	F	M	A	M	J	J	A	S	O	N	D
Chichester Harbour	261	44	79	40	40	-	14	364	415	71	128	147
East Hayling	55	1	-	-	-	-	-	-	15	157	10	-
Langstone Harbour	136	151	60	16	18	42	42	162	260	210	217	394
Portsmouth Harbour	-	-	5	-	-	-	-	-	52	80	1	34
Titchfield Haven/Brownwich	43	21	3	2	1	1	-	-	40	-	70	90
Hamble Estuary/Warsash	34	2	-	-	-	-	-	52	87	65	-	-
Langdown/Fawley/Calshot	16	24	3	-	3	-	2	-	3	70	12	5
Lepe/Inchmery	30	-	13	-	-	2	-	60	70	62	20	80
Needs Ore/Beaulieu Estuary	-	19	2	24	8	-	9	7	22	10	-	-
Sowley-Lymington	6	-	4	2	6	-	-	-	60	50	50	12
Lymington/Hurst	140	80	30	24	26	22	-	96	112	112	138	67
APPROX COUNTY TOTAL	**460**	**298**	**120**	**68**	**62**	**67**	**53**	**377**	**721**	**816**	**518**	**682**

Elsewhere the highest counts were of 100 at Southsea on Nov 22nd and 20 at Weston Shore on Dec 14th.

A leucistic individual returned to the Hurst area for its seventh consecutive year.

Golden Plover   *Pluvialis apricaria*

A common winter visitor and passage migrant; very scarce in summer.

Monthly maxima at various localities and the approximate monthly totals for the county are tabulated below. The monthly totals for the county also include figures from other localities:

	J	F	M	A	M	J	J	A	S	O	N	D
Chichester Harbour	2436	1390	1284	1	-	-	-	11	56	242	1048	958
East Hayling	650	120	734	-	-	-	-	11	-	80	-	5
Langstone/North Hayling	2250	756	-	-	-	-	-	-	-	-	100	300
Langstone Harbour	61	1	1	-	-	-	-	1	17	1	14	1
Cams Bay, Portsmouth Hbr	320	110	-	-	-	-	-	-	22	160	400	173
Hamble Estuary	120	-	-	-	-	-	-	-	-	360	280	198
Lymington/Hurst	460	391	500	-	-	-	-	-	-	150	307	300
Wide Lane, Eastleigh	90	377	-	32	-	-	-	-	1	254	420	1100
Winchester SF/Chilcomb	85	70	-	-	-	-	-	1	-	448	40	-
Alresford	200	60	125	7	-	-	-	-	-	-	-	-
Wootton St Lawrence/Ibworth	-	-	-	-	-	-	-	-	-	279	352	5
Odiham area	100	346	42	-	-	-	-	-	-	80	3	400
APPROX COUNTY TOTAL	**4736**	**2601**	**2295**	**1049**	**-**	**-**	**-**	**13**	**40**	**1812**	**2166**	**2582**

Other counts to exceed 100 in the early year were as follows: 200 at Kilmeston on Jan 15th, 200 at Warnford on Jan 19th, 370 near Basingstoke on Feb 9th, 113 at Medstead on Mar 5th, 250 at Sparsholt on Mar 8th, 330 at Romsey on Mar 15th, 200 at Cliddesden on Mar 16th, 500 at Long Down on Apr 1st (a large flock was there from Mar 19th-Apr 23rd), 310 at Hambledon (Big West End Farm) on Apr 14th and 340 on 20th and 170 was the last spring record at Sparsholt on Apr 24th.

The first return was a flock of 11 birds seen at South Hayling on Aug 9th and presumably the same birds on East Hayling on Aug 12th. Single birds were seen inland at Winchester SF on Aug 21st and 27th. Birds appeared in ones and twos until a flock of 30 was recorded near Ropley on Sep 24th. Other counts to exceed 100 in the late year were of 250 at Charity Down Farm on Nov 3rd, a flock of 240 east at Titchfield Haven on Nov 24th (probably the Hamble flock) and 100 at South Wonston on Dec 1st.

Grey Plover   *Pluvialis squatarola*

A common winter visitor and passage migrant, with a varying (usually small) summering population.

Numbers wintering in the county in the early year were high, with peak counts of **1838** at East Hayling, *819* in Langstone and *708* in the Beaulieu Estuary in January and *1124* on East Hayling in March. High counts were also made in the second winter period at both Langstone and East Hayling.

Spring passage was very light. An early record of 24 east at West Hayling on Mar 29th may have been a local movement. Otherwise, only 39 were recorded moving east between Apr 6th and May 20th, with a peak count of 10 at Hurst on May 13th.

Monthly maxima at the main localities and the approximate monthly totals for the county are tabulated overleaf.

	J	F	M	A	M	J	J	A	S	O	N	D
Chichester Harbour	2477	3180	1576	43	25	-	69	570	1408	603	1618	1700
East Hayling	1838	530	1124	7	21	-	66	370	510	202	832	1083
Langstone Harbour	819	361	58	31	40	28	13	500	800	798	385	937
Portsmouth Harbour	4	2	2	-	-	-	-	-	-	1	52	4
Titchfield Haven	2	8	5	1	9	-	-	-	-	-	-	3
Hamble Estuary	69	80	2	-	1	-	-	7	19	27	62	110
Langdown/Fawley/Calshot	32	24	5	-	-	-	-	1	-	3	12	16
Needs Ore/Beaulieu Estuary	708	456	416	12	1	-	-	22	101	123	188	180
Sowley/Lymington	150	100	-	17	6	-	19	50	250	200	250	30
Lymington/Hurst	40	117	222	33	14	-	30	33	135	77	90	93
APPROX COUNTY TOTAL	**3662**	**1678**	**1834**	**101**	**92**	**28**	**128**	**983**	**1815**	**1431**	**1871**	**2456**

There were no inland records for the year.

Lapwing   *Vanellus vanellus*

A common but decreasing breeder and numerous winter visitor.

Numbers of birds present were somewhat lower then previous years, but featured a gathering of about 2500 in the Beaulieu Estuary in January and February and 1100 at Eversley GP in January. Late year numbers were normal, until the last few weeks of the year, when numbers in the Avon valley grew substantially to over 8500. This was probably due to extensive flooding as a result of a period of very mild, wet weather. Apart from the main areas in the table, the largest flocks reported were of 600 at Testwood Lakes on Dec 22nd, 300 near Odiham on Jan 1st, 260 at Brockenhurst on Dec 18th, 260 near Testwood Lakes on Jan 14th, 250 at Houghton on Jan 12th and 250 at Lee on Feb16th.

Monthly maxima at various localities are tabulated below. The approximate monthly totals for the county also include figures from other localities:

	J	F	M	A	M	J	J	A	S	O	N	D
Chichester Harbour	3586	2397	549	83	29	-	168	397	486	805	1040	1882
East Hayling	377	881	233	4	5	-	41	53	41	103	200	481
Langstone Harbour	1100	650	260	57	56	122	160	205	172	313	650	1000
Portsmouth Harbour	611	41	-	-	-	-	34	37	45	107	164	222
Titchfield Haven area	300	300	87	25	10	16	54	90	156	150	300	400
Hamble Estuary	568	288	64	-	-	-	32	17	44	42	160	460
Lower Test/Eling/Bury Marshes	1500	80	14	2	-	20	23	-	1	6	292	1000
Langdown/Fawley/Calshot	80	100	-	-	-	1	22	-	29	-	60	84
Beaulieu Estuary	2500	2500	503	91	84	37	185	93	96	56	524	1000
Sowley/Lymington	385	-	150	-	-	-	1	-	-	160	-	510
Lymington/Hurst	620	590	40	3	-	-	6	25	102	100	400	800
Sopley/Avon Causeway	100	300	250	-	-	-	-	-	-	-	400	1000
Avon Causeway/Ringwood	384	1414	317	33	-	67	-	-	-	85	1250	6645
Blashford Lakes/Bickton	1150	150	96	-	-	75	196	380	280	-	398	1100
Eastleigh area	200	62	-	-	-	-	-	-	-	32	106	161
Winchester SF	500	801	70	9	5	42	102	156	156	523	283	17
The Vyne	100	-	25	25	-	-	209	325	241	121	42	60
Eversley GP	1100	700	151	13	16	170	250	475	200	253	465	350
APPROX COUNTY TOTAL	**13900**	**9620**	**2410**	**260**	**175**	**530**	**1530**	**2130**	**1560**	**2230**	**5960**	**17250**

There was evidence of inland cold weather movement in early January, with 150 west over Fleet Pond on Jan 2nd and 86 west and 14 west there on the next two days. On Jan 3rd, there were 16 south-west at Stratfield Saye and 11 south-west over Ashley Walk, with nine south-west at Overton, the following day. A flock of 170 flew south-west over Whitchurch on Jan 9th. There were about 300 flying south along the Test valley between Oct 21st and Nov 1st, during a period of often stormy weather.

Breeding season reports were substantially lower from the Avon valley, compared to 2001. There were 27 territorial pairs at seven sites, compared to at least 75 pairs last year. Elsewhere, at least 102 territories were reported from 32 sites. Sites with five or more pairs were located at Kilmeston (15 pairs), Hook-with-Warsash (eight), Long Down (eight), Titchfield Haven (eight), Brambridge (seven) and Hipley (five). Only eight records were received giving information about breeding success. These indicated at least 28 fledged. Highlights were four pairs with seven young at The Vyne and three pairs with eight young at Chidden.

Knot   *Calidris canutus*

A moderately common winter visitor (to the eastern harbours) and passage migrant.

A below average year, with the largest numbers noted in Langstone Harbour with a peak count of 539 on Jan 12th. Monthly maxima at the main localities and the approximate monthly totals for the county are tabulated below:

	J	F	M	A	M	J	J	A	S	O	N	D
Chichester Harbour	505	162	101	-	5	-	-	-	36	-	31	411
East Hayling	210	150	100		5						10	70
Langstone Harbour	539	210	150	1	7	4	4	16	155	56	160	382
Lymington/Hurst	35	10	-	7	1	-	-	9	18	20	22	41
APPROX COUNTY TOTAL	**800**	**370**	**250**	**8**	**30**	**4**	**4**	**25**	**175**	**90**	**200**	**490**

Elsewhere, the peak counts were of 35 at Needs Ore on Jan 13th, 14 at Cams Bay on Oct 2nd and 150 at Tanners Lane on Mar 3rd. The last two-figure count was 25 in Langstone Harbour on Mar 7th and the last of the early year also there with five on June 8th. Spring coastal passage was poor with only 25 observed heading east with seven past Hurst Beach on Apr 6th and one on May 8th and 17 past Sandy Point on May 17th.

The first returning bird was noted at Langstone Harbour on July 30th. Double-figure counts resumed with 16 at Lepe and 10 at Farlington Marshes on Aug 28th. Records other than those tabulated in the late year were:

Portsmouth Harbour- Cams Bay: 1, Sep 7th; 14, Oct 2nd; 3, Oct 17th.
Titchfield Haven/Hill Head: 2, Aug 25th; 1 juv, Aug 30th; 5, Nov 29th.
Hook-with-Warsash: 1, Sep 14th; 1-3, between Nov 14th and 26th; 1, Dec 31st.
Weston Shore: 1, Nov 30th.
Needs Ore: 4 W, Sep 9th.
Sowley Shore/Pylewell Saltings: 4, Sep 12th; 26, Oct 2nd; 6, Oct 6th; 15, Oct 30th; 40, Dec 2nd.

Sanderling   *Calidris alba*

A moderately common passage migrant and winter visitor.

The numbers of wintering Sanderling have been slowly increasing over the last five years. The peak count for the year was 360 on the Hampshire side of Chichester Harbour at Black Point, Hayling on Feb 2nd. This general increase in numbers is reflected in the westerly spread of birds from the Hayling stronghold. A count of 220 was noted along Southsea Beach, with 10 at Southsea Castle on Jan 14th. In the latter part of the year 41 were observed at Gilkicker Point on Dec 24th. The movements between Southsea, Hayling Bay and Chichester Harbour warrant further study so the approximate county total, derived from the monthly maxima at the main sites tabulated below, may be an over estimate:

	J	F	M	A	M	J	J	A	S	O	N	D
Chichester Harbour	12	360	86	119	49	-	3	160	9	4	1	62
East Hayling/Black Point	300	360	-	-	15	-	-	-	-	14	4	-
Hayling Bay/Sandy Point	24	165	-	35	41	-	-	93	4	60	340	75
Eastney/Southsea	230	4	120	-	-	-	-	-	-	18	-	100
APPROX COUNTY TOTAL	**560**	**370**	**132**	**200**	**260**	**25**	**18**	**102**	**4**	**95**	**344**	**217**

Spring coastal passage (between Mar 17th to May 21st) was detected at five sites (Sandy Point, Stokes Bay, Hill Head, Needs Ore and Hurst Beach). The total east at Hurst Beach between Mar 17th and May 20th was 76. Movements of up to 150 noted at Stokes Bay, in the middle two weeks of April, may relate to local tidal movements to and from Browndown Spit. Taking into account possible duplication, it seems that about 210 were noted on passage along the Hampshire coast, with the peak occurring during the second week of May. Notable records in late spring came from Langstone Harbour (max. 22, June 1st), Lymington/Hurst (15, May 16th), Titchfield Haven/Hill Head (max. 12, May 18th), Needs Ore (max. five, July 23rd.), Hordle Cliff (max. five, May 17th).

There was an unusual inland record of one at Meadow Lake (Lower Test) on Apr 26th.

Little Stint
Calidris minuta

A scarce passage migrant, particularly so in spring. Very scarce winter visitor.

It was a poor year with approximately 65 individuals recorded compared with 117 in 2001, although the presence of long-staying juveniles from mid September onwards makes it difficult to assess the true total passing through the county.

One at Black Point, East Hayling on Jan 29th was the only record from a group of 13 that over wintered on the Sussex side of Chichester Harbour area from Jan 12th-Mar 2nd. Also, an adult and a first-winter remained in the Lymington/Hurst area from Jan 1st-Apr 11th, with one lingering until May 4th. The only spring records were two at Titchfield Haven on June 5th/6th.

A protracted autumn passage involved about 48 between July 31st and Oct 20th, with nine in the Lymington/Hurst area on Aug 26th being the highest count. Only one was recorded inland. In the late year, one was seen in the Lymington/Hurst area on Nov 7th and Dec 1st and four were noted in Chichester Harbour in December. Records for each site are summarised below followed by annual autumn passage numbers 1993-2002:

Juvenile Little Stint, Farlington Marshes (Jason Crook)

Coastal sites
Chichester Harbour: 9-13, Jan 12th-Mar 2nd; 2, Sep 7th; 1, Oct 5th; 3-4, Nov 9th-Dec 7th.
Farlington Marshes /Langstone Harbour: 1-3, Aug 1st-4th; 1, Aug 8th-10th; 1, Aug 18th/19th; 1,

Sep 7th; 2, Sep 23rd; 2, Oct 12th; 1-2, Oct 12th-15th.

Titchfield Haven: 2, June 5th/6th; 1-2 Aug 23rd-28th; 1, Aug 30th; 1, Sep 11th-26th.

Lymington/Hurst area: 1-2, Jan 1st-May 4th; 2, July 31st; 1, Aug 25th; 9, Aug 26th; 3, Sep 25th; 1-2, Sep 27th/28th; 1-2, Oct 2nd/3rd; 3-4, Oct 4th-6th; 4-6, Oct 9th/10th; 1, Oct 20th; 1, Oct 26th; 1, Nov 7th; 1, Dec 1st;

Inland sites
Winchester SF: 1, Sep 29th-Oct 3rd.

Autumn passage	1993	1994	1995	1996	1997	1998	1999	2000	2001	2002
Little Stint	140	31	73	400	28	175	64	29	113	48

Temminck's Stint   *Calidris temminckii*

A very scarce passage migrant (6,112,2).

There were just two records, one in the spring and the other in autumn. The spring bird was seen at Titchfield Haven on June 20th (BSD), while the autumn individual was at Farlington Marshes on Aug 4th (m.o.).

White-rumped Sandpiper   *Calidris fuscicollis*

A rare vagrant (0,15,1).

One was at Testwood Lakes on Sep 15th/16th (PDW, TR). The bird was very elusive and only seen for two short periods on the 15th and again briefly the following day. A photograph was taken. The record has been accepted by *British Birds* and is the 16th for Hampshire.

Pectoral Sandpiper   *Calidris melanotus*

A rare passage migrant (0,65,1).

An adult female in summer plumage was at Farlington Marshes on May 16th (finder unknown but m.o. *per* JCr). This record brings the Hampshire total to 66.

Curlew Sandpiper   *Calidris ferruginea*

A scarce passage migrant, particularly so in spring. Rarely winters.

About 145 were recorded during the year, making 2002 the second best year in the last decade. Unusually, one was recorded in winter at Titchfield Haven on Jan 27th. There was only one spring record, incidentally the only inland record, of two at Woolmer Pond on Apr 19th. Autumn passage was typical with a brief pulse of adults in late July to mid August, then the main migration of juveniles from late August to October. Records for each site are summarised below followed by annual autumn passage numbers 1993-2002:

Coastal sites
Farlington Marshes /Langstone Harbour: 1, July 18th-24th; 1, Aug 1st; 1, Aug 8th-12th; 2, Aug 22nd; 4, Aug 23rd-25th; 2-3, Aug 26th-28th; 1-3, Aug 30th/31st; 7, Sep 5th; 1-6, Sep 7th-16th; 1-5, Sep 17th-24th; 5, Sep 25th/26th; 3, Sep 28th; 1, Oct 4th-6th.

Cams Bay: 2, Oct 2nd.

Titchfield Haven: 1, Jan 27th; 1, Sep 5th-8th; 1, Sep 19th/20th; 1, Oct 9th.

Hook-with-Warsash: 3-8, Sep 11th/12th; 2, Sep 16th.

Needs Ore: 4-6, Aug 24th-27th; 9-14, Aug 29th-31st; 2, Sep 7th/8th.

Pennington/Keyhaven Marsh: 1, July 29th; 1, July 31st; 1, Aug 3rd; 3-11, Aug 19th-26th; 2-6, Aug 29th-31st; 2, Sep 7th; 1-8, Sep 10th-14th; 1-4, Sep 18th-21st; 1, Oct 10th; 1-7, Oct 19th-21st; 2, Oct 26th.

Inland sites

Woolmer Pond: 2 N, Apr 19th (1800 hrs).

Autumn Passage	1993	1994	1995	1996	1997	1998	1999	2000	2001	2002
Curlew Sandpiper	79	60	70	190	60	105	135	95	89	138

Purple Sandpiper   *Calidris maritima*

A very scarce winter visitor and passage migrant to the coast.

It was a poor year with just 13 recorded. In the early year just one was seen at Southsea Castle on Jan 22nd, with one in the Hurst/Milford on Sea area between Jan 3rd and Feb 11th.

Spring records included a single at Hurst Castle on Apr 28th and again 30th.

In the late year two were briefly at Hurst in November and up to five were present at Southsea Castle from Dec 14th until the years end. The records are summarised below:

Southsea Castle: 1, Jan 22nd; 1-5, Dec 14th-28th (max. on Dec 14th).

Hurst Beach/Milford on Sea: 1, Jan 3rd-Feb 11th; 1W, Apr 28th; 1, Apr 30th; 1, Sep 8th; 2, Nov 14th-20th.

Becton Bunny: 1, Nov 17th (flew E and could have been one of the Hurst birds)

Dunlin   *Calidris alpina*

An abundant winter visitor and common passage migrant; small numbers summer.

Overall, numbers recorded remained at the same level as the last few years, but several thousand down on the large counts of the mid 1990's. This may possibly reflect smaller populations but could also result from more rigorous estimating techniques. Internationally important wintering numbers were counted in Langstone Harbour in January and November. Monthly maxima at the main localities and the approximate monthly totals for the county are tabulated below:

	J	F	M	A	M	J	J	A	S	O	N	D
Chichester Harbour	12084	5202	11370	165	160	-	29	1705	2228	557	2704	15661
East Hayling	3020	210	3378	16	20		12	100	23	123	1480	7993
Langstone Harbour	**16742**	7396	12760	59	293	7	400	967	554	716	**15000**	8654
Portsmouth Harbour	2269	1078	1097	-	-	-	-	-	5	60	2175	1152
Southampton Water												
Hamble Estuary	685	1250	-	-	-	-	2	32	49	112	1377	2300
Weston Shore	150	189	4	-	-	-	-	-	-	-	409	95
Dibden Bay-Calshot	850	750	59	-	-	-	-	4	-	53	550	500
Needs Ore/Beaullieu E.	4500	2306	1689	27	26	-	-	2	55	48	1000	1471
Sowley-Lymington	1000	470	400	7	4	-	-	2	70	50	800	850
Lymington-Hurst	960	3400	1600	122	118	-	16	96	68	300	2000	2050
APPROX TOTAL	30180	14970	20990	230	490	37	460	1280	820	1460	24790	25140

Elsewhere, significant counts included 2000 at Cams Bay on Dec 16th, 1500 at Southseaon Nov 22nd, 190 flying west at Stokes Bay on Jan 29th and 70 at Hill Head on Aug 23rd.

Spring movement was light and reported from three areas. The heaviest passage was at Hurst, with a total of at least 382 noted moving east. Records of spring coastal passage are summarised below:

Hayling Bay/Sandy Point: 13 E between May 8th and 17th.
Hill Head/Stokes Bay: 156 E between Apr 9th and May 13th.
Hurst Beach: 382 E between Apr 6th and July 12th.

Inland records were received for nine sites, mostly for the passage periods, but including a notable flock of 70 at Avon Causeway in December. All inland records are summarised below:

Ibsley Water: 1, Nov 3rd.
Avon Causeway: 1, May 2nd; 70, Dec 14th; 25, Dec 19th; 40, Dec 22nd.
Lakeside CP: 1, Jan 7th.
Winchester SF: 1, Apr 24th; 1, May 15th; 1, May 19th/20th.
Meadow Lake: 1, May 6th.
The Vyne: 2, Aug 24th/25th; 1, Oct 11th/12th.
Fleet Pond: 1, Sep 12th/13th; 1, Oct 9th.
Eversley GP: 1, May 25th/26th; 2, Aug 6th; 1, Aug 12th/13th.
Bourley North: 1, May 15th.

Ruff   *Philomachus pugnax*

A scarce but regular passage migrant and winter visitor.

Much higher passage numbers contributed to the highest annual bird-month total since the 1980s. Only two sites held wintering birds in the first two months of the year, with maxima of six in the Lymington/Hurst area on Feb 17th and two at Needs Ore on Jan 29th.

A significant spring passage took place between mid-March and mid-April, involving about 120, with the peak occurring during March 24th-28th. The last spring record was one at Titchfield Haven on May 17th.

Return passage commenced on July 17th with a moulting male at Keyhaven Marsh and one at Titchfield Haven. Small numbers, mostly one or two, were then noted throughout the autumn. A small influx occurred in mid-September, when a maximum count of ten was noted at Lower Test Marshes on Sep 12th. In the late year several wintering birds were present in the Avon valley, Chichester Harbour and the Lymington/Hurst area.

The records from each locality are summarised below:

Coastal sites
Farlington Marshes : 1, Mar 28th-Apr 2nd; 1, Apr 5th-8th; 1, Apr 15th; 1, Apr 26th-28th; 1, Aug 4th; 1, Aug 22nd-24th; 2, Aug 27th; 1, Sep 3rd.
Titchfield Haven: 1, Mar 13th; 20, Mar 22nd; 3-16, Mar 24th-31st; 1, Apr 1st; 1, Apr 5th; 1, Apr 7th; 1, Apr 11th; 2, Apr 24th/25th; 2, Apr 27th; 1, May 15th-17th; 1, July 17th-28th; 1, Aug 22nd-30th; 1, Sep 14th-22nd; 1, Oct 16th; 1, Nov 3rd.
Weston Shore: 1, Mar 28th.
Lower Test Marshes: 10, Sep 12th.
Dibden Bay: 21, Mar 24th-25th.
Needs Ore/Park Shore: 2, Jan 4th-29th; 2, Mar 29th; 2-3, Apr 1st/2nd; 1-2, Apr 5th-7th; 2, Apr 14th; 1, Apr 17th-20th; 1, Sep 11th.
Pennington/Keyhaven Marsh: 1-6, Jan 6th-Feb 28th; 3-4, Mar 3rd-7th; 6-10, Mar 26th-29th; 3-8, Apr 1st-14th; 1, Apr 17th; 1, Apr 20th; 1, July 17th; 1, July 22nd/23rd; 2, Aug 25th; 1-3, Sep 8th/9th; 4-5, Sep 15th-19th; 1-5, Sep 22nd-25th; 1 E, Nov 9th; 2-3, Nov 16th-Dec 31st.

Hurst Beach: 18 E, Mar 24th.
Barton on Sea: 1 E, Sep 15th.

Inland sites
Avon Causeway-Bisterne area: 1, Dec 19th; 2, Dec 22nd.
Ibsley: 2, Dec 28th.
Meadow Lake: 1, Aug 27th.
Winchester SF: 1, Oct 23rd-25th.
The Vyne: 1, Aug 24th-30th; 1, Sep 11th.
Woolmer Pond: 1, Apr 28th.
Pale Lane, Winchfield: 1, Apr 28th.

Approximate monthly totals and annual totals of bird-months 1993-2002 are as follows:

J	F	M	A	M	J	J	A	S	O	N	D
5	6	94	31	1	0	3	9	28	2	4	7

Bird-months	1993	1994	1995	1996	1997	1998	1999	2000	2001	2002
Ruff	118	125	124	164	112	120	119	76	61	197

Stilt Sandpiper   *Micropalama himantopus*
A very rare vagrant (0,0,1).

A splendid adult moulting out of summer plumage was found at 0800 hrs on Butts Lagoon, Pennington Marsh on July 21st (RBW). It remained in the area until Aug 3rd, allowing many hundreds of observers to catch up with this fascinating *Nearctic* species. It was undoubtedly the bird of the year for many who saw it. This record has been accepted by *British Birds* and is the first for Hampshire. It is the 56th species of wader to be recorded in the county. A paper on the finding of this bird is included in this Report.

Jack Snipe   *Lymnocryptes minimus*
A scarce but overlooked winter visitor and passage migrant.

In the early year a minimum total of 59 was reported, with 22 at ten coastal sites and 37 at 12 inland sites. Counts exceeding two were reported at Long Valley (5, Feb 14th and Mar 15th; 3, Mar 16th; 8, Mar 29th), Hillside (6, Mar 3rd), Itchen Valley CP (3, Feb 26th), Itchen Valley between Bishopstoke and Brambridge (10, Feb 24th) and Langstone Harbour Islands (3, Mar 16th). The last was at Titchfield Haven on Apr 23rd.

The first return was one at Lower Test Marshes from Sep 19th followed by single birds at Farlington Marshes on Sep 26th and at Eversley GP on Sep 30th. Birds were then seen in small numbers at a variety of sites. Late in the year a minimum of 52 were seen, with 20 at six coastal sites and 32 at twelve inland sites. Counts exceeding two were as follows: Long Valley (5, Dec 7th; 7, Dec 14th; 10, Dec 27th), Itchen Valley CP (5, Dec 29th; 7, Dec 31st) and Farlington Marshes (12, Dec 7th).

The approximate monthly totals are tabulated below:

J	F	M	A	M	J	J	A	S	O	N	D
17	36	21	4	0	0	0	0	3	6	3	45

Common Snipe
Gallinago gallinago

A moderately common but declining breeder, common passage migrant and winter visitor.

Numbers remained at the generally low level of recent years. In the first winter period counts reached or exceeded 50 at six sites as follows:

Farlington Marshes : 60, Mar 29th.
Titchfield Haven: 50, Jan 27th.
Hook-with-Warsash: 70, Feb 27th.
Bishopstoke: 53, Mar 3rd.
Lower Test Marshes: 55, Jan 12th; 50, Feb 2nd; 62, Feb 9th.
Hillside (Odiham): 53, Jan 13th; 100, Feb 10th; 70, Mar 3rd.

In April there was only one count exceeding ten: Farlington Marshes , 14 (partial count), Apr 2nd. During the breeding season drumming males were reported from the New Forest as follows: one at Shatterford Bottom, two at both Anthony's Bee Bottom and Holmsley Bog. Other New Forest records, with no evidence of breeding activity, were four at Rowbarrow and one at Furzey Lodge. In the Avon valley one was drumming at Hucklesbrook Lakes. Non-breeding birds, in small numbers, were reported from several coastal sites during June and July. There were 25 at Hucklesbrook Lakes on July 21st.

Small numbers were reported from coastal sites during August and September. Inland there were 22 at The Vyne on Sep 15th and 34 at Woolmer Pond on Sep 28th.

In the second winter period counts exceeded 50 at five sites as follows: Upper Hamble Estuary (55, Dec 30th); Needs Ore/Beaulieu Estuary (81, Dec 12th); Lower Test Marshes (107, Dec 7th); Bishopstoke (150+, Dec 31st); Hillside (64, Nov 17th; 65, Dec 9th and 127, Dec 29th). During the course of the *Wintering Great Grey Shrike Survey* in the New Forest on Dec 14th, a total of 110 was found at six of 29 sites covered, including 92 at Plaitford Common.

Woodcock
Scolopax rusticola

A common resident and winter visitor.

Just 77 records were received which seriously under represents the county population that was last estimated at 950-1500 roding males in 1991 (*BoH*). There were a mere seven reports from the New Forest, one of the strongholds of this species. In the first quarter, 42 were reported from 17 sites, including five at Woolmer Forest on Feb 14th and six at Roydon Woods on Mar 4th.

The total number of roding males reported was 35 at 20 sites, predominantly in the north-east. Highest counts were of five at Bricksbury Hill and Havant Thicket with just three reported from the New Forest.

The only records from July to September were single birds at Pond House, Liss Forest on Aug 6th and 25th. In the final quarter, 27 were reported from 16 sites with four reports of two and the rest singles.

Black-tailed Godwit   *Limosa limosa*

A common passage migrant and winter visitor. Small numbers summer.

*Juvenile Black-tailed Godwit (ssp. islandica),
Langstone Harbour (Jason Crook)*

Unlike 2001 with drier conditions there was no repeat of the large numbers found in the Avon valley in the early winter. However flooding at the end of the year led to December counts between Sopley and Bisterne of *600* on 10th, **2000** on 12th and **1980** on 22nd; the county population estimate was in excess of 3000. Apart from the December influx, numbers for the rest of the year followed the normal pattern.

Monthly maxima at the main localities and approximate monthly totals for the county are tabulated below:

	J	F	M	A	M	J	J	A	S	O	N	D
Chichester Harbour	500	197	347	181	6	-	131	503	477	688	**715**	260
East Hayling	105	47	45	0	0	-	6	0	0	47	220	38
Langstone Harbour	190	150	189	165	90	45	363	620	612	670	225	165
Portsmouth Harbour	40	185	-	-	-	-	-	-	130	109	196	81
Titchfield Haven	350	550	200	110	142	110	90	100	41	46	400	350
Hamble Estuary	23	14	129	103	83	9	3	61	123	126	60	25
Lower Test/Eling/Bury M'shes	85	74	70	-	-	2	-	-	21	34	5	53
Hythe/Fawley/Calshot	-	-	-	-	-	-	44	81	47	80	-	3
Needs Ore/Beaulieu Estuary	-	**725**	508	71	34	32	40	6	28	7	-	150
Lymington/Hurst	311	117	**722**	214	10	20	66	132	156	235	334	149
Sopley-Bisterne, R. Avon	-	19	3	-	-	-	-	-	-	-	57	**2000**
APPROX COUNTY TOTAL	1100	1880	1890	660	360	220	610	1000	1160	1350	1500	3020

Elsewhere in the Avon valley, three were at Bickerley Common on Jan 5th, 10-19 were at Hucklesbrook Water Meadows from Mar 1st-21st, one was there on July 21st and one was at Ibsley on Dec 28th. In the north, two were at Eversley GP on July 11th and one was at The Vyne on Oct 6th.

Bar-tailed Godwit   *Limosa lapponica*

A moderately common passage migrant and winter visitor. Small numbers summer.

Just three sites regularly held wintering birds during the year, with the bulk of the population at Chichester and Langstone Harbours and small numbers at Lymington/Hurst. Monthly maxima at the main localities and the approximate monthly totals for the county are tabulated below:

	J	F	M	A	M	J	J	A	S	O	N	D
Chichester Harbour	840	708	910	45	132	-	27	47	364	105	872	930
East Hayling	834	683	910	-	60	-	9	43	260	104	870	71
Langstone Harbour	465	490	295	18	62	38	75	60	400	500	315	600
Lymington/Hurst	20	35	11	10	20	1	-	-	-	2	1	-
APPROX COUNTY TOTAL	**930**	**720**	**1210**	**148**	**300**	**39**	**75**	**60**	**410**	**500**	**880**	**620**

1 Note that, because of the regular daily movements of birds between Chichester and Langstone Harbours, the approximate monthly totals normally include just the higher of the East Hayling or Langstone Harbour's peak monthly counts; the combined count was used when occasionally both WeBs counts were conducted on the same day at East Hayling and Langstone Harbour and exceeded the peak number recorded at either site during the month

Elsewhere the only double-figure counts were from Needs Ore/Beaulieu Estuary (14 on Apr 27th); Langdown/Hythe (10, May 10th), Titchfield Haven (10, May 15th); Hordle (10 SW, Sep 6th) and Tanners Lane (12, Nov 27th; 23, Dec 9th).

Diurnal spring passage along the coast was recorded at four sites from Mar 27th to May 20th. Individual site totals and peak counts of birds moving east or north-east were as follows:

Sandy Point/Hayling Bay: 87 E from Apr 7th-May 17th (peak 41, Apr 7th).
Langstone Harbour: 31 E, May 11th.
Hill Head/Stokes Bay: 176 E or NE from Apr 11th-May 20th (peak 48 NE, May 8th).
Lymington/Hurst: 222 E from Mar 27th-May 16th (peak of 77 E, May 6th).

The only inland record, although not very far north, was at Lakeside CP (3 SW, Aug17th with 11 Whimbrel).

Whimbrel   *Numenius phaeopus*

A common passage migrant. Rare in winter.

During the first three months of the year single birds were reported occasionally from Langstone Harbour between Jan 6th and Mar 23rd, Bury Marshes on Jan 26th and Feb 23rd and at Keyhaven Harbour on Feb 24th and Mar 1st. Spring passage was light. The first double-figure count was of 21 at Needs Ore on Apr 16th. Most other reports were of small numbers on easterly passage with 21 briefly at Testwood Lakes on Apr 28th, 48 past Hill Head on May 6th and 65 past Needs Ore on May 16th. The last double-figure count of spring was on May 20th when 17 flew north at Southampton Old Docks.

A few were seen throughout the summer along the coast. Numbers of birds in double-figures appeared from mid July as follows: Langstone Harbour (34, July 13th), Lymington/Hurst (16, July 18th), Hayling Oysterbeds (22, July 26th) and East Hayling (45, Aug 12th). Numbers declined during August and September, from early October into December there were just singles at several coastal sites including East Hayling, Langstone Harbour, Bury Marshes and Keyhaven Harbour.

The largest counts for coastal movement and of grounded birds are listed below followed by all inland records, of which there were many more than in 2001:

Selected spring coastal movement
Sandy Point: 36 E, between May 4th and 16th.
Hill Head: 109 E, NE or N between Apr 15th and May 19th.
Needs Ore/Beaulieu Estuary: 76 E between May 4th and 16th.
Hurst Beach/Milford on Sea: 240 E between Mar 27th and May 16th.

Selected off passage, coastal sites
Langstone Harbour: 69, May 11th.
Portsmouth Harbour: 10, May 11th.
Curbridge: 25, May 5th.
Dibden Bay: 24, May 1st.
Lymington/Hurst: 40, May 5th and 70, May 7th.

Inland sites
Wootton Coppice Inclosure: 20 over, May 1st.
Sway: 1N, Apr 29th; 6, July 31st.
Testwood Lakes: 21, Apr 28th.
Timsbury: 3 W, Apr 25th.
Lakeside CP: 5 N, Apr 27th; 1 N, May 8th; 4 NE, May 17th; 11 SW, Aug 17th.
Itchen Valley CP: 11, Apr 27th.
Allbrook: 1 N, May 2nd.
Overton: 1, July 15th.
Clamp Kiln Farm, Wickham: 15, Apr 29th.
Hipley: 9, Apr 29th; 3, Apr 30th.
Lye Heath: 2, Apr 29th.
Long Down: 2 NE, Apr 28th.
Petersfield: 6 alighted in ploughed field, May 11th.
Woolmer Pond: 3, Apr 21st.
Woolmer Forest: 1 over, May 10th.
Fleet Pond: 1 N, Apr 25th.

Curlew   *Numenius arquata*

A common passage migrant and winter visitor. Breeds in small numbers, mainly in the New Forest.

Numbers wintering in the early and late year were about average. The peak count at Langstone Harbour was 1817 on Sep 7th, exceeding the 2001 peak of 1703 on Aug 18th.

Spring coastal passage was heavier than usual. A minimum total of 333 moved east through The Solent between Feb 18th and May 2nd (peaks 148 E, Hurst, Apr 13th and 135 E, Stokes Bay, Apr 14th) and in addition a total of 301 was noted leaving east from Langstone Harbour at dusk on seven dates between Mar 25th and Apr 19th (peak 116, Apr 15th).

In the breeding season single pairs were noted from the New Forest at Hatchet Pond, Fawley Inclosure, Beaulieu Heath, Bisterne Common, Pipers Wait and Pig Bush. No records of successful breeding were received. One pair probably bred Woolmer Forest.

Records of 29 sightings were received from 16 inland sites outside the New Forest. All records were of six or less apart from a gathering of up to 31 at Hucklesbrook Lakes from Mar 3rd-21st (max on 9th) and 16 at Burgate Meadows on Mar 24th.

Monthly maxima at the main localities and the approximate monthly totals (of grounded birds) for the county are tabulated below:

	J	F	M	A	M	J	J	A	S	O	N	D
Chichester Harbour	808	760	996	433	142	-	1650	1764	1654	1737	1414	770
East Hayling	179	372	347	95	50	-	501	395	456	618	323	257
Langstone Harbour	1250	670	796	309	176	450	1115	1676	1817	982	531	429
Portsmouth Harbour	250	220	546	-	-	-	-	-	38	241	225	254
Hamble Estuary	74	153	73	-	-	-	13	18	69	121	103	87
Lower Test/Eling/Bury Msh	25	48	23	-	-	-	44	35	47	51	45	30
Dibden Bay - Calshot	88	121	144	84	-	56	81	103	177	187	338	122
Needs Ore/Beaulieu Estuary	212	630	338	17	13	-	184	286	250	250	185	315
Sowley/Lymington	89	-	17	7	-	-	32	40	50	50	15	26
Lymington/Hurst	208	270	69	27	11	31	176	214	139	189	121	200
APPROX COUNTY TOTAL	2380	2480	2350	-	-	-	2150	2770	3040	2690	1890	1720

Spotted Redshank   *Tringa erythropus*

A moderately common passage migrant and scarce winter visitor.

Needs Ore held the majority of 12 wintering birds recorded in January with up to seven present; there were also two at Keyhaven/Pennington Marshes and single birds at Hayling Oysterbeds, Hook-with-Warsash and Calshot. In March numbers increased to a maximum of 13 at Needs Ore; single birds were still wintering at Farlington Marshes , Calshot and Keyhaven/Pennington Marshes.

Spring passage was recorded between Apr 8th and May 5th as follows:

Farlington Marshes : 1-2, almost daily Apr 8th-28th
Titchfield Haven: 1, Apr 21st.
*Needs Ore:*1, Apr 17th, 21st and 27th; 1, May 5th
Keyhaven/Pennington Marshes: 1, Apr 7th and 25th.

The first return was one at Titchfield Haven on June 9th. Two summer plumaged birds were at Pylewell Saltings on June 18th. From the middle of July there was a regular passage at:

Farlington Marshes : monthly maxima July-October 2,4,5,6.
Needs Ore: monthly maxima July-October 1,4,9,9

Inland, passage was noted from just one site with one flying west over Eversley GP on Oct 10th.

There were 13 wintering in December, with ten at Needs Ore and single birds at Farlington Marshes , Hamble Estuary and Ashlett Creek.

The minimum monthly totals are tabulated below:

J	F	M	A	M	J	J	A	S	O	N	D
12	7	16	10	1	4	3	12	16	19	2	13

Redshank   *Tringa totanus*

A moderately common but declining breeder, common passage migrant and winter visitor.

In the early year the eastern harbours held 1270, over 70% of the county total, with the rest distributed along the coast to the west except for singles inland at Tundry and Fleet Ponds and Lakeside CP (Eastleigh). Early year numbers were 550 less than December 2001, principally because of a lower count from East Hayling. Peak counts in the late year were similar to 2001. Monthly maxima at the main high tide roosts and approximate monthly totals for the county are tabulated below:

	J	F	M	A	M	J	J	A	S	O	N	D
Chichester Harbour	1264	736	1675	333	36	-	853	1827	1633	1911	1829	1332
East Hayling	256	245	353	-	2	-	28	65	331	430	185	289
Langstone Harbour	481	424	351	170	-	115	594	748	943	918	480	401
Portsmouth Harbour	484	671	593	-	-	-	-	-	457	733	859	680
Hamble Estuary	57	42	36	8	-	-	41	40	117	77	69	66
Lower Test/Eling/Bury Msh	88	40	73	5	4	5	9	5	60	87	50	70
Langdown/Fawley/Calshot	100	85	-	3	1	-	-	37	28	-	85	120
Beaulieu Estuary	70	67	105	57	28	-	34	56	77	84	85	45
Lymington/Hurst	98	121	140	47	18	12	72	186	262	160	90	116
APPROX COUNTY TOTAL	1740	1850	1800	350	150	250	800	1200	2100	2400	1800	1700

In the Avon valley, 18 pairs were located with three nearby at Blashford Lakes. Breeding was also confirmed at Winchester SF (one/two pairs) and The Vyne (three pairs). Single pairs were also reported between March and early May at Ashe, Avington Lake, Brown Candover, Hatchet Pond, Headbourne Worthy CB, Timsbury and Woolmer Pond but none stayed to breed. On the coast, 17 pairs held territory on Langstone Harbour Islands, six at Keyhaven Marsh, three at Hurst Castle and three at Hook-with-Warsash.

Inland records away from breeding areas included single birds at Tundry Pond (Jan 1st), Lakeside (1 S, Jan 6th), Fleet Pond (Jan 12th), East Worldham (Mar 17th), Odiham Airfield (July 9th) and Itchen Valley CP (1 NE, Sep 10th).

Greenshank   *Tringa nebularia*

A moderately common passage migrant; scarce winter visitor.

Approximately 30 wintered at coastal sites during the first quarter. All were at coastal sites with the exception of a single at Eversley GP on Feb 15th.

Spring passage was as usual light, with the majority passing through between mid April and mid May. Birds were recorded at five locations where none had wintered. Inland records were single birds at Sparsholt College Apr 24th and Winchester SF from Apr 27th-30th and Bisterne on May 12th. The last bird in spring was at Farlington Marshes on June 2nd.

The first returning bird was recorded from Farlington Marshes on June 21st. Three were there by June 24th and numbers there quickly built up to 15 at the same location by July 15th. Autumn passage was prolonged with significant numbers still passing through into the first week of November. Inland records came from eight sites with a minimum total of 36 including four at The Vyne on July 26th and eight there from Aug 25th-29th, six at Eversley GP on Aug 7th and four there between Aug 21st and Aug 23rd.

In December around 25 were present, all at coastal locations.

Monthly maxima at the main localities and the approximate county totals are tabulated below:

	J	F	M	A	M	J	J	A	S	O	N	D
Chichester Harbour	11	1	17	15	13	-	78	191	142	90	34	15
East Hayling	1	1	0	0	0	0	2	0	2	0	0	0
Langstone Hbr/Farlington	1	1	0	6	6	3	44	60	53	23	11	2
Portsmouth Hbr/Fareham Creek	4	4	3	0	0	0	5	10	13	5	2	1
Titchfield Haven	3	0	0	2	1	0	4	4	2	1	8	1
Hook-with-Warsash	1	7	1	1	0	0	3	14	10	11	8	8
Curbridge	5	5	10	9	2	0	20	5	7	0	1	2
Ashlett Creek/Calshot	0	0	0	0	0	0	2	2	2	0	0	0
Needs Ore/Beaulieu Estuary	3	1	2	2	1	0	6	18	11	10	2	1
Lymington/Hurst	3	2	5	6	3	0	13	16	17	18	7	5
APPROX COUNTY TOTAL	25	22	22	30	15	3	106	134	137	72	54	25

Green Sandpiper   *Tringa ochropus*

A passage migrant, scarce in spring and moderately common in autumn. Small numbers winter.

In the first quarter of the year approximately 45 were wintering, with ten at six coastal localities and 35 at 17 inland sites.

The last spring bird was at Overton Lagoons on May 17th. The first return was at Lower Test Marshes on June 1st. Autumn passage extended to around the middle of October and over that period 171 birds were recorded at 12 coastal sites and 128 at 31 inland sites.

In November and December, around 39 were wintering. Eight were at four coastal locations and 31 were at ten inland sites.

Monthly maxima at the main localities and the approximate county totals are tabulated below:

	J	F	M	A	M	J	J	A	S	O	N	D
Farlington Marshes	0	0	2	1	0	1	3	4	4	2	1	1
Titchfield Haven	1	0	0	1	0	3	7	10	8	6	1	1
Hook-with-Warsash	1	2	1	0	0	0	1	2	1	0	0	1
Lower Test Marshes	5	5	9	6	0	11	20	25	14	8	2	5
Needs Ore	0	0	1	1	0	0	6	6	4	1	0	0
Blashford Lakes	1	2	2	1	0	2	2	4	2	2	10	6
Overton Lagoons	2	3	2	1	1	0	1	1	0	0	0	0
Winchester SF	0	1	3	3	0	1	0	6	5	5	1	0
Eversley GP	1	4	5	1	0	2	4	5	3	3	1	1
APPROX COUNTY TOTAL	33	40	47	23	1	27	75	90	66	45	28	33

Other significant counts were as follows:

Sopley-Avon Causeway: 4, Feb 10th; 4, Dec 22nd.
Hucklesbrook Lakes: 6, July 4th; 15, July 16th; 6, July 21st.
Lymington Hurst: 4, July 20th.
The Vyne: 5, Aug 16th.
Timsbury: 5, Nov 17th.

Wood Sandpiper   *Tringa glareola*

A scarce passage migrant; more numerous in the autumn.

It was an average year with just two in spring, on a small gravel pit at Pennington Marsh on May 4th and at Lower Test Marshes on May 9th. The first was at Eversley GP on Apr 24th followed by one at Keyhaven Marsh on May 4th and another at Lower Test Marshes on May 9th.

Autumn passage involved about 20 between July 15th and Sep 19th. On the coast 13 were recorded:

Farlington Marshes : 2 juv, Aug 1st; 1, Aug 4th; juv, Aug 8th-19th; 1, Sep 3rd.
Titchfield Haven: 1, July 20th.
Needs Ore/Lepe: 1-2, Aug 4th -17th; 1-2, Sep 3rd-14th.
Lymington/Hurst: 1, July 15th-26th; 1, Aug 6th; 1, Aug 17th-29th; 1 E, Sep 5th.

Inland migration was notable with around seven involved:

Timsbury: 1, Aug 30th.
Woolmer Pond: 1, Aug 9th-10th; 1-2, Aug 13th-19th; 1, Sep 10th; 1, Sep 19th.
Bourley North: 1, Aug 4th.

The approximate monthly totals are shown below followed by annual autumn passage numbers 1993-2002:

J	F	M	A	M	J	J	A	S	O	N	D
0	0	0	1	2	0	2	12	5	1	0	0

	1993	1994	1995	1996	1997	1998	1999	2000	2001	2002
Wood Sandpiper	18	19	29	27	25	17	13	12	16	20

Common Sandpipers (David Thelwell)

Common Sandpiper   *Actitis hypoleucos*

A moderately common passage migrant; a few regularly winter; has attempted breeding at least once.

During the early year 11 were recorded from eight sites. Riverside Park, Southampton held birds throughout the period with four on Mar 18th and 28th. Other records all involving single birds were from Allbrook (Jan 1st), Spinnaker Lake, Blashford (Jan 5th-9th), Sopley (Jan 5th, Mar 3rd), Curbridge (Jan 5th, Feb 23rd), Lower Test Marshes (Jan 6th-20th) and Broadmarsh/Budds Farm SF (Jan 24th-Apr 14th).

Wintering birds at Riverside Park and Budds Farm lingered into early April. A single at Woolmer Pond on Apr 1st was possibly an early migrant. Singles were reported from Titchfield Haven on Apr 7th and Lower Test Marshes on Apr 11th. A more general passage began on Apr 17th with records from ten sites over the next three days. Spring passage was generally light, especially on the coast with only 38 at 12 sites and a highest count of just four at Titchfield Haven on Apr 23rd. There were 58 recorded from 26 inland sites. Passage was heaviest in the last week of April and first week of May. The last was a single at Lower Test Marshes on June 1st.

Four at Woolmer Pond on June 11th could have been failed breeding birds returning. Coastal return passage began with a single at Hayling Oysterbeds on June 21st. Approximately 300 were subsequently recorded from 21 coastal sites and 95 from 25 inland sites. Peak counts from the main coastal sites were as follows: Hayling Oysterbeds (27, July 26th; 10, Aug 21st), Farlington Marshes (11, July 14th; 16, Aug 4th), Fareham Creek (12, Aug 4th; 12, Sep 3rd), Hook-with-Warsash (12, July 24th), Lower Test Marshes (11, Aug 10th) and Cams Bay (12, Sep 3rd). The peak inland count was from Winchester SF where up to seven were recorded on various dates in July and August.

During November and December around nine were present, with records from Broadmarsh/Budds Farm (at least 2, throughout), Sopley-Avon Causeway (1, throughout), Riverside Park (1-4, throughout), Curbridge (1, Nov 23rd; 1, Dec 1st) and Portsmouth Harbour (1, Dec 7th).

The approximate monthly totals are tabulated below:

J	F	M	A	M	J	J	A	S	O	N	D
8	3	6	42	42	12	126	182	91	16	8	9

Turnstone   *Arenaria interpres*

A moderately common passage migrant and winter visitor. Small numbers summer.

Autumn counts were well above average, but as last year, it is difficult to conclude that this represents an increasing trend in numbers rather than better coverage of known roosts. As usual part of the Langstone Harbour roost moved to Hayling Bay in late autumn. Unfortunately there was no count for Hayling Bay in December.

Monthly maxima at the main localities are tabulated below:

	J	F	M	A	M	J	J	A	S	O	N	D
Chichester Harbour	52	82	173	137	5	-	14	52	40	164	75	100
East Hayling	-	17	47	-	-	-	-	-	-	2	6	3
Hayling Bay	100	150	1	-	-	-	-	-	-	70	159	-
Langstone Harbour	62	63	30	112	48	5	41	271	470	566	208	71
Portsmouth Harbour	23	15	44	-	-	-	-	-	29	-	119	46
Titchfield Haven/Chilling	15	41	60	45	34	7	25	53	64	56	62	70
Hamble Estuary	45	35	-	-	-	-	-	-	32	76	50	48
Langdown/Fawley/Calshot	6	-	-	-	-	-	-	-	-	15	2	2
Beaulieu Estuary/Lepe	56	43	40	10	11	-	2	56	96	39	60	44
Lymington/Hurst	66	73	63	67	49	4	11	61	78	49	47	48
APPROX COUNTY TOTAL	**450**	**500**	**300**	**250**	**110**	**17**	**75**	**450**	**800**	**900**	**750**	**400**

Spring movement was extremely light with one east off Sandy Point on Mar 23rd and a total of five and four flew east there on May 7th and 8th respectively. A total of nine flew east off Hurst Beach on May 7th and are likely to be in addition to those seen the same day at Sandy Point. Two groups totalling 24 left Langstone Harbour at dusk on May 3rd and five on June 2nd; all flew in a WNW direction.

A few non-breeders remained including four at Titchfield Haven from June 28th-July 18th but 41 at a roost in Langstone Harbour July 24th were presumably returning birds. Numbers increased in August with 230 were in Langstone Harbour on 30th and 467 by Sep 7th. Inland, an adult was at Eversley GP on July 31st.

Red-necked Phalarope   *Phalaropus lobatus*

A rare passage migrant (3,33,1).

An adult female in summer plumage was found on the evening of June 7th in Langstone Harbour (JCr). Later, the same evening, it flew onto Farlington Marshes, where it fed on the Deeps for a while before relocating to the Lake at dusk.

Grey Phalarope   *Phalaropus fulicarius*

A very scarce autumn and early winter visitor, usually occurring after gales. Very rare in December-February (?,237,2).

A first-winter was on the IBM Lake on Oct 15th/16th (GF). This was after a period of heavy rain and gales in the south-west of the country. Another was seen at close range on Janesmoor Pond, NF for an hour from 1015hrs on Nov 28th (MRC).

Pomarine Skua   *Stercorarius pomarinus*

A scarce passage migrant.

A relatively poor year by recent standards with a maximum of 21 birds recorded in the spring, including an early bird on Apr 7th (MPM, TP, RBW) and only a single in the autumn. All records are listed below:

Hurst Beach: 1 E, Apr 7th; 13 E, May 6th; 2 E, May 7th; 1 W, June 24th.
Sandy Point/Hayling Bay: 2 W, May 17th.
Hill Head: 1, May 12th; 1 E, May 17th; 1, Nov 10th.

Arctic Skua   *Stercorarius parasiticus*

A scarce passage migrant, recorded in every month except February.

Spring passage numbers were slightly up on 2001 with around 117 recorded between Apr 2nd and June 29th. After the first at Sandy Point on Apr 2nd no more were seen until Apr 17th. Peak counts were again made in late April/early May with only a few stragglers passing through after the third week of May. Spring records are summarised below:

Sandy Point/Hayling Bay: 20 E on 9 dates Apr 2nd - May 13th. The only multiple counts were 3 E, May 7th and 6 E, May 13th.
Hill Head/Stokes Bay: 12 E on eight dates Apr 17th - May 28th. Peak of 4E , May 13th.
Hook-with-Warsash: 1, Apr 26th; 1 NW, Apr 30th.
Needs Ore: 1 E, Apr 27th.

Hurst Beach/Milford on Sea: 85 E on 29 dates from Apr 17th-June 29th. Double-figures counts were: 11 E, Apr 28th; and 19 E, Apr 30th.

Autumn passage was again protracted with the first recorded at Hurst Beach on July 9th and the last there on Nov 20th. Approximately 34 were recorded in the county at six coastal sites. Records are summarised below:

Black Point/Sandy Point/Hayling Bay: 1 W, Aug 30th; 1 E, Sep 24th.
Farlington Marshes : 1 S, Aug 22nd; 1 W, Aug 30th.
Hill Head/Stokes Bay: 1, Aug 19th; 2 W, Sep 6th; 1, Sep 11th; 1, Sep 20th; 2, Sep 21st/22nd; 1, Oct 5th/6th.
Browndown: 1 E, Aug 18th.
Hook-with-Warsash: 1, Sep 22nd.
Hurst Beach/Milford on Sea: 4 E, July 9th; 1 E, July 11th; 1, Aug 7th; 2 E, Aug 9th; 1 E, Aug 19th; 1 W, Oct 24th; 1, Nov 10th; 1E, Nov 12th; 1 W, Nov 20th.

Surprisingly there were no records in the Hurst area between Aug 20th and Oct 23rd. As with Great Skua, a significant proportion (30%) of the birds was seen moving east. Most likely these were local movements in response to changing feeding conditions or sheltering in The Solent from autumn storms.

Approximate monthly totals are given below:

J	F	M	A	M	J	J	A	S	O	N	D
0	0	0	56	57	4	5	7	8	2	3	0

Long-tailed Skua   *Stercorarius longicaudus*

A rare spring and autumn passage migrant, also reported twice in winter (1,22,1).

One flew east past Hill Head at 1300 hrs on May 17th (IC).

Great Skua   *Stercorarius skua*

A very scarce passage migrant, most frequent in spring and autumn but recorded in all months.

A good year with two or three in the early winter period, seven in spring and a minimum of 14 in the autumn.

During February birds were recorded at Eastney and Hurst (two) on 1st and at Hill Head the next day. Subsequent sightings of single birds at Hurst on 5th, 9th, 11th and 26th probably related to one of the earlier birds.

Spring passage was ordinary by recent standards. All records are listed below:

Black Point/Hayling Bay: 1, May 13th; 1, May 16th.
Hill Head/Stokes Bay: 1, May 18th.
Hurst Beach/Milford on Sea: 4 E, Apr 29th.

After an early bird east past Hurst Beach on July 27th there were a further 13 up to Nov 21st. Interestingly, nine of these were noted moving east. All autumn records are listed below:

Hill Head: 1, Oct 15th.
Frater: 1, Nov 12th.
Hurst Beach/Milford on Sea: 1 E, July 27th; 1, Aug 7th; 1 E, Sep 16th; 1 E, Oct 15th; 1 E, Oct 24th;

1 E and 1 found dead, Oct 27th; 1 W, Nov 10th; 1 E, Nov 12th; 1 E, Nov 21st.
Barton on Sea: 1, Oct 26th.

Skua *sp*   *Stercorarius sp*

Five unidentified skuas were noted in the Hurst area on five dates from Apr 30th to Nov 12th. A single was at Hill Head on May 16th with a further two there on May 20th.

The annual totals of bird- months 1993-2002 for all skua species are as follows:

	1993	1994	1995	1996	1997	1998	1999	2000	2001	2002
Great Skua	5	13	14	10	15	27	15	32	38	24
Arctic Skua	95	141	125	169	122	101	120	115	139	151
Pomarine Skua	66	44	31	33	119	9	25	61	45	22
Long-tailed Skua	2	3	-	2	-	1	-	1	1	1

Mediterranean Gull   *Larus melanocephalus*

A scarce but increasing visitor and scarce breeder.

In the early winter period around 30 were resident on the coast with a further seven seen on a few dates only. The peak count was of ten in Portsmouth Harbour on Feb 14th. As in previous years, an early spring build up at the north-west end of Chichester Harbour and in Langstone Channel was most marked, with 35 in Chichester Harbour on Mar 11th and 51 in Langstone Harbour on Apr 13th, the highest of five double-figure counts. This probably represents pre-breeding concentrations of the Langstone colony.

During the breeding season 19 pairs fledged 11 young on the Langstone Harbour Islands. This is well down on the 20 young raised by 46 pairs in 2001. Elsewhere, up to six pairs were present but there was no indication that any young were produced.

In the late winter around 27 were resident with a further 11 wandering. The highest count was of 11 in Portsmouth Harbour on Dec 10th.

Few were seen inland and all the records are listed below;

Havant: 3 adults, Mar 9th; 2 adults SW, June 19th; adult, July 13th.
Lakeside CP, Eastleigh: first-winters, Jan 4th and 9th; second-winter, Jan 6th; first-winter, Mar 12th.
Petersfield Heath Pond: second-winter, Jan 15th.
Long Road, Soberton: second-winter, Dec 12th.
Fleet Pond: second-winter left E, Jan 1st
Waterlooville: adult hawking insects, Aug 14th.

Peak monthly counts at the main localities are tabulated below:

	J	F	M	A	M	J	J	A	S	O	N	D
Emsworth-Langstone Bridge	2	5	35	29	1	4	3	1	-	1	5	6
Black Point/Sandy Pt/Hayling Bay	3	1	3	4	4	3	4	1	1	1	2	-
Langstone Harbour	1	5	31	51	38	38	52	1	1	1	1	2
Portsmouth Harbour/Southsea	7	10	5	4	1	1	1	1	1	1	4	11
Gilkicker Point/Stokes Bay/Hill Hd	-	1	4	5	1	2	1	-	-	-	-	-
Weston Shore/Woolston/Itchen Est.	2	3	2	1	1	-	-	2	-	1	1	-
Inchmery/Lepe	1	-	10	1	2	5	2	-	-	-	-	-
Needs Ore/Beaulieu Estuary	-	5	7	12	2	6	-	-	-	-	-	-

Little Gull   *Larus minutus*

A scarce sometimes moderately common visitor, recorded in all months but most numerous in spring and autumn.

Approximately 300 were recorded during the year (*cf* 232 in 2001) and this high total was almost entirely due to unseasonal numbers in the late autumn in the wake of stormy weather.

1st summer Little Gull, Testwood Lakes, 27th Apr (Dan Philpott)

In the early year single figures were resident along the coast with a few more being recorded on single dates only. Spring passage commenced in mid March but numbers were well down on the previous year. The highest single day count was 12 east at Sandy Point on Apr 17th but passage had fizzled out by mid May. After the traditional summer and early autumn lull numbers picked up in October in association with storms mid month. A second, larger, peak was noted in November with the majority of birds in the Hurst area. 85 moved west there on Nov 12th but only single birds were noted elsewhere. Inland eleven birds were noted at six sites through the year.

Monthly maxima at the main coastal sites are tabulated below:

	J	F	M	A	M	J	J	A	S	O	N	D
Langstone Harbour	1	1	1	-	1	-	1	1	-	2	1	-
Hayling Bay	1	-	4	12	-	-	-	1	-	-	-	-
Hill Head/Stokes Bay	-	1	3	2	1	-	1	-	1	11	-	-
Lymington/Keyhaven	-	2	7	1	-	-	-	-	1	3	1	1
Hurst Beach/Milford on Sea	2	1	5	4	-	-	-	-	-	17	85	1

All inland records were as follows:

Ibsley Water: 3 adults, Mar 23rd, 1 still present Mar 30th; adult and first-winter, Oct 27th and Nov

24th.

Testwood Lakes: 1 first-winter, Apr 26th-28th.
Lakeside CP, Eastleigh: 1 first-winter, Feb 6th; 1 first-winter, Dec 28th/29th.
Alresford Pond: 1 first-winter, Jan 17th and 19th.
Fleet Pond: 1 first-summer, Apr 22nd.

Approximate bird month totals are given below:

J	F	M	A	M	J	J	A	S	O	N	D
6	6	25	30	21	0	2	2	2	58	142	3

Sabine's Gull   *Larus sabini*

A rare autumn passage migrant (1,142+,0).

2001 addition: One flew east at Stokes Bay between 0858-0910hrs on Oct 8th (PR).

Black-headed Gull   *Larus ridibundus*

A numerous resident, passage migrant and winter visitor.

Selected counts of over 1000 are listed below:

Coastal sites
Farlington/Langstone Harbour: 5400, Mar 29th; 4250, Apr 25th; 1000, July 16th/17th; 3000
    hawking insects, Aug 7th (but see breeding data for size of colony).
Portsmouth Harbour/Paulsgrove Reclamation: 3000, Jan 31st; 3000, Feb 9th; 4900, Mar 2nd; 1100,
    Sep 9th; 1160, Oct 5th; 8133, Nov 16th; 12,000, Dec 7th.
Eling (low tide feeding counts): 1000, Jan 26th; 1000, Feb 9th; 1000, Aug 17th.
Oxey Lake: 1700, Oct 18th.

Inland sites
Sopley-Avon Causeway: 1155 N, Dec 22nd.
Ibsley Water/Mockbeggar Lake (roost counts): 4500, Jan 4th; 3400, Mar 3rd; 1800, Oct 26th; 3000,
    Nov 24th.
Denmead/Waterlooville: 1500 hawking insects, Aug 14th.
Rowland's Castle: 1000, Dec 11th & 16th.
Ropley: 1000, Sep 1st.
Broadlands, Romsey: 1300 N, Nov 17th.
Lakeside CP, Eastleigh: 1000, Jan 23rd.
Queens Parade, Aldershot: 1070, Dec 30th.

Breeding records:
Langstone Harbour Islands: 2906 pairs raised 345 young.
Titchfield Haven: 1 pair bred – the first ever at this site.
Needs Ore: 6524 pairs, all failed due to wash out by high tides when the young were large.
Lymington/Hurst area: 3000 pairs raised large numbers of young despite storms in early July.

A 'white' bird with normal black primaries was at Tipner Lake on Nov 20th and 25th
and an albino was at Portsmouth Guildhall on June 12th.

Ring-billed Gull   *Larus delawarensis*

A very scarce visitor seen annually since 1991 (0,33,0).

Three were seen in the early year and one very late in the year. The adult, first seen on Feb
22nd 1998, returned again to Langstone Harbour and was seen regularly from Jan 22nd to

Mar 26th (m.o.). It returned once more from Dec 28th (JCr). A second-winter was seen briefly at Farlington Marshes on Jan 27th (JCr) and may have been one of two first-winters seen in the Langstone Harbour area in 2001. A further adult, or third-summer, was in Hayling Bay from April 9th-13th (SJW, TAL). This followed a second-summer present there in 2001. It is thus possible, indeed probable, that none of these birds were new to the county total, as the species exhibits surprising site fidelity in its choice of winter and spring quarters.

Common Gull   *Larus canus*

A common winter visitor and passage migrant; small numbers summer.

In the early year counts in excess of 250 were made on seven occasions with a cold weather influx of 900* leaving north from Ibsley Water at dawn on Jan 4th and notably 4000 south down Broom Channel, Langstone Harbour on Jan 23rd.

Evidence of spring passage was noted at six coastal sites. Farlington Marshes had the highest count with 103 on Mar 18th. Inland, feeding flocks were larger and reached three figures on eight occasions. A count of 600 at East Meon on Mar 4th was the highest of these although 700 were noted moving south at Petersfield, presumably to roost, on Mar 22nd.

During the breeding season a pair was resident at one site but there was no evidence of nesting.

In the late year the highest count was of 1000 at Ropley on Sep 1st with no other sites recording more than 400. Single leucistic/albino birds were again present in the Langstone Harbour area on Jan 10th and from June 30th to July 7th.

Lesser Black-backed Gull   *Larus fuscus*

A common visitor, which occurs in all months; the first successful breeding attempt was in 2001. It is most numerous in autumn and increasing in winter.

This species again bred in 2002. At Chickenhall Lane Industrial Estate in Eastleigh two pairs nested with unknown success and in Southampton a pair raised one young from a nest in the old docks area.

Outside the breeding season the Avon valley now appears to have taken over from Eling as the county's premier site for this species although no pre-roost counts appear to have been made at Eling. The county record was again beaten when 5500 were counted leaving Ibsley Water at dawn on Oct 26th (JMCk). At Blackbushe Airfield pre-roost numbers peaked at 692 on Aug 26th. The highest count away from these sites was of 400 at Wootton St Lawrence on Sep 16th. Counts for the three main sites are tabulated below:

	J	F	M	A	M	J	J	A	S	O	N	D
Ibsley Water	7	1	-	-	-	4	-	820	3100	5500	1070	45
Eling	8	5	3	-	-	-	-	28	-	54	-	18
Eversley/Blackbushe	-	-	-	-	-	1	30	692	557	512	0	

Presumed passage was noted as follows:

Sandy Point: 6 E, Apr 17th; 5 E, May 13th.
Farlington Marshes : 62 E, 16 dates between Mar 12th and Mar 6th.
Hurst Beach: 5 E, Mar 18th.

Petersfield: 22 NE, June 3rd.
Woolmer Pond: 7 E, Apr 26th.

Herring Gull   *Larus argentatus*

A common winter visitor and passage migrant with a scarce but increasing breeding population; small numbers (mostly immatures) summer.

Records were received from only eight coastal sites and a further nineteen inland. Numbers were highest in the eastern harbours with 1500 in Langstone Harbour on Jan 2nd and 1073 in Portsmouth Harbour on Dec 7th being the only totals over 1000.

Inland, 50 roosting at Ibsley Water on Jan 4th, 280 at Eastleigh SF on Mar 2nd, 250 at Long Down on July 4th and 62 at Winchester SF on Oct 27th were noteworthy but no other counts above 50 were made.

In the breeding season a minimum of 52 pairs was located at the five sites listed below:

Burrfields, Portsmouth: 1 pair raised 2 young.
Southampton Old Docks: 4 pairs, 2 failed but the others raised 3 young each.
Chickenhall Lane Ind Est, Eastleigh: Several pairs bred but success unknown due to difficulties with viewing the nesting area.
Langdown/Hythe MOD base: 33 occupied nests.
Fawley Refinery: 11 occupied nests but some sites from previous years were not checked.

Yellow-legged Gull   *Larus cachinnans*

A scarce visitor, mostly occurring in autumn.

The taxonomy of the Herring Gull complex is still under review by the BOU. In accordance with recent studies and literature, this *Report* represents Yellow-legged Gull as a full species with two distinct taxons, the western race, *L.c.michahellis* and the eastern race *L.c.cachinnans*. Most authorities currently refer to the eastern race as Caspian Gull.

Western Yellow-legged Gull *(L. c. michahellis)*

A scarce but regular visitor, mostly occurring in autumn.

Sightings were made at 14 coastal and nine inland areas. The late summer and early autumn build-up was, as always, most pronounced in the Eling/Redbridge area. Numbers peaked on the rather late date of Oct 5th. The 104 counted at high tide on that day represent the first three-figure count for the county (SSK). The only other sites where an autumn peak was noticeable were both inland. In the Fleet/Eversley area birds were recorded from the third week of July through to November peaking at six on Aug 25th and Sep 22nd. At Ibsley Water numbers built up from late August and continued through to the year's end. After a high of 22 on Nov 10th numbers rapidly dwindled to single figures.

Elsewhere no counts of more than three were made and many were just single birds. Several of these made protracted stays. For example adults in the Hook-with-Warsash and Sturt Pond areas stayed for three months from the end of June and early July respectively. A few movements were noted at Farlington Marshes (1 W, Sep 8th and 2 W, Oct 15th) and Hurst Beach (1 E, Sep 9th).

Monthly totals for the county are summarised below:

	J	F	M	A	M	J	J	A	S	O	N	D
Eling	1	1	1	0	1	0	73	94	69	104	2	2
Others	11	4	1	1	0	1	4	10	18	10	28	10
Total	12	5	2	1	1	1	77	104	87	114	30	12

Caspian Gull (*L. c. cachinnans*)
A very scarce autumn and winter visitor.

A first-winter was the only record as follows:

Keyhaven/Pennington Marshes: first-winter, Sep 25th & 27th (MPM, RBW), and the same individual Oct 5th.

[Note that all records of this taxon require detailed supporting notes for acceptance. The identification characteristics of *L. c. cachinnans* are becoming more widely known and identification of sub-adult birds such as this first-winter above are now better understood; developments in identification are well covered in the birding press e.g. *Birding World* Vol. 13, No. 2 and 11.]

Iceland Gull   *Larus glaucoides*
A very scarce visitor, usually in winter but recorded in all months except June (3,69,4).

A maximum of four was seen in the early year - the highest total since 1994. A third winter was at Weston Shore on Jan 13th (RB). An adult was seen from Hurst Castle on Jan 26th (MPM). A well watched second or third-winter bird frequented Southampton Water from Feb 2nd to Mar 15th (RB *et al*). It was most often seen between Netley and Weston Shore but visited Hook on Feb 4th and 10th (TFC) and Hill Head on Feb 7th, 10th and 11th (PDW). A first-winter was off Lee-on-the-Solent for 25 minutes on Feb 11th (PR).

Glaucous Gull   *Larus hyperboreus*
A very scarce visitor, usually in winter but recorded in every month (3+,89,2).

An adult was off Hurst Beach on Mar 23rd (MPM). A first-winter moved west off there on Nov 14th (AL).

Great Black-backed Gull   *Larus marinus*
A moderately common winter visitor and passage migrant; small numbers (mostly immatures) summer; occasionally breeds.

The regular breeding pair reappeared in the Avon valley in March but failed to raise any young. Other inland counts were made in a further eight areas with double-figure counts of ten roosting at Ibsley Water on Jan 3rd/4th, 17 at Alresford Pond on Jan 6th and 13 at Fleet Pond on the same date.

Birds were recorded along the length of the coast but only reached three figures as follows:

Langstone Harbour: 500, Jan 2nd.
Portsmouth Harbour/Paulsgrove Reclamation: 138, Oct 30th; 144, Nov 16th; 304, Dec 7th; 242, Dec 26th.

Keyhaven: 125, July 18th; 126, Dec 27th.

During the spring, eastward migration was noted in the Hurst area with seven on Mar 17th and 12 on Mar 18th. In the autumn, 25 west at Stokes Bay on Sep 6th was the only indication of return movement.

Kittiwake   *Rissa tridactyla*

A passage migrant and winter visitor, usually scarce but sometimes occurring in large numbers after gales.

Early year counts reached double-figures on 11 occasions in association with stormy weather, particularly in February. Seven of these counts were made in the Hurst area, the highest of which was 60 west on Feb 26th; in the Hill Head/Stokes Bay area 120 moved east on Feb 24th with a further 88 east on 26th.

Spring passage east through The Solent was light (*cf* Little Gull) and all records are summarised below:

Sandy Point/Hayling Bay: 20 E, 4 dates between Apr 17th and May 17th. Peak count 13, May 13th.
Hill Head/Stokes Bay: 2 E, May 13th; 5 E, May 17th.
Hurst Beach/Castle: 8 E, 6 dates between Mar 17th and June 6th.

Stormy weather in November was responsible for the high total in that month with most birds recorded in the Hurst area. All double-figure records for the late year are given below:

Hurst Beach/Castle: 41 W, Nov 9th; 46 W, Nov 12th; 121 S behind The Needles, Nov 20th; 33 E, Nov 21st; 11 W, Nov 24th.

The only birds to be recorded inland were single adults at Lakeside CP (Eastleigh) on Nov 10th and Dec 31st. The monthly county totals were:

J	F	M	A	M	J	J	A	S	O	N	D
103	435	13	6	22	4	1	1	1	15	307	2

Sandwich Tern   *Sterna sandvicensis*

A moderately common summer visitor and passage migrant; rarely recorded in winter.

The first of the year was seen off Hurst Beach on Mar 17th and was followed by records at a further four sites by the month end. Eastward passage through The Solent was slow with lower than average numbers recorded in the west, all sightings are summarised below:

Black Point/Hayling Bay/Sandy Point: 775 E between Mar 23rd and May 17th. Peak count 254 E on May 13th.
Stokes Bay: 333 E between Apr 5th and May 13th. Peak count 76 E on May 13th.
Hill Head: 154 E between Mar 21st and May 21st. Peak count 41 E on May 13th.
Hurst Beach/Castle: 97 E between Mar 17th and Apr 30th. Peak 27 E on Apr 21st.

Breeding was recorded at Langstone Harbour Islands where 29 pairs raised one young, Needs Ore where 226 pairs bred but failed to raise any young due to high spring tides and the Pitts Deep/Hurst area where 147 pairs in two colonies raised 16 young. There were no counts of 50+ after the spring until the build up of post-breeding birds in Langstone Harbour that peaked at 100 on Sep 5th.

Autumn passage was even quieter than spring and the only recorded movements were from Stokes Bay with 65 west on Sep 6th and 17 west on Sep 10th. Inland, three were seen at Lakeside CP, Eastleigh on Sep 13th and an adult was at Fleet Pond on Sep 21st. In October 20 records were received involving 49 birds including a peak of ten in Langstone Harbour on Oct 6th and inland a juvenile flying north-east at Fleet Pond on 3rd. During November, one bird remained in Langstone Harbour until 26th and it was joined by a second from Nov 4th-9th. It is perhaps the wanderings of this bird that account for the records from Portsmouth Harbour and Hill Head between Nov 16th and 18th. There were two records in December at Hurst Castle of a first-winter on 1st and an adult on 25th.

Roseate Tern   *Sterna dougallii*
A very scarce passage migrant, which occasionally breeds.

There was an early spring record when one moved west at Hill Head on Apr 24th. Subsequently, a minimum of 13 was noted moving east through The Solent between May 5th and 17th with totals of eight at Sandy Point (peak four, May 13th), four at Hurst, three at Stokes Bay and one at Hill Head. Reports of resting passage birds included up to three at Titchfield Haven/Hill Head between May 5th and 19th. Further reports from there involved one from June 23rd-29th and two on June 30th.

The now familiar run of late summer/autumn records was again a feature. In Langstone Harbour an adult was recorded on eight dates between July 14th and Aug 10th and two adults flew into the harbour at dusk on Aug 23rd. At Titchfield Haven/Hill Head, a minimum of four different adults was recorded between July 6th and Sep 1st although no more than two were recorded on any one date. A ringed juvenile was present between Aug 9th and 19th. Single adults were in Hayling Bay on July 22nd and at Hook Spit on Aug 4th. The last record relates to a late adult at Hill Head on Sep 22nd.

Common Tern   *Sterna hirundo*
A moderately common summer visitor and common passage migrant.

The first was one off Hurst Beach on Mar 17th (MPM). This is the earliest ever for Hampshire by eight days. The next were two again at Hurst Beach and one at Needs Ore on Apr 6th, but only eight more were recorded up to mid April. In common with other sea birds, eastward passage really got going from Apr 17th. From then until the end of May approximately 5600 moved through The Solent with heaviest passage recorded on May 13th, when counts of over 1000 were recorded at two watch points. Sea-watch records are summarised below:

Sandy Point/Hayling Bay: 2345 E, 9 dates between Apr 17th and May 17th. Peak count was 1045, May 13th.
Stokes Bay/Gilkicker Point: 456 E on 7 dates between Apr 17th and May 13th. The only three-figure count was 261 E, May 13th.
Hill Head: 1529 E, 8 dates between May 6th and May 21st. Peak count 648 E, May 13th.
Hurst Beach: 1672 E, between Mar 17th-May 28th. Peak count 1273 on May 13th.

Inland, about 171 birds were recorded in spring with 26 at Eversley GP on May 17th and 14 at Fleet Pond on Apr 26th being the highest counts.

In the breeding season the following counts of pairs were made:

Langstone Harbour Islands: 88 pairs raised 7 young.

Hayling Oysterbeds: 7 pairs raised 2 young.
Titchfield Haven: 1 pair.
Needs Ore: 20-30 pairs, breeding failed.
Pitts Deep-Hurst: 300 pairs raised 17+ young.
Blashford Lakes: 4 pairs raised at least 5 young.

A large post-breeding gathering was established in Langstone Harbour. The flock built up from 300 in late July, reaching 2000 on Aug 23rd, before peaking at 2300 on Sep 5th. A movement of 331 west past Stokes Bay from 0700-0900 hrs on Sep 6th could have been part of this flock. Three-figure counts were recorded at Hill Head/Titchfield Haven on ten occasions, the peak being 500 on Aug 3rd. Notable counts elsewhere included 300: at Chichester Harbour on July 23rd and at Hurst Beach with 120 E on July 12th. A total of 22 birds was recorded during October with the last two at Portsmouth Harbour on Oct 23rd.

Inland, 87 were recorded during the autumn from thirteen sites, including nine at Fleet Pond on July 7th and 30 roosting at Eversley GP on July 14th.

Arctic Tern
Sterna paradisaea

A scarce passage migrant.

Numbers reported in spring were down on recent years with a total of 48 passing east through The Solent between Apr 17th and May 20th. Peak counts were 15 at Stokes Bay on Apr 17th and 14 at Hill Head on May 20th. No other double-figure counts were received. All coastal spring records are given below:

Hayling Bay/Sandy Point: 1 E, Apr 17th; 2 W, Apr 30th; 1 E, May 13th.
Stokes Bay: 15 E, Apr 17th; 2 E, Apr 21st.
Hill Head/Titchfield Haven: 1, May 17th; 14 E, May 20th.
Needs Ore: 4 E, May 7th.
Hurst Beach: 1 E, Apr 17th; 1, May 8th.

Inland spring records were received from Winchester SF with one on Apr 30th and four on May 13th. There was also one at Fleet Pond on May 1st.

Autumn passage extended from July 20th to Oct 17th during which time 51 birds were seen, 41 of which were in a single flock on Aug 18th. There was only a single inland record, one at Fleet Pond on Oct 3rd. All coastal autumn records are given below:

Langstone Harbour: 1, Aug 15th; 41 SW in one flock at 1500 hrs on Aug 18th (JCr, RAC) - by far the largest number ever recorded in autumn.
Titchfield Haven: 2, July 20th; 1, Aug 18th.
Southampton, Itchen Bridge: 1, Aug 13th.
Southampton, Mayflower Park: 3, Aug 14th.
Hurst Beach: 1, Oct 17th.

Little Tern
Sterna albifrons

A moderately common summer visitor and passage migrant; recorded once in winter.

The first records were on Apr 10th with one east at Keyhaven and five at Hayling Oysterbeds. Numbers increased rapidly from mid April as passage began. From then until May 17th approximately 220 moved east through The Solent. Records from the main sea-watching sites are summarised below:

Sandy Point/Hayling Bay/Black Point: 134 E, 7 dates between Apr 17th and May 17th; peak 37, May

13th.
Stokes Bay: 14 E, 3 dates between Apr 21st and May 7th, with peak of 9 E, May 7th.
Hill Head/Browndown: 71 E, 7 dates between Apr 24th and May 17th, with peak 36 E, May 13th.
Hurst Castle and Beach: 66 E, 4 dates Apr 24th to May 10th, with peak 31 E, May 5th.

During the breeding season 175 pairs were present at three sites as follows:

Langstone Harbour Islands: 14 pairs, no young raised.
Hayling Oysterbeds: 122 pairs raised 27-31 young.
Lymington/Hurst: 39 pairs raised 12 young.

During the autumn, the highest counts were of 80 in Langstone Harbour on Aug 1st and 70 there on Aug 6th. As always, numbers dropped off quickly in September with only two recorded on two dates. The last record was one in Langstone Harbour on Sep 12th.

The table below summarises annual numbers of breeding pairs of tern species 1993-2002 indicating that populations, whilst fluctuating from year to year, appear to show long term stability:

Breeding pairs	1993	1994	1995	1996	1997	1998	1999	2000	2001	2002
Sandwich Tern	277	298	233	219	246	250	334	356	271	402
Common Tern	348	418	352	363	338	332	457	311	418	430
Little Tern	155	96	123	150	160	136	145	154	192	165

Black Tern   *Chlidonias niger*

A moderately common passage migrant.

2002 marked a return to more normal numbers, with about 234 recorded between Apr 21st and May 17th then again between July 23rd and Oct 2nd, of which only five were seen inland. The heaviest spring coastal passage occurred between May 8th and 17th, when the only inland bird was seen. Spring records are summarised below:

Coastal sites
Sandy Point: 1 E, May 7th; 1 E, May 8th; 6E, May 13th; 3E, May 17th.
Langstone Harbour: 2, May 10th; 1, May 18th.
Stokes Bay: 1E, May 13th.
Hill Head/Titchfield Haven: 1E, Apr 24th; 7E, May 8th; 8E, May 13th; 1E, May 16th; 1E, May 17th.
Hurst Beach: 1E, Apr 21st; 4E, May 8th; 9E, May 13th.
Pennington Marsh: 1, June 2nd.

Inland sites
Winchester SF: 1, May 17th.

Return passage started with a trickle from July 23rd, picking up pace in mid August. The peak passage was in late August and early September and had almost ceased by mid month. The last bird was recorded at Hill Head on Oct 2nd. All autumn records are summarised below:

Coastal sites
Sandy Point/Black Point/Hayling Bay: 1, July 23rd; 1, Aug 13th; 1, Aug 15th; 7, Aug 18th; 7, Aug 22nd; 9, Aug 31st; 1, Sep 13th.
Langstone Harbour: 104 bird-days between July 26th and Sep 8th including 12, Aug 5th; 9, Aug 25th.
Lee on Solent: 3, Sep 4th.
Hill Head/Titchfield Haven: 2, July 31st; 1, Aug 2nd; 2, Aug 3rd; 1, Aug 5th; 2, Aug 21st; 4, Aug 22nd; 1, Aug 30th; 2, Aug 31st; 3, Sep 1st; 8, Sep 6th; 1, Oct 2nd.
Hook-with-Warsash: 3, Aug 3rd; 2, Aug 19th.

Pennington/Keyhaven Marsh: 1, Aug 10th; 4, Aug 25th; 1, Aug 28th.
Hurst Beach: 1, July 31st; 3, Aug 9th; 2, Aug 10th; 2, Aug 17th.

Inland sites
Testwood Lakes: 1, Sep 13th.
The Vyne: 1, Aug 25th; 2, Sep 1st.

The table below summarises spring passage numbers (measured as the annual totals of bird-days for eastbound spring passage through the Solent) for all regularly occurring tern species:

Spring passage	1993	1994	1995	1996	1997	1998	1999	2000	2001	2002
Sandwich Tern	408	1092	940	516	292	269	923	819	1005	1059
Roseate Tern	5	6	4	7	1	4	16	5	8	13
Common Tern	2063	2717	3440	2887	931	2398	5930	3916	4600	5600
Arctic Tern	109	25	4	49	19	29	48	95	95	48
Little Tern	205	412	197	273	42	54	238	296	247	220
Black Tern	102	142	68	183	45	74	69	86	89	36

Guillemot *Uria aalge*

A scarce but increasing winter visitor and passage migrant.

An unusually high total of 201 was seen during the year although, sadly, 18 of these were tide line corpses. Numbers peaked in late January and early February, with a total of 121 being seen, although there may be some duplication of records in The Solent. Double-figure counts were made at both Hurst and Stokes Bay.

A count of 40 on Feb 3rd at Hurst Castle (MPM) is the highest day total ever reported in the county. Four sites had counts exceeding the previous day maximum of ten on Oct 23rd 1981. The majority of corpses was also found during this period although relatively few were oiled. The early year passage reduced to more normal numbers in spring and the only record for the summer months was of a juvenile seen from Hurst Beach on July 12th.

In the late year, only 22 were seen including two dead or dying birds. The peak count was 15 east at Hook-with-Warsash on Nov 9th. Of interest, a single record of the bridled form was received from Hurst Castle on Oct 21st.

Monthly totals for the county follow:

J	F	M	A	M	J	J	A	S	O	N	D
72	88	4	3	13	0	1	0	0	2	8	10

Razorbill *Alca torda*

A scarce but increasing passage migrant and winter visitor.

It was a well above average year, perhaps reflecting the health of breeding colonies of this species elsewhere on the south coast. A total of 117 was seen throughout the year. Even allowing for some duplication, this number far exceeds that of any previous year. Peak counts were at the end of January and early February when 44 were seen. The count from Hurst Beach of 20 on Feb 2nd is the highest day total for Hampshire (MR), exceeding the previous maximum of 17 on Oct 4th 1981. Unfortunately, 15 corpses were also found during the first three months of the year although only a few appeared to be the result of oil spillage.

During the summer, two moulting juveniles were in the Hurst/Keyhaven area from July 31st-Aug 27th.

In late autumn/early winter, 33 were seen. The peak count was five at Hurst Beach on Dec 16th. Monthly totals for the county follow:

J	F	M	A	M	J	J	A	S	O	N	D
23	51	3	2	1	0	2	2	1	14	6	12

Little Auk   *Alle alle*

A very scarce winter visitor, usually appearing following storms (10+,103+,5)

A total of five was seen at three different sites including three individuals early in the year in Stokes Bay following gales in the last week of January. The other two were seen in the more typical month of November. The records were as follows:

Stokes Bay: 2, Jan 31st (NM); 1 E, Feb 3rd (GC, IC).
Hill Head: 1, Nov 23rd (SI).
Hurst Beach/Castle: 1, Nov 12th (MPM, AL, RBW).

Auk sp.   *Uria/Alca sp.*

Total records of 115 unidentified auks, either Guillemot or Razorbill, were received from four different sites. The total of 50 reported from Stokes Bay on Jan 27th was noteworthy as the highest county day count for either of the two species or a mix thereof; monthly bird totals of unidentified auks follow:

J	F	M	A	M	J	J	A	S	O	N	D
62	48	0	0	5	0	0	0	0	0	0	0

The table below summarises the annual totals of bird-months 1993-2002 of the four auk species:

Annual bird-months	1993	1994	1995	1996	1997	1998	1999	2000	2001	2002
Puffin	0	0	0	3	0	2	0	3	0	0
Guillemot	32	35	59	32	24	39	56	54	33	201
Razorbill	13	28	24	26	23	21	29	30	30	117
Little Auk	3	1	13	9	3	14	1	1	3	5

Feral Pigeon   *Columba livia*

A common resident.

Five observers submitted 18 records of this species. The maximum count was of 490 at Posbrook Lane, Titchfield on Nov 15th. Of the four other counts reaching 400, three were from the Southseaarea and the other was from Crondall – all were in the winter periods.

Stock Dove
Columba oenas

A numerous resident and winter visitor.

Just three gatherings reached three figures all year: 100 at Winchfield Moor on Feb 5th, 106 at Long Down on Mar 24th and 114 at Gander Down on Apr 17th (mirroring the spring 2001 gathering there). Just 32 other reports were received of flocks and none greater than 75 were seen in the latter part of the year.

Only thirteen territorial pairs were reported, indicative of the paucity of records for this common species. Movements were also poorly reported: 60 flew north over Petersfield on Feb 2nd, 30 flew west at Bedhampton on Nov 1st and 40 flew south-west over Strodgemoor Bottom on Dec 14th.

Wood Pigeon
Columba palumbus

An abundant resident and winter visitor.

Large flocks in the early year included 1500 at Overton on Jan 1st, 3000 at Popham on Jan 12th, 2000 at Hambledon on Mar 9th and 1000 as late as Apr 19th at Idsworth. On the latter date, the spring counts of feeding birds at Farlington Marshes reached a maximum of 110.

A leucistic bird was at Ashe Park Lake on two dates in the early year.

Few indicators of movement were noted in the first half of the year, peak counts included 260 moving south-west at Southington Lane on Jan 4th and 220 also south-west over Whitchurch eleven days later.

Very few records of breeding were received. The highest total was 48 pairs in the Lower Test Marshes NR CBC plots. Interestingly a pair held territory and may have bred on the Langstone Harbour Islands.

Autumn passage commenced on Oct 23rd when 116 flew south-west over Fleet Pond. Just over 23,000 were then noted up to Nov 17th, mostly moving west or south-west, with a maximum count of 9350 west at Hook-with-Warsash on Nov 4th. Inland, 482 moved south-east at Fleet Pond on Nov 2nd and 1000 flew east in two hours at Plaitford Common, NF on Nov 16th. However, some subtle aspects of autumn movements remain to be clarified, as 1400 moved north-east over the Broadlands Estate on Nov 17th.

Few large winter gatherings were noted at the year's end, the maximum was only 600 at Morestead on Dec 31st.

Collared Dove
Streptopelia decaocto

A numerous resident and passage migrant.

Only fifteen records were submitted. No count reached three figures (maximum 95 at Cams Bay on Sep 25th), there was no record indicative of movements and the only counts of breeding pairs were 14 at Lower Test Marshes NR CBC plots. A leucistic bird was at Overton in early April.

Turtle Dove
Streptopelia turtur

A moderately common, but declining, summer visitor and passage migrant.

The first arrivals noted were singles at Lakeside CP and Petersfield on Apr 21st and a further four singles were seen by the month's end. Passage was poorly recorded on the coast, with just four reports from non-breeding sites. Most inland territories were reoccupied by the end of the first week of May.

Just over 100 breeding season records were received involving some 90 territories, with eight at Ringwood Forest (down from 11 in 2001), six at Noar Hill and just six at Martin Down (12 in 2001). Along the Basingstoke Canal, none were present in an area where they had been recorded in previous surveys undertaken in 1978 and 1991 and there were also none noted in the Timsbury/Romsey area. The table below summarises the reported totals of breeding pairs 1993-2002:

Breeding pairs	1993	1994	1995	1996	1997	1998	1999	2000	2001	2002
Turtle Dove	40	60	78	70	90	70	80	81	90	90

After mid-August only twelve reports were received of ones and twos to a total of 14. The last were singles at Titchfield Haven and Sinah Common on Sep 21st and 22nd respectively.

Ring-necked Parakeet
Psittacula krameri

A very scarce visitor, possibly resident.

This species remains very scarce in Hampshire. Only one record is considered sufficiently detailed to be included here, one was at Sway on Dec 21st. (SGK)

Cuckoo
Cuculus canorus

A moderately common summer visitor.

A very early arrival was heard singing at Liss on Mar 21st, a fortnight ahead of the next, at Lower Test Marshes on Apr 4th. One at Warnford was on the more expected date of Apr 11th, but the main arrival started from Apr 15th. It seems likely that migration continued well into May: A single male was at Farlington Marshes from May 8th-28th, but up to three were singing there in late May and early June.

About 77 records indicative of breeding were submitted, including seven territories in the Lower Test Marshes NR CBC plots, five males singing around Liss and three territories at Titchfield Haven. On a negative note, none were found breeding at Abbotts Ann for the first time in 15 years.

Just ten (at least seven of them juveniles) were noted after the beginning of July, the last being a juvenile at Farlington Marshes on Sep 21st.

Barn Owl
Tyto alba

A moderately common resident.

Based on the number of records received, the population of Barn Owls in the county seems to be fairly stable. As in recent years, records came from about 60 sites with the majority in the south-west, the main river valleys and the north-east. Approximately one third were from Titchfield Haven, illustrating the concentration of observers rather than number of Barn Owls on the site! Breeding was confirmed for 16 pairs and, of these, six pairs raised 15 young mainly in nest boxes.

Little Owl   *Athene noctua*

A common resident.

During the Tetrad Atlas Survey (1986-91), Little Owls were found in 531 or 52% of Hampshire tetrads and this was almost certainly an under-estimate. In 2002, reports were received from just 66 sites, mainly on the coast and in the east and north-east. It is scarce in the New Forest but there is very little information about numbers in the centre and north-west of the county, where only 14 were reported from the block of 11 ten km squares, SU33-35, 43-45, 53-55, 63 and 64 (a total area of 1100 square km). No records were received at all from four of these squares, and the species is clearly under-recorded.

Little Owl, Needs Ore Point (Rosemary Watts/Powell)

Tawny Owl   *Strix aluco*

A common resident

As with the previous owl species, most of the records received were from known breeding sites, however a few were from areas where breeding was not confirmed during the Tetrad Atlas Survey (1986-91). These included proven breeding at Milford on Sea, Curbridge, Drayton and East Meon. One at Needs Ore on Sep 3rd is also noteworthy because Tawny Owls are scarce on the coast and were not found at this location during the Tetrad Atlas Survey. Adults are generally sedentary but there is some dispersal of juveniles and the Needs Ore bird may have moved into the area from a breeding site elsewhere.

Observers are asked to submit all breeding season (February-July) records of this species and records in other months from areas where it is not normally recorded. Non-breeding records need to be qualified with a note to the effect that the species is not normally recorded at the site otherwise it will not be input to the database.

Short-eared Owl   *Asio flammeus*

A scarce but regular winter visitor and passage migrant that occasionally breeds.

After the relatively poor showing in recent years, 2002 was better with records in all months other than July and August. The first was at Farlington Marshes on Jan 11th and 12th. On Jan 13th one was at Ashley Warren and on Jan 18th another, or possibly the same bird, was flushed from maize at nearby Hare Warren Farm. Back in Langstone Harbour one was on North Binness Island on Jan 30th/31st. In February and March records continued from Langstone Harbour with regular reports of single birds from Farlington Marshes and the Islands. Two birds were seen at Farlington Marshes on Feb 3rd and Mar 24th and on

North Binness Island on Feb 9th. Elsewhere during this period, one was at Dibden Bay on Mar 19th and Cheesefoot Head on March 24th. Records of one or two birds continued from Farlington Marshes and the Islands until Apr 24th, then of one at Farlington Marshes from May 1-10th. There were three late spring records with one at Tidgrove Airstrip on May 9th, another at Farlington Marshes on June 1st and the last at Keyhaven Marsh on June 6th.

In autumn some early records were of birds moving west along the coast. The first were again from Langstone Harbour with one at Farlington Marshes on Sep 1st and Sep 4th and two on the Islands on Sep 2nd. One was seen flying high west at The Kench on Sep 4th. There were no further records until Sep 24th when one was seen at Needs Ore at 1400 hrs and, possibly the same bird, flying west along Hurst Beach at 1750 hrs. One was at Farlington Marshes on Sep 26th. In October and November most records continued to be from the coast with single birds at Lymington/Hurst on Oct 5th and Nov 4th, Titchfield Haven on Oct 5th and 19th, Brownwich on Oct 6th, Farlington Marshes on Nov 9th, 29th and 30th, Dibden Bay/Hythe Marina on Nov 17th and Broadmarsh/Bedhampton on Nov 18th. Records continued from the Langstone Harbour area into December with the last seen arriving at Langstone South Moor from the RSPB Islands on Dec 12th.

The first inland records of the second winter period were from the New Forest where a roost was discovered on Nov 17th. Three were seen on Nov 19th and at least one remained in the area to at least Dec 22nd. All other inland records were in December. One was at Martin Down on 19th, Ashley Warren on 21st, Old Winchester Hill on 22nd and 28th and Droxford on 28th. There were two at Leckford on 28th.

Approximate monthly totals are tabulated below:

J	F	M	A	M	J	J	A	S	O	N	D
4	3	4	2	1	2	0	0	3	4	7	8

Nightjar   *Caprimulgus europaeus*
A moderately common summer visitor and passage migrant.

The first records were all from known breeding sites in the north-east. One at Hazeley Heath on May 9th was followed by records from Abbots Wood Inclosure and Longmoor Inclosure on May 10th, Yateley Heath Wood on May 12th and Tweseldown on May 15th. The only record of visible migration was of two, probably just in off the sea, flying low over playing fields at HMS Daedalus Airfield at 0930 hrs on May 20th. Away from known breeding sites, there was also a record of a bird on the road at dusk at Teglease Down on May 26th.

As usual for this species, counts during the breeding season were far from complete. Records of 28 territories/churring males were submitted from the New Forest, including counts of five churring males at both Fields Heath and Holmsley Walk. On the Thames Basin and Wealden Heaths 75 territories/churring males were counted from 16 sites but important locations such as Warren Heath, Woolmer Forest and Yateley Common were not surveyed. Although incomplete, the counts suggest that the north-east population is being maintained although probably no longer growing. In the south-east ten territories/churring males were reported from three sites including four at Havant Thicket and three at West Walk. A bird was also seen on the road at Clanfield at dusk on July 18th. Elsewhere, ten birds were reported from four sites, two of which, Blackfield Totts Down and Burton Common, were on the edge of the New Forest. No counts were received from Ringwood

Forest.

Available counts at sites outside the New Forest are tabulated below:

Thames Basin Heaths		Wealden Heaths	
Bourley Heath/Long Valley	8	Alice Holt Forest	7
Bramshill Plantation	6	Broxhead Common	3
Bricksbury Hill	11	Liss Forest	1
Eelmoor Marsh/Pyestock Wood	2	Lichett Plain, Thames Basin	1
Eversley Common/Castle Bottom	2	**South-east**	
Hawley Common	2	Botley Wood	2
Hazeley Heath	7	Havant Thicket	4
Longmoor Inclosure, Wealden	16	West Walk	3
Tadley Common	1	Wickham Hundred Acres	1
Tweseldown	2	**Elsewhere**	
Velmead Common	3	Blackfield Totts Down	4
Yateley Heath Wood	3	Burton Common	4
		Martin Down	1

There were three September records all from the New Forest or close by. Singles were at Wootton Coppice Inclosure on Sep 5th, in Denny Wood on Sep 11th and the last was at Blackfield on Sep 13th.

Swift
Apus apus

A numerous summer visitor and passage migrant.

The first records were unusual in that they included a double-figure count; ten were seen over Avon Causeway and one at Cams Bay on Apr 20th. Over the following week small numbers were seen at several sites, mainly on the coast, with the next double-figure counts of ten at Farlington Marshes and Titchfield Haven on Apr 27th. The largest counts in early May were again from Farlington Marshes where there were 75 north-east on May 3rd. Counts from this well-watched site showed peaks of 160 on May 25th, 130 on May 29th and 150 on June 9th. Elsewhere, three-figure counts were made at Fleet Pond (100 on May 26th) Winchester SF (100 on May 30th) Titchfield Haven (100 on June 4th) and latterly at Hook-with-Warsash (292 north-west on June 27th, the highest count of the spring).

High numbers continued into July at Farlington Marshes with the monthly maximum of 100 on July 11th. Inland, the only three-figure count was at Woolmer Pond with 120 on July 21st. Return migration was noted from late July including a maximum of 120 SSW over Fleet on July 27th. The last three-figure count of the year was 200 at Langstone Harbour entrance on Aug 5th. Passage continued throughout August although numbers were generally very low. The last double-figure count was ten at Southsea on Aug 15th. There were eight September records and the last was at Pylewell Saltings on Sep 19th.

Kingfisher
Alcedo atthis

A moderately common resident whose numbers may be severely depleted during harsh winters.

Over 500 records were received from 145 sites (compared with 365 records from 120 sites in 2001). Most came from the main river valleys, lakes, gravel pits and ponds, including garden ponds, and, particularly outside the breeding season, from the coast. More surprisingly, one was seen flying down East Street in central Southampton on Jan 3rd. The highest count at any single location was seven at Blashford Lakes on Nov 24th. There were six at Yateley GP on Nov 18th and five at the same site on Sep 10th and Dec 9th.

Regular counts at well-watched coastal sites demonstrated the familiar pattern with birds moving to and becoming much more obvious on the coast after the breeding season. Noteworthy was one seen flying across the mouth of Chichester Harbour from Sandy Point, Hayling to East Head in West Sussex on July 28th. Bird days at selected coastal sites are given below:

	J	F	M	A	M	J	J	A	S	O	N	D
Farlington Marshes	0	0	1	0	0	0	0	2	19	14	5	0
Bedhampton Creek	1	1	0	0	0	0	2	3	7	8	11	12
Hook-with-Warsash	2	1	3	2	0	0	3	8	9	5	1	2
Titchfield Haven	1	0	0	0	1	5	8	22	18	25	11	18

Out of the total 500 records, approximately one quarter were during the breeding season (March–July) and the majority of these would refer to birds on territory. Counts of actual territories included four on the River Itchen up to Allbrook and 12 north of Winchester. There were five territories at Somerley Park in the Avon valley and two along the River Blackwater at Eversley GP. Elsewhere there were seven reports of occupied nests or recently fledged young.

Bee-eater   *Merops apiaster*

A rare vagrant (0,8,2).

One was heard and seen at Longstock at 1855 hrs on Aug 15th (MJ). It was relocated hawking for insects over the village early on Aug 16th and seen again later that morning (MJ, BG). Another flew over the observer's house at Ashley on Aug 26th (PS). These are the ninth and tenth records for Hampshire.

Hoopoe   *Upupa epops*

A very scarce passage migrant; bred on eight occasions during 1953-59 but not since (?,176,3).

Three were recorded, all in April. The first was at Densome Corner, NF on Apr 7th (EN) and presumably the same individual was nearby at Godshill on 9th (JA). One was present in a garden at Hythe on Apr 15th/16th (CR) with the last at Barton on Sea on 22nd (SW).

2001 addition: One was in horse paddocks at Sinah, Hayling Island from 1225-1234 hrs on Apr 29th before it was disturbed by a Magpie and flew off (JCr).

Wryneck

Jynx torquilla

A very scarce passage migrant; formerly bred.

A good year with 19 records referring to 12 individuals including one in spring and one during the breeding season:

The Mill Field, Barton's Mill, Old Basing: 1, Apr 13th.
New Forest: 1, June 26th. This bird was behaving territorially and singing throughout the morning but was not seen subsequently.
Farlington Marshes : 1, Aug 26th, identified as a juvenile/first-winter.
Abbotts Barton: 1, Aug 28th.
Sandy Point: 1, Aug 29th.
Slufters Inclosure, NF: 1, Aug 31st.
Markway Inclosure, NF: 1, Sep 3rd.
Bramshott Common: 1, Sep 4th.
Eastleigh: 1, Sep 6th.
Lymington/Hurst: 1, Sep 7th.
Hampton Ridge, NF: 1, Sep 19th.
Monxton: 1, Sep 26th.

Wryneck, Farlington Marshes, Aug 26th
(Jason Crook)

Green Woodpecker

Picus viridis

A common resident.

The majority of records came from the north-east where the species is surveyed as part of the monitoring programme on the Thames Basin and Wealden Heaths. Examples of counts included 18 territories on the Bourley/Long Valley/Tweseldown and Velmead Common area, six on Hazeley Heath and 20 in Longmoor Inclosure. A survey of the Basingstoke Canal (see paper elsewhere in this report) located six territories. Elsewhere, four territories were counted on Hayling Island and three at Lower Test Marshes NR and Hook Valley, Warsash.

The species was seen more frequently than usual at Farlington Marshes , a non-breeding site. Records were obtained in all months other than June with monthly bird-day totals as follows:

	J	F	M	A	M	J	J	A	S	O	N	D
Farlington Marshes	5	4	12	10	10	0	4	14	6	13	7	12

On most occasions only one bird was seen but two were present occasionally including an adult and a juvenile on July 7th. This all suggests probable breeding close by, just to the north or north-east of the reserve. The only other records from a non-breeding site were of single birds at Horsea Island, Portsmouth Harbour on July 13th and Aug 10th.

Great Spotted Woodpecker

Dendrocopos major

A common resident.

As with the previous species, most records came from the north-east heaths. They included counts of 17 territories on Bourley /Long Valley and Tweseldown and 14 in Longmoor Inclosure. A survey of the Basingstoke Canal located 11 territories. Elsewhere there were six territories at Lower Test Marshes NR, five on Hayling Island and three at both Hook Valley, Warsash and on the Longstock WBS.

Records from coastal non-breeding sites included several from Farlington Marshes , where the monthly bird-day totals were as follows:

	J	F	M	A	M	J	J	A	S	O	N	D
Farlington Marshes	2	0	2	0	0	0	2	4	2	3	2	12

All sightings were of single birds other than on Dec 11th when at least three individuals were present. On Mar 12th one flew east and was seen to land on North Binness Island and on Oct 6th one left high to the west. Elsewhere, single birds were seen at Horsea Island on Jan 12th, Mar 2nd and Nov 16th, also at IBM Lake on June 15th and regularly from Aug 15th to Oct 16th (when two were present) and at Lymington/Hurst on July 11th, 17th and Sep 7th with two on 8th.

Lesser Spotted Woodpecker   *Dendrocopos minor*
A moderately common resident.

A total of 83 records was submitted from 53 sites, continuing the strong downward trend noted in recent years. Whether this represents a real reduction in population or simply reflects a fluctuation in the level of recording is unclear. However the fact that only 21 records were from the New Forest, the stronghold of the species in the county, suggests that the level of recording is low. Many records referred to territorial, calling or drumming, birds in the February-June period but the only evidence of confirmed breeding was a juvenile caught in Fareham on June 24th. One encouraging aspect of the breeding season records is that at least 11 were from sites where breeding was not confirmed during the Tetrad Atlas Survey (1986-91). These included two or three males in a 40 ha wood at South Boarhunt. A record of one at Titchfield Haven on Jan 19th was the first there for over a year.

Woodlark   *Lullula arborea*
A moderately common but local resident and passage migrant.

There were relatively few records of overwintering birds at the beginning of the year. The largest flock was at Wickham Hundred Acres, which peaked at 13 on Jan 12th. There were also four at Prince's Marsh, Liss from Jan 8th until Apr 14th. In contrast, there were several early records from known breeding sites in the New Forest and the north-east. These included a bird at Bourley and Long Valley on Jan 14th and a singing male at Longmoor Inclosure on Jan 15th with records from a further 11 sites by the end of February. The only records of possible spring migrants were from Hook-with-Warsash where single birds were seen on Mar 8th and Apr 8th.

During the breeding season, 98 pairs/singing males were located on the Thames Basin and Wealden Heaths in the in the north-east but several important sites were either not covered at all (e.g. Ludshott Common) or not covered fully (e.g. Warren Heath/Heath Warren and Woolmer Forest). If allowance is made for this under-recording, the area total was probably around 120 pairs/singing males.

More records were received from the New Forest than in recent years, although the coverage was still very patchy. About 40 pairs/singing males were reported (compared with

180-184 in the 1997 survey). Away from the New Forest and north-east, small populations were reported from Ringwood Forest and the Test, Itchen and Meon Valleys. Some of these birds were on chalk downland. For example up too three males were present from mid February to early May in stubbles, game strips and young plantations at Winters Down near Warnford. Unfortunately no proof of breeding was obtained.

Counts of pairs/singing males outside the New Forest are tabulated below:

Thames Basin Heaths		Wealden Heaths continued	
Blackbushe Airfield	8	Liss Nurseries/Prince's Marsh	3
Bourley Heath/Long Valley	18	Longmoor Inclosure	11
Bramshill Plantation	8	The Warren, Oakhanger	1
Bricksbury Hill	7	Woolmer Forest	6
Eelmoor Marsh/Pyestock Wood	1	**Ringwood Forest**	2
Hawley Common	1	**Test valley**	
Hazeley Heath	2	Casbrook Common	1
Silchester Common	3	Mottisfont	1
Tadley Common	1	Pittleworth	1
Tweseldown	2	**Meon Valley**	
Velmead Common	3	Chappetts Copse, West Meon	1
Warren Heath/Heath Warren	1	Wickham	1
Yateley Common	8	Wickham Hundred Acres	1
Yateley Heath Wood	2	Winters Down, Warnford	2/3
Wealden Heaths		**North-east**	
Bramshott Chase	2	Eversley GP	1
Bramshott Common	2	Greywell	1
Broxhead Common	4	**East**	
Hammer Common	1	Temple Manor	1

Birds continued to sing at known breeding sites well after the breeding season with records from Broxhead Common on Oct 5th, West Meon on Oct 6th, Winters Down, Warnford on Oct 7th, Longmoor Inclosure on Oct 15th and Nov 3rd and very late records from Bourley and Long Valley and Islands Thorns Inclosure on Dec 28th. Up to three seen over farmland at Cufaude Lane north of Basingstoke on Oct 10-12th also included a singing male. These are included below as probable migrants but it is possible that they were breeding nearby.

There were few notable post-breeding gatherings. The highest count was nine at Stoney Cross Plain in the New Forest on Sep 27th. Autumn movement was noted at both inland and coastal sites as listed below:

Coastal sites
Lower Test Marshes: 1, Sep 30th.
Hill Head: 1 SE, Oct 3rd.
Milford on Sea: 2 W, Oct 4th; 1W, Oct 24th.
Titchfield Haven: 1 W, Oct 19th; 1 S, Nov 14th.
Hook-with-Warsash: 4 NW, Nov 3rd; 1 NW, Nov 9th.
Keyhaven Marsh: 1 W, Nov 3rd; 1, Nov 7th.

Inland sites
Beacon Hill, Warnford: 3 NW, Sep 25th.
Itchen Valley CP: 1 S, Oct 18th.

Cufaude Lane: 1, Oct 10th; 3, Oct 12th.
Tweseldown: 1 E, Oct 19th.

The largest gathering during the second winter period was at Wickham Hundred Acres, where nine were present on Nov 2nd, 11 on Nov 13th and ten on Nov 18th. Seven were at Brownwich on Nov 15th. Other winter records, all in the north-east, included single birds at Longmoor Inclosure on Dec 5th and 28th, Hartley Wintney on Dec 27th and The Warren, Oakhanger on Dec 28th.

Skylark   *Alauda arvensis*

A numerous resident, passage migrant and winter visitor.

During the first-winter period there were just two three-figure flocks reported, both of 100, at Keyhaven Marsh on Jan 2nd and Malthouse Farm, Sleaford on Jan 25th and Feb 2nd.

The only record of spring movement was one flying north at Hurst Castle on Mar 8th.

Significant counts during the breeding season included 15 territories on Langstone Harbour Islands, 22 in the Oxey/Normandy area, 20 at Martin Down and 16 at Butser Hill where only half the hill was surveyed. In the north-east there were five territories on Odiham Airfield and, after their disappearance in 2001, three pairs returned to Bourley and Long Valley SSSI, following heathland reclamation work.

In autumn, weak diurnal movement was logged at both coastal and inland sites between Sep 28th and Nov 7th. The only three-figure count during this period was of 110 at Tunworth on Nov 1st. Half-monthly totals of moving birds and grounded flocks are tabulated below:

Skylark	Sep 15-30	Oct 1-15	Oct 16-31	Nov 1-15
Movements	8	0	80	50
Flocks on the ground	0	45	165	265

During the second winter period there was just one three-figure count; 110 were at Gander Down on Dec 25th.

Sand Martin   *Riparia riparia*

A common breeding summer visitor and numerous passage migrant.

The first were two at Alresford Pond on Mar 9th, with the main arrival from 16th onwards, although the highest count for March was only 30 at Timsbury on 29th. Numbers remained generally low during April, with the largest count being 200 at Bisterne on 6th.

Details of breeding colonies were received from only a few localities, as follows: Barton on Sea, 50 holes in a new cliff-top site; East Wellow, 158 holes; Eversley GP, 37 holes; Fair Oak SP, 120 nests (250-300 in 2001); Hamer Warren, one pair excavating hole; Hordle, 8 occupied nests; Kimbridge, 700 pairs (950 in 2001); Woolmer Pond, up to 240 present but holes not counted.

Autumn migration commenced early with 44 west at Farlington Marshes on June 25th. Numbers in July and August were average, but peak counts of moving birds and feeding flocks included 400 north-east at Needs Ore on July 13th and 140 still inland at Woolmer Pond on July 21st. There were still 50 at Titchfield Haven on Sep 1st, but after 29 east at Stokes Bay on Sep 11th there were only eight further reports, with the last for the year being one between Bishopstoke and Brambridge on Sep 29th.

Swallow
Hirundo rustica

A numerous summer visitor and abundant passage migrant.

The first for the year was one at Titchfield Haven on Mar 15th, with the main arrival being from Mar 27th with reports from thirteen sites by the end of the month. As with several other spring migrants passage was light picking up in late April. Peak counts included 398 north at Hurst Castle between 0708-1903 hrs on Apr 28th. Inland there were 200 at Alresford Pond on Apr 30th. During May migration continued with a maximum of 100 at Petersfield Heath Pond on 13th.

The only breeding data received was of two pairs nesting at Hurst Castle and one pair nesting in a canal-side building during the Basingstoke Canal survey.

Post-breeding a large flock building to 1000 strong was found feeding over bean fields at Riplington from July 16th-26th. The autumn roost at Farlington Marshes began to build up from mid-July with 500 present on July 18th, rising to 850 on Aug 15th, but the maximum count there in September was just 95 on 1st. At Timsbury numbers roosting in a maize field peaked at 350 on Sep 11th.

Swallows (Rosemary Watts/Powell)

In direct contrast to the spring, large numbers were observed on autumn migration. The heaviest passage occurred on Sep 21st, with an estimated 35,000 moving over the coast between Keyhaven/Pennington Marshes and Barton on Sea alone. Four-figure counts from well-watched coastal sites are as follows:

Farlington Marshes : 1000 E, Sep 20th.
Langstone Harbour: 1000 E, Sep 19th.
Stokes Bay: 1500 E, Sep 11th and 12th.
Lymington/Hurst area: 1260, Sep 5th; 15,000 E, Sep 21st; 1500 E, Sep 22nd.
Hurst Beach: 2000 SE, Sep 12th; 1000, Sep 17th; 2500 E,　Sep 20th; 5000 S, Sep 21st;
Barton on Sea: 1000 E, Sep 15th; 7000(3000 E,　　4000W), Sep 20th; 15,000 E, Sep 21st.

Another notable inland count included 3000 south at Lakeside CP, Eastleigh on Sep 21st causing aircraft at nearby Southampton Airport to be grounded until the birds had moved through. Passage continued throughout October, with a peak of 100 at Sandy Point on 22nd. In November there were 21 reports totalling 51 birds at 14 sites, but the last for the year were three at Titchfield Haven on Dec 6th.

House Martin
Delichon urbica

A numerous summer visitor and abundant passage migrant.

The first for the year was one at Bisterne on Mar 17th, but there were only another three sightings by the end of the month. The main arrival was from mid-April, but spring passage was very light with the only three-figure count being 100 at Tundry Pond on May 6th.

During the breeding season records received indicated 714 occupied nests at 51 sites. Colonies included 113 nests at Sparsholt College (140 in 2000), 65 at Compton Manor Estate (76 in 2001), 52 at Bickton, 36 at Southwick and 26 at Bramshill. The potential of artificial nests was illustrated by five out of six on the Post Office stores in Selborne being occupied.

Autumn feeding flocks began to build up from late August onwards with a peak count of 228 at Colemore Church on Aug 24th. Visible migration began in early September with 200+ west at Ashford Hangers on 1st, but the main movement took place during the period Sep 12th-29th with a particularly strong passage on 21st-22nd. Four-figure counts included 5000 over Lymington/Hurst between 0915-1800 hrs on 21st, with 1500 east there on 22nd; and 1000 at Titchfield Haven on 22nd. At Woolmer Pond numbers rose from just 20 on Sep 12th to 1600 on 16th, dropping to 1200 on 17th, 400 south-west on 23rd and 200 on 25th. In October, 500 were feeding over Fleet Pond on 2nd and left south-east but all counts decreased thereafter. The last for the year were six at Ibsley on Oct 27th.

Richard's Pipit
Anthus novaeseelandiae

A rare passage migrant (0,21,2).

One showed well on the golf course at Taddiford Gap from Oct 5th-7th (SGK *et al*) and another was at Pennington Marsh on Nov 9th (RBW). These records bring the county total to 23.

Tree Pipit
Anthus trivialis

A moderately common summer visitor and passage migrant.

The first was one in song-flight at Longslade Bottom, NF on Mar 16th and equals the earliest ever arrival date for the county (FJ). In the north-east the first return to a breeding site was on Apr 1st with two singing males at Bourley Heath.

On the Thames Basin and Wealden heaths in the north-east a total of 126 pairs/singing males was located at 19 sites during the breeding season. Counts were not received from several localities and only partial coverage was received for Woolmer Forest. Coverage in the New Forest was, as usual, very patchy, with a total of 16 pairs/singing males at 14 sites. Elsewhere, reports of possible breeding came from only six sites, including an unusual record of a pair seen collecting food at Needs Ore on June 11th. Counts of pairs/singing males away from the New Forest, are tabulated overleaf.

Thames Basin Heaths		Wealden Heaths	
Bramshill Plantation	2	Bramshott Common	5
Bramshot Heath	1	Broxhead Common	1
Bricksbury Hill	15	Hammer Common	1
Bourley Heath/Long Valley	17	Longmoor Inclosure	33
Castle Bottom	2	The Warren, Oakhanger	1
Eelmoor Marsh/Pyestock Wood	3	Woolmer Forest	15
Hawley Common	3	**Other sites**	
Hazeley Heath	9	Alice Holt Forest, Lodge Inclosure	2
Tweseldown	1	Carpenters Down Wood	1
Velmead Common	2	Chawton Park Wood	2
Warren Heath	3	Martin Down	1
Yateley Common	3	Medstead	1
Yateley Heath Wood	6	Needs Ore	1

Autumn passage covered the period Aug 15th to Oct 6th, with an approximate total of 112 at 29 sites, of which less than half were seen on the coast. The highest count by far was 23 at Old Winchester Hill on Aug 26th. There were four records in October with the last for the year being one at Langley on Oct 6th.

Meadow Pipit   *Anthus pratensis*

A locally common resident, numerous passage migrant and winter visitor.

Between January and early March flocks exceeding 20 totalled only 381 at 11 sites, with a peak count of 100 at Lower Test Marshes on Mar 15th, although this probably included some migrants.

Spring passage was generally light. At Hurst Beach a total of 439 flew north between Feb 18th and Apr 16th, with a peak of 101 on Apr 6th, while movement elsewhere included a maximum count of 50 north at Broadmarsh/Bedhampton on Mar 22nd.

During the breeding season a total of 54 pairs/singing males was found at 13 sites, including 27 on the Langstone Harbour Islands (18 in 2001). The only pairs located on the north-east heaths were three on Blackbushe Airfield, one at Bourley/Long Valley and one on Eelmoor Marsh. No counts were received of breeding densities in the New Forest, but several pairs were located at downland sites, including five at Butser Hill and three at both Magdalen Hill Down and Windmill Hill.

Autumn migration was concentrated into the period Sep 14th-24th, with a very noticeable passage on 21st and 22nd (*cf* Swallow and House Martin). At Farlington Marshes a total of 1950 moved north/east during this period, with 643 being counted in 2.25 hours on Sep 21st and an estimated 1500 passing over by mid afternoon. In the west of the county at Barton on Sea an impressive peak count of 2060 flew east there between 0645-0845 hrs on Sep 21st. Inland, at Testwood Lakes 1024 flew south-west between 0745-1800 hrs on Sep 22nd. Passage continued at a lower ebb into October, when the only three-figure count was 155 at Stoke Wood, West End Down on 8th.

During November and December flocks in excess of 20 totalled 759 at 21 sites, with a maximum of 80 at Oxey Barn Fields on Nov 7th. In addition, surveys of the New Forest produced totals of 643 at 19 sites on Nov 17th and 399 at 26 sites on Dec 14th.

Rock Pipit   *Anthus petrosus*

A very scarce resident, scarce passage migrant and winter visitor.

Records for January to March totalled approximately 60 at 19 sites. As usual the majority of records came from the south-west coastline, with maxima of 12 at Hurst Castle on Feb 28th, six at Barton on Sea on Feb 15th and six at Milford on Sea on Feb 16th and Mar 6th. The maximum count east of Southampton Water was five at the Hamble Estuary on Jan 13th. At Needs Ore, four present on Mar 3rd were thought to be possibly of the Scandinavian subspecies *littoralis*.

During the breeding season five/six pairs were present at Hurst Castle, one pair bred at Lepe and an adult and juvenile were seen at Tanners Lane on July 3rd.

With the exception of breeding birds the first returns to wintering localities occurred from Sep 16th onwards, with records from six sites by the end of September. A very unusual inland record was of three at Woolmer Pond on Sep 25th. During the period October to December there was an approximate total of 91 at 20 localities. The maximum count was 25 in the Lymington/Hurst area on Oct 26th, with other notable counts being 15 at North Binness Island, Langstone Harbour on Dec 3rd, seven at Park Shore on Oct 19th and seven at the Hamble Estuary on Nov 17th.

Water Pipit   *Anthus spinoletta*

A scarce winter visitor and passage migrant.

In the early year the maximum count was 28 at Lower Test Marshes on Jan 15th and Feb 28th, while the highest count at Titchfield Haven was 15 on Mar 2nd. Elsewhere, a total of 26 was present at six localities. This included the only inland record of one at Chawton on Mar 3rd.

One or two probable spring migrants were noted at all of the well-watched coastal sites, with the last for the early year being one at Farlington Marshes on Apr 13th.

The first return was one at Winchester SF on the early date of Oct 2nd, with the next being at Pinglestone CB on Oct 20th, this being the only report during the year from the former cress-bed stronghold in the Alresford area. Thereafter, the majority of records came from the two main localities, with peak counts of 25 at Lower Test Marshes on Dec 24th and six at Titchfield Haven on Nov 9th. The only other sites to record the species were Farlington Marshes , where there were 20 bird-days between Oct 26th and Dec 28th (with two on six dates) and Keyhaven/Pennington Marshes where single birds were seen on Oct 27th, Nov 7th and Dec 13th.

Monthly maxima at the main localities are tabulated below:

	J	F	M	A	M	J	J	A	S	O	N	D
Farlington/Langstone Harbour	1	1	1	1	0	0	0	0	0	2	2	2
Lower Test Marshes	28	28	15	8	0	0	0	0	0	2	13	25
Pennington/Keyhaven Marsh	1	3	2	1	0	0	0	0	0	1	1	1
Titchfield Haven	13	8	15	0	0	0	0	0	0	0	6	2

Yellow Wagtail   *Motacilla flava*

A very scarce and declining summer visitor and common passage migrant.

The first for the year was one flying north-east over Farlington Marshes on Mar 29th, followed by one flying north there on Apr 1st. During spring passage there were approximate totals of 57 at 11 coastal sites and 22 at 16 inland sites up to May 12th. Apart from eight flying north at Titchfield Haven on Apr 6th counts did not exceed four. Half-monthly totals are tabulated below:

Apr 1-15	Apr 16-30	May 1-15
26	24	29

For the second year running no breeding occurred at Farlington Marshes . A female was present from May 7th-21st and was even seen carrying nesting material, but any attempt at breeding was frustrated by the lack of any males. Elsewhere, one pair bred at West Park Farm, Sandleheath, although the outcome was unknown; and a male was seen taking food into a bean-field at Sleaford on two dates in early July, indicating that young were being fed.

The table below summarises reported breeding pairs in Hampshire 1993-2002:

	1993	1994	1995	1996	1997	1998	1999	2000	2001	2002
Yellow Wagtail	9	16	12	12	2	9	6	5	1	2

Autumn migration began early with the first return being one at Keyhaven Marsh on July 17th, followed by another 12 at five sites by the month-end. Peak numbers occurred in late August and early September, with the highest count being 440 roosting at Titchfield Haven on Sep 7th. This is the highest total since 460 roosted at the same locality on Sep 8th, 1981. Passage was recorded at 32 inland sites, with the maximum count being 50 at Chidden on Aug 30th. The last one for the year was at Empress Dock, Southampton on Oct 16th. Counts in excess of 25 are summarised below, followed by the minimum half-monthly totals:

Farlington Marshes : counts exceeded 25 on seven dates between Aug 31st and Sep 17th, with a peak of 57 flying to roost on Sep 9th.
Sinah Common: 30, Sep 13th.
Stokes Bay: 43, Sep 12th.
Titchfield Haven: 70, at reed-bed roost, Aug 23rd; 150, Sep 1st; 440, Sep 7th; 350, Sep 8th; 150, Sep 12th.
Chilling: 60, Aug 24th; 34, Sep 8th; 50, Sep 14th.
Hook-with-Warsash: counts exceeded 25 on 15 dates between Aug 21st and Sep 20th, with a peak of 101 on Sep 12th.
Needs Ore/Beaulieu Estuary: 30, Aug 27th.
Pylewell: 30, Sep 11th.
Keyhaven Marsh: 35 SW, Aug 24th.
Barton on Sea: 60, Sep 1st, with a separate report of 44 W on the same date.

July 16-31	Aug 1-15	Aug 16-31	Sep 1-15	Sep 16-30	Oct 1–16
12	10	467	1123	137	14

Grey Wagtail   *Motacilla cinerea*

A moderately common resident, passage migrant and winter visitor.

In January and February a minimum of 65 was reported at 43 sites, with the peak count being of only six, flying in to roost at Alresford Pond on Feb 8th.

During the breeding season a total of 23 territories was found along the River Itchen north of Durngate, Winchester and eight pairs were found along the Basingstoke Canal. The latter count is a major improvement on the 1991 survey when only one pair was found, but still well down on the 16 pairs found in 1978 before the canal was restored for the use of waterborne traffic. Elsewhere, one or two pairs/singing males were reported from 56 sites, of which 18 pairs were known to have bred successfully.

Counts of eight at Mapledurwell CB on Aug 10th and ten at Winchester SF on Aug 12th were presumably local birds.

As in previous years autumn passage was most noticeable at Farlington Marshes where there were 69 bird-days between Aug 17th and Oct 18th. In November and December a minimum of 79 individuals was reported at 55 sites, with maxima of only four at Springhead, Greywell on Nov 4th and at Broadmarsh/Bedhampton on Nov 24th.

Pied Wagtail   *Motacilla alba*

A numerous resident, abundant passage migrant and winter visitor.

Three-figure counts, mostly involving roosts*, were recorded as follows:

Waterlooville Precinct*: 300, Nov 4th.
Chilling Cliffs: 100, Nov 30th.
Lakeside CP, Eastleigh: 120, Aug 7th.
Calmore*: 100, Oct 31st.
Ringwood*: 126, Feb 15th.
Lymore Lane, Pennington: 200, Jan 12th.
Alresford Pond*: 200, Jan 17th.
Oakley: 123, Feb 1st.
Basingstoke Town Centre*: early-year maxima 494, Mar 21st; late-year maxima 659, Dec 7th.
Darby Green SF: 100, Jan 2nd.
Eversley GP*: 100, Oct 3rd.
Camp Farm SF: 100, Jan 13th.
Petersfield Town Centre*: 120, Mar 15th.

Three territories were located on the Basingstoke Canal survey, compared to four in 1991.

Spring passage was recorded from Hurst Beach with 25 flying north-east between Mar 1st-24th. Movement in autumn was far more pronounced than normal. At Barton on Sea GC 65 flew east on Sep 21st and at Hurst Beach a total of 44 flew south between Sep 21st and 28th (max. 30 on 28th). At Keyhaven/Pennington Marshes 28 flew south on Sep 30th, followed by an impressive 315 flying ESE there on Oct 3rd, a record day count of passage in the county (RBW). Another 45 moved over Pennington Marsh on Oct 5th and at Taddiford Gap 41 flew west on Oct 5th and 50 west on 6th. At Farlington Marshes a total of 98 moved mainly east between Sep 17th and Oct 1st (max. 23 on Sep 22nd) and at Stokes Bay 46 flew east on Oct 9th.

White Wagtail *(M. a. alba)*

A scarce spring and autumn passage migrant.

Records of birds showing characteristics of this race began with one at Hurst on Feb 28th, the earliest ever for the county (NM). This was followed by a light spring passage involving a minimum of 18 individuals, with the last being on May 7th. In the autumn 14 were noted between Sep 8th and Oct 7th and included the only inland sighting of one at Woolmer Pond.

An interesting record involved a probable male White/Pied Wagtail intergrade that was present at Farlington Marshes intermittently from Apr 10th to July 18th. During this period it was seen with a female Pied Wagtail and observed feeding young on June 9th.

Individual records are listed below:

Farlington Marshes : 1-2, Apr 10th-24th (minimum of five involved); plus probable intergrade male visiting from nearby breeding site; 1, Sep 8th; 1 NE, Oct 6th; 4, Oct 7th.
Milton playing fields: 1, Mar 14th.
Titchfield Haven: 1, May 3rd.
Chilling: 1, Mar 3rd.
Hook-with-Warsash: 1, Mar 11th-13th; 1 Apr 7th and 9th.
Lower Test Marshes: 1, Sep 27th.
Needs Ore: 1, May 7th.
Park Shore: 1, Apr 14th.
Keyhaven/Pennington Marshes: 2, Apr 13th; 1 juv, Sep 8th; 2-3 juvs, Sep 12th; 1, Sep 14th; 2, Sep 22nd.
Hurst Castle/Hurst Beach: 1, Feb 28th; 1 NE, Mar 29th; 1 N, Apr 13th.
Barton on Sea: 1 E, May 4th.
Woolmer Pond: 1, Sep 17th-21st.

Wren   *Troglodytes troglodytes*

An abundant resident, passage migrant and winter visitor.

Evidence of long term population trends came from the survey along the Basingstoke Canal, a total of 162 territories was located, a moderate increase on the 144 pairs/singing males found during 1991. Also, 103 territories were located at Titchfield Haven and 75 at Longmoor Inclosure. The abundance and dispersive nature of this species is illustrated by up to three being present on North Binness Island, Langstone Harbour, on Dec 12th.

Dunnock   *Prunella modularis*

An abundant resident, passage migrant and winter visitor.

Few records were received for this species. Counts included a total of 40 territories located during the survey of the Basingstoke Canal, compared with the 25 pairs/singing males found during 1991. Also, 23 territories were located at Titchfield Haven and 12 at Longmoor Inclosure. Evidence of autumn migration came from Keyhaven/Pennington Marshes, with a marked arrival of 25 on Sep 7th/8th.

Robin   *Erithacus rubecula*

An abundant resident, passage migrant and winter visitor.

Just ten records were received. During the breeding season counts of territories included 151 along the Basingstoke Canal, an estimated 90 in Longmoor Inclosure, 87 at Lower Test Marshes (78 in 2001 and 96 in 2000) and 40 at Titchfield Haven.

An erythristic bird (i.e. abnormal red plumage) was noted at St. Lucia Woods, Bordon on Apr 18th.

Nightingale   *Luscinia megarhynchos*

A scarce and declining summer visitor, previously moderately common.

The first was early, a singing male at Bassett on Apr 10th, followed by one at Botley Wood on Apr 13th, on the same day as the first at this site in 2001. The main arrival was from Apr 21st onwards, with singing males being recorded from ten sites by the end of the month.

During the breeding season a total of 40 singing males was reported from 21 widespread locations. This figure continued the downward trend, for example, only three territories were located on Martin Down, which held ten in 1999. The maximum recorded at any site was seven at Botley Wood.

No records were received for the second half of the year, the last bird being noted at Blackbushe Airfield on June 13th.

Bluethroat   *Luscinia svecica*

A rare passage migrant (2,24,2).

A male of the white-spotted form (*L.s.cyanecula*) was at Hook-with-Warsash on Mar 30th (SM) and a juvenile was ringed at Titchfield Haven on Sep 1st (PC, TDC, BSD). These records bring the Hampshire total to 28.

Black Redstart   *Phoenicurus ochruros*

A scarce passage migrant and winter visitor; occasionally breeds.

A minimum of four was present during the first winter period. Three were on the coast with one inland at Darby Green on Jan 2nd. Spring passage was particularly light and involved only two individuals on Mar 19th and Apr 10th.

Records received for the breeding season were of a pair, which probably bred successfully in the north of the county and a male at Farlington Marshes on July 13th.

Autumn passage, or more likely post-breeding dispersal, commenced with one on Aug 15th, another three days later and a third on Sep 9th; more typical dates for passage were from Oct 11th. Two remained into December, including a long-staying first-winter present at Burrfields, Portsmouth from Oct 26th.

All records are summarised below, followed by approximate monthly totals:

Coast and immediate hinterland
Beachlands, Hayling: 2, Nov 3rd.
Farlington Marshes : 1, July 13th.
Widley Farm: 2, Oct 24th.
Burrfields, Portsmouth: 1, Oct 26th-Dec 31st.
Fareham: 1, Nov 17th.
Posbrook Lane, Titchfield Haven: 1, Nov 15th.
Solent Breezes: 1, Nov 17th.
Winsor: 1, Sep 9th.

Southampton Area: 1, Oct 11th; 1, Nov 2nd.
Hounsdown, Totton: 1, Nov 17th-25th.
Lepe: 1, Nov 16th.
Lymington/Hurst area: 1, Jan 1st-10th; 1, Feb 10th; 1 on six dates between Oct 14th and Dec 28th.
Barton on Sea GC: 1, Jan 11th.

Inland Sites
Darby Green: 1, Jan 2nd.
Long Down: 1, Mar 19th.
Hoe Cross: 1, Nov 30th-Dec 28th.
Old Winchester Hill: 1, Aug 15th.
South Wonston: 1, Aug 18th; 1, Oct 18th.
Magdalen Hill Down: 1, Apr 10th.
Aldershot: 1, Nov 1st.

J	F	M	A	M	J	J	A	S	O	N	D
3	1	1	1	3	1	2	2	1	6	13	2

Redstart   *Phoenicurus phoenicurus*

A locally common summer visitor (mostly to the New Forest) and passage migrant.

The first arrival was a male at Bishop's Dyke on Mar 29th. Subsequent records of migrants at non-breeding sites involved eight at six coastal sites in April/early May and an inland bird at Odiham Airfield on Apr 14th.

Redstart (Dan Powell)

Breeding season coverage in the New Forest was sparse, but included 18 singing males at Denny Wood, ten at Emery Down and Knightwood Oak Inclosure and eight at Bolderwood, Matley Wood and Latchmore Bottom. On the north-east heaths a total of 13 pairs/singing males was located at seven sites as follows: Bourley Heath/Long Valley, 2;

Longmoor Inclosure, 5; Woolmer Forest, 2; Bramshott Common, 1; Birch Piece, Liphook, 1; Waggoners Wells, 1; and Yateley Heath Wood, 1. The north-east heaths total was a dramatic decrease from the 48 pairs/singing males, at six sites, reported in 2001, largely due to poor coverage at Woolmer Forest.

The first evidence of post-breeding dispersal was of a bird at Meadow Lake, Test valley on July 9th. There ensued a steady stream of migrants mainly from coastal and downland sites throughout the county, with numbers peaking in late August/early September. The approximate half-monthly totals for the autumn passage period are tabulated below:

Aug 1-15	Aug 16-31	Sep 1-15	Sep 16-30
5	54	49	6

At Old Winchester Hill 14 bird-days were recorded on eight dates between Aug 15th and Sep 9th, with a maximum of four on Aug 24th. Elsewhere, the highest counts were four at Lower Test Marshes on Aug 27th, Sandy Point on Sep 4th and Farlington Marshes on Sep 12th. The last record for the year was one at Lakeside CP, Eastleigh on Sep 28th.

Annual reported totals for 1993-2002 of spring and autumn numbers and breeding pairs follows:

Redstart	1993	1994	1995	1996	1997	1998	1999	2000	2001	2002
Spring bird-months	30	26	24	110	90	16	21	17	18	12
Breeding pairs	-	-	34	49	131	77	130	136	75	75
Autumn bird-months	77	105	115	94	184	109	57	121	136	114

Whinchat   *Saxicola rubetra*

A very scarce summer visitor and common passage migrant.

The first was at Farlington Marshes on Apr 21st with a further 15 recorded in April and 38 in May, the last being on 15th. Of these, 15 were found inland. The maximum recorded at any site was four at Farlington Marshes on May 3rd and again on 7th.

The first evidence of post-breeding dispersal was of males at Keyhaven Marsh and Farlington Marshes on July 17th. There was a peak to autumn passage in early/mid September. The table shows half-monthly peak numbers for Farlington Marshes and the minimum half-monthly total for other sites:

	Aug 1-15	Aug 16-31	Sep 1-15	Sep 16-30	Oct 1-15	Oct 16-31	Nov 1-15
Farlington Marshes	0	10	26	11	3	0	0
Other sites	4	134	402	152	7	3	2

As in previous years heaviest passage was recorded at Farlington Marshes , with 46 bird-days in August (max.10 on 28th), 195 bird-days in September (max. 26 on 4th) and 13 bird-days in October (max. 3 on 3rd/4th). Counts from elsewhere included 20 at Oxey Marsh on Sep 12th, 17 at Soberton on Sep 16th, 15 at Titchfield Haven on Sep 9th and Lower Test Marshes on Sep 13th, 13 at Barton on Sea GC on Sep 15th, 12 along the canal path at Titchfield Haven on Sep 15th and 11 at Keyhaven/Pennington Marshes on Sep 7th. The last for the year were singles at Titchfield Haven on Nov 3rd and 9th and possibly the same individual at nearby Stubbington on Nov 18th.

Annual reported totals for 1993-2002 of spring and autumn passage numbers and breeding pairs follows:

Whinchat	1993	1994	1995	1996	1997	1998	1999	2000	2001	2002
Spring bird-months	52	34	41	70	45	41	25	27	21	55
Breeding pairs	3	0	0	2	3	2	0	0	0	0
Autumn bird-months	451	375	476	324	181	284	349	330	304	794

Stonechat *Saxicola torquata*

A moderately common but local resident and partial migrant.

Wintering birds in January and February totalled 33 at 14 coastal sites and 72 at 27 inland sites. The majority of those found inland were located on downland or river valley sites.

Spring passage commenced in early February with two at Hazeley Heath on Feb 6th. Passage continued throughout March with birds returning to various heathland sites during the month. The maximum number recorded at the coast was six at Dibden Bay on Mar 4th.

During the breeding season recording was far from comprehensive with little data received from the New Forest and only partial coverage of Woolmer Forest. Just 127 pairs were reported from 53 sites. Of these, 95 were at 19 sites on the north-east heaths (where fuller coverage in 2001 reported a total of 122 pairs at 18 sites); at least 14 pairs were at nine coastal sites and at least 18 pairs at a further ten inland sites. Confirmed breeding records are summarised below.

Thames Basin Heaths

Blackbushe Airfield	4
Bramshill Plantation	3
Bricksbury Hill	6
Castle Bottom	1
Eelmoor Marsh/Pyestock Wood	5
Hammer Common	4
Hazeley Heath	5
Tadley Common	1
Tweseldown	3
Warren Heath	1
Yateley Common/Yateley Common South	12
Yateley Heath Wood	1

Wealden Heaths

Bourley Heath	7
Bramshott Common	2
Broxhead Common	2
Longmoor Inclosure	15
The Warren, Oakhanger	2
Warren Hill, Liss	1
Woolmer Forest	20

Coastal sites

Barton on Sea GC	1
Chilling	1
Hook-with-Warsash	1
Hordle	1
Lepe	3
Lymington/Hurst	4+
Park Shore	1
Taddiford Gap	1
Titchfield Haven	1

Other sites

Bisterne Common	1
Dunsbury, Havant	1
North End Farm, Harbridge	1
Horndean	1/2
Hucklesbrook Lakes	1
Martin Down	9
Toyd Down	1
Tundry Pond	1
Winchester SF	1

The first evidence of autumn movement was on July 23rd when a male was in Dogmersfield Park. Significantly higher numbers were involved than in the previous three years with minima of 94 at 16 sites in August, 248 at 58 sites in September, 189 at 43 sites in October and 223 at 69 sites in November. The latter included a total of 86 at 19 New Forest sites out of 29 checked during the course of the Wintering Great Grey Shrike

Survey.

During December there was a minimum of 149 present at 51 sites, including 53 at 16 sites in the New Forest on 14th and a maximum of eight in the Lymington/Hurst area on 19th and 31st. On the north-east heaths, only 15 were located at four sites.

Wheatear   *Oenanthe oenanthe*

A scarce summer visitor and common passage migrant.

Wheatears (David Thelwell)

First arrivals were on Mar 11th with three at Sinah Common and one at Sandy Point. Inland there were three reported at Rhinefield Inclosure on Mar 16th. The first double-figure count was not until Apr 16th when 16 were present at South Hayling. Records in this area later in the month included 25 at Sinah and 12 at Sandy Point on Apr 25th. A total of 209 bird-days was recorded at Farlington Marshes between Mar 12th and May 20th with peak counts of 12 on Mar 27th and 29th, 16 on May 1st and 13 on 7th. Birds were reported daily to May 16th with only four subsequent records to 31st. The minimum half-monthly totals are tabulated below:

Mar 1-15	Mar 16-31	Apr 1-15	Apr 16-30	May 1-15	May 16-31
5	439	36	48	23	4

Evidence of breeding was obtained for only one pair in the New Forest.

The first returning migrant was a female at Langstone South Moor on July 18th, with the next not being until 27th when one was at Lepe. Passage peaked in late August/early September, but was generally light with the maximum count being 41 at Barton on Sea GC on Sep 1st. The minimum half-monthly totals are tabulated below:

July 16-31	Aug 1-15	Aug 16-31	Sep 1-15	Sep 16-30	Oct 1-15	Oct 16-31
15	89	217	77	101	34	18

Records from sites with double-figure counts are summarised below:

West Hayling Shore: 12, Sep 5th.
Fort Nelson: 13, Sep 9th.
Hook-with-Warsash: 23, Aug 21st; 15, Aug 22nd.

Park Shore: 11, Aug 10th; 12, Aug 24th.
Needs Ore/Beaulieu Estuary: 12, Aug 27th.
Lymington/Hurst area: 23, Aug 21st; 10, Aug 24th; 11, Aug 26th; 12, Sep 4th; and 12, Sep 8th.
Hordle: 19, Aug 21st.
Barton on Sea GC: 12, Aug 25th; 41, Sep 1st.

The last record for the year was one at Black Gutter Bottom, NF on Nov 2nd.

Annual reported totals for 1993-2002 of spring and autumn passage numbers and breeding pairs follows:

Wheatear	1993	1994	1995	1996	1997	1998	1999	2000	2001	2002
Spring bird-months	264	456	445	798	525	441	308	385	554	555
Breeding pairs	3	1-4	4	5	4	6	5	1	3	1
Autumn bird-months	294	371	372	368	429	419	555	399	551	551

Greenland Wheatear (*O. o. leucorhoa*)

A very scarce spring and autumn passage migrant.

There was a single spring record of a bird showing characteristics of this race: a male in the Lymington/Hurst area on May 12th (RBW, SGK).

Ring Ouzel   *Turdus torquatus*

A scarce passage migrant; has wintered.

It was a very good year with an estimated total of 33 from records received, the highest total since 1989. Records were from mainly inland sites, with only nine reports from the coast. In spring eight were noted between Mar 16th and Apr 21st as follows:

Black Gutter Bottom: 1 male, Mar 16th.
Dibden Bay: 1 male, Mar 29th.
Black Dam NR: 1male, Apr 1st.
Lakeside CP, Eastleigh: 1, female, Apr 1st.
Browndown: 1 male, in off the sea, Apr 3rd.
Jacks Bush, Porton: 1, Apr 7th.
Funtley: 1 male, Apr 16th.
Old Winchester Hill: 1 male, Apr 21st.

The first autumn passage record was on Oct 6th, there was then almost daily reporting through to Oct 23rd mostly of singles as follows:

Titchfield Haven: 1, Oct 6th.
Milford on Sea cliffs: 1, Oct 7th.
Black Gutter Bottom: 1, Oct 10th; 2, Oct 11th/12th; 4, Oct 17th.
IBM Lake, Cosham: 1, Oct 10th-12th.
Old Winchester Hill: 1, Oct 10th-12th; 1, Oct 17th.
Butser Hill: 1, Oct 11th.
Beaulieu Heath West: 2, Oct 12th.
Farlington Marshes : 1, Oct 15th.
Itchen Valley CP: 1, Oct 16th/17th.
Sandy Point: 1, Oct 17th; 2, Oct 22nd.
Cheesefoot Head: 3, Oct 18th.
Sinah GP: 1, Oct 23rd.

The last of the year, two late males, were singles at Farlington Marshes on Nov 16th and Ocknell Plain on Dec 4th (APSH). The December record is particularly unusual and is only the second record for the month, the first being seen on Dec 31st 1983. Passage (bird months) is summarised below for the last ten years:

Ring Ouzel - Passage	1993	1994	1995	1996	1997	1998	1999	2000	2001	2002
Spring.	9	4	6	8	4	6	6	6	2	8
Autumn	20	11	2	6	10	25	8	19	15	25

Blackbird   *Turdus merula*

An abundant resident, passage migrant and winter visitor.

A total of 30 records was submitted. As with previous years, significant winter numbers were at Petersfield, where one observer noted early and late maxima in his garden of 57 on Jan 3rd and 46 on Dec 19th. Other noteworthy early year counts included: 20 in Connaught Road, Fleet on Jan 1st, 27 on Wilverly Plain on Jan 17th and 34 at Sarisbury Green on Feb 14th. Breeding records included 87 territories along the Basingstoke Canal, an estimated 30 territories at Longmoor Inclosure, 22 at Titchfield Haven and 83 at Lower Test Marshes.

Autumn produced four significant records of migrants: a fall of 60 at Casbrook Common on Oct 11th, 28 at Itchen Valley CP on Oct 18th, 30 at Lakeside CP on Oct 19th and 20 at Farlington Marshes on Oct 31st.

Female Blackbird
(Rosemary Watts/Powell)

Fieldfare   *Turdus pilaris*

A numerous to abundant winter visitor and passage migrant.

Numbers were above average in both the early and late year. The approximate monthly totals are tabulated below:

J	F	M	A	M	J	J	A	S	O	N	D
4935	4049	2548	799	0	0	0	0	1	841	7752	5442

Flocks in excess of 100 were reported from 14 sites in January, with the largest flocks being 600 to roost at Springhead, Greywell on 13th, 400 on the Leckford Estate on 16th and 350 at South Wonston on 19th. In February there were a further 18 locations with three-figure counts, the largest being 350 both at Hartley Mauditt and Sleaford Malt House on 2nd. Five additional locations held three-figure flocks in March, the largest being 350 at South Wonston and 300 at Exton, both on 16th. Two further sites held three-figure flocks into April, the largest gatherings being 300 at Somerley Park on 3rd and 160 at Coombe on 14th. The last birds of the early year were 12 at Somerley Park and four north over Timsbury on Apr 21st.

The first bird of the autumn was at Long Down on Sep 27th. The first substantial arrival was 50 at Brockenhurst on Oct 16th. By the end of October there were reports from thirteen sites, including a total of 195 at Coopers Hill on 29th. In the late year three-figure flocks on the ground were reported from 36 sites: including 350 at Gander Down on Nov 16th, 300 at Long Down on Nov 29th, 300 at Temple Manor on Dec 7th and 920 at Four Lanes End on Dec 22nd. Small movements were noted including on Dec 10th 400 west over Testwood Lakes and 383 north, with 19 west, over Black Gutter Bottom.

Song Thrush   *Turdus philomelos*

A numerous resident, passage migrant and winter visitor.

A total of 35 records was submitted compared with 25 for 2001, the majority being breeding and autumnal passage records. The increase in records was mirrored by an increase in territories at several sites: 18 at Lower Test Marshes (14 in 2001) and 24 at Bricksbury Hill-Bourley Heath, (17 in 2001). Along the Basingstoke Canal 36 territories were recorded and there were an estimated 14 at Longmoor Inclosure and 10 at Bramshill Plantation.

The first arrival of the autumn at Farlington Marshes was five on Sep 20th, with 10 there on the 29th. A night movement was heard over Barton on Sea on Oct 31st, with about 20 in 20 minutes. Further arrivals / flocks of 20 or more birds were noted at the following sites:

Farlington Marshes : 30, Oct 18th; 37, Oct 31st; 20, Nov 3rd; 20, Nov 16th.
Itchen Valley CP: 25, Oct 18th.
Old Winchester Hill: 39, Oct 1st.
Ashford Hangers: 30, Oct 7th.
Casbrook Common: 40, Oct 11th; 10W Nov 7th.
Empshott: 20, Nov 17th.
Soal Farm, Steep: 24, Dec 17th.

Redwing   *Turdus iliacus*

A numerous to abundant winter visitor and passage migrant.

Numbers were average in the early year with increases reported in the second winter period. The approximate monthly totals are tabulated below:

J	F	M	A	M	J	J	A	S	O	N	D
1246	252	754	12	0	0	0	0	18	1704	7041	2806

In the early year flocks in excess of 100 were seen at just nine sites. The largest concentration was 300 at Albury Farm, Blackmoor on Mar 10th. There was little evidence of movement during the period with the only double-figure counts being 50 north-east over Petersfield on Jan 13th and 40 over the same site on Mar 12th. Numbers fell off noticeably after this date with the last double-figure count being 25 at Bisterne on Mar 17th. The last spring record was of one at Humbers Wood, Kings Somborne on Apr 18th.

Reports in September came from five sites, with the first on 21st when 12 were at Old

Winchester Hill. Most October records were of birds passing overhead, with the majority occurring from 8th, when 84 moved south over Timsbury, with the largest counts being 125+ moving WSW over Riverside Park, Southampton on 28th and 124 moving north over Casbrook Common on 20th. Substantial numbers on the ground started to appear on Oct 28th (160 at Itchen Valley CP) and further heavy nocturnal passage was noted over Gosport with a total of c.1500 on 31st. Movements continued to be reported during November, with the largest being 629 moving south over Hinchelsea Bog, NF on Nov 17th. Reports of flocks on the ground increased to the years' end with the largest concentration being 600 at Ocknell Plain, NF on Nov 30th. No movements of birds were reported after Nov 30th when six moved south-west over Whitchurch.

Mistle Thrush

Turdus viscivorus

A numerous resident and passage migrant.

A single double-figure flock was reported in the early year: 35 at Cutler's Farm on Mar 6th. During the breeding season the maximum number of territories recorded at any site was seven, along the Basingstoke Canal. Double-figure flocks of post-breeding birds between July and August were recorded from nine sites, with the highest being 56 at Lakeside CP, Eastleigh on Aug 5th, 45 at Newlands Farm, Purbrook on July 8th and 35 on Gander Down on July 23rd. The only significant visible movement was 16 south over Petersfield on July 26th. Concentrations later in the year included 22 at Sherborne St. John on Sep 9th, 25 at Sparsholt on Sep 14th and 29 at Bisterne on Dec 7th.

Cetti's Warbler

Cettia cetti

A moderately common resident; first bred in 1979.

Reports in the first winter period came from nine sites (15 in 2001) and in the late year from 14 sites (17 in 2001). A record December count came from Titchfield Haven where 26 were heard on Dec 16th. The north-east had its first record since 1998, with a bird singing at Springhead, Greywell from Oct 4th-19th.

Breeding was reported from 37 sites (46 in 2001), a minimum total of 180 singing males shows an increase over the 150 of 2001. Titchfield Haven reported 43 pairs (35 in 2001) and 106 were caught and ringed during the season. Other significant counts came from the Itchen Valley where 41 singing males were counted upstream from Winchester on Apr 30th and from Lower Test Marshes where there were 38 territories compared with 24 the previous year.

Grasshopper Warbler

Locustella naevia

A scarce summer visitor which has declined considerably since 1970.

The first of the nine spring records was at Hook-with-Warsash on Apr 7th, the other eight follow in chronological order:

Farlington Marshes : 1, Apr 19th.
Keyhaven Marsh: 1, Apr 20th; 1 Apr 23rd; 1 Apr 28th.
The Kench: 1, Apr 21st.
Broadmarsh/Bedhampton: 1, Apr 23rd.
Hermitage Stream, Bedhampton: 1, Apr 27th.
Titchfield Haven: 1, Apr 27th.

Record numbers of Grasshopper Warbler were caught at Titchfield Haven in 2002 (Trevor Codlin)

Confirmation of breeding is difficult. Single birds were heard reeling at Titchfield Haven on six dates between Apr 27th and June 2nd, with two reported on May 5th. Additionally, in the Itchen Valley single birds were heard at one site on June 3rd and at another between July 16th and Aug 4th. A late record perhaps involving one of these birds was a reeling male reported from Allbrook on three dates between July 16th and Aug 4th.

Autumn records came from seven sites, with the last at Titchfield Haven on Sep 25th. The ringing results at Titchfield Haven were truly amazing: 232 caught, of which 221 were juveniles.

Autumn
Titchfield Haven: 232 trapped between July 27th and Sep 25th. Capture occurred on 34 dates, with 14 in July, 134 in August and 84 in September. The peak day was 19 on Aug 23rd and there were a further ten days with 10+ birds. The peak period was the 13 days between Aug 20th and Sep 1st when 121 birds were ringed.
Allbrook: 1, Aug 4th.
Pylewell Saltings: 2 juveniles ringed, Aug 21st; with 2 on 25th and 1 on 29th.
Fareham Creek: 1, Aug 28th.
Farlington Marshes : 1, Sep 7th.
Needs Ore/Beaulieu Estuary: 1, Sep 11th.
Lower Test Marshes: 1, Sep 13th.

Aquatic Warbler   *Acrocephalus paludicola*
A rare autumn passage migrant (1,67,2).

Single juveniles were trapped at Titchfield Haven on Aug 10th and Aug 20th (BSD).

Sedge Warbler

Acrocephalus schoenobaenus

A common summer visitor and passage migrant.

The first of the year was one at Farlington Marshes on Mar 30th. During April there were reports from 18 sites, including an early inland record of one at Eversley on 1st. The only significant numbers were from Farlington Marshes , with 20 singing males on Apr 20th and 30 on 25th.

Few counts of breeding pairs/singing males were submitted, the most significant being 56 at Lower Test Marshes, 60 territories up the Itchen Valley to Allbrook and an estimate of 162-185 upstream from Winchester, both counted on June 1st.

Autumn records came from ten sites, with ringing activities a Titchfield Haven providing a total of 1356 trapped on 40 dates from July 27th until Oct 8th, the latest county date (BJD). The maximum daily catch was 161 on Aug 11th and there were catches of 50+ on another nine dates. Elsewhere, few were reported with the maximum being four at Hook-with-Warsash on Aug 31st.

Reed Warbler

Acrocephalus scirpaceus

A common but local summer visitor and passage migrant.

The first of the year was one at Titchfield Haven on Apr 4th, closely followed by one next day at Hook-with-Warsash. Reports in April came from a further four coastal locations plus eight inland, the first of which was one at Fleet Pond on 14th. One was singing in thick fog on Old Winchester Hill on Apr 24th.

Counts of pairs/singing males during the breeding season included 103 at Lower Test Marshes (110 in 2001) and 34 from Fleet Pond (40 in 2001). On June 1st there were 82 territories counted up the Itchen Valley to Allbrook, with 149-159 above Winchester.

Autumn records came from five coastal and four inland sites, mostly of one or two birds, apart from a total of 766 trapped at Titchfield Haven between Aug 1st and Oct 8th. The last record was two at Farlington Marshes on Oct 19th.

Melodious Warbler

Hippolais polyglotta

A very rare passage migrant (0,11,1).

One was at Park Shore, Needs Ore on Aug 24th (MJWH). This is the 12th county record, and the first since one at Farlington Marshes from Sep 12th-27th 1992.

Dartford Warbler

Sylvia undata

A moderately common resident, largely confined to the heaths of the New Forest and north-east.

Coverage on the Thames Basin and Wealden heaths was less complete than usual, with only 135 pairs/singing males located. However, if allowance is made for a few pairs missed and estimates of 30 for Ludshott Common and 40 for Woolmer Forest, the true total was around 200 pairs, (189 in 2001). Coverage of coastal sites was incomplete, with only 15 pairs/singing males reported. No survey work was carried out in the species' stronghold in the New Forest.

Counts of pairs/singing males away from the New Forest are tabulated below:

Thames Basin Heaths		Wealden Heaths continued	
Blackbushe Airfield	5	Longmoor Inclosure	37
Bourley Heath/Long Valley	5	Ludshott Common	nc
Bramshill Plantation	2	The Warren, Oakhanger	1
Bricksbury Hill	24	Woolmer Forest	10+
Eversley Common/Castle Bottom	5	**Coastal sites**	
Hawley Common	nc[1]	Sandy Point, Hayling Island	2
Hazeley Heath	2	Sinah Common	2+
Pyestock Heath	3	Gilkicker Point	nc
Tadley Common	1	Browndown	1
Tweseldown	6	Hamble Common	1+
Warren Heath	1+	Dibden Bay	nc
Yateley Common (HCC)	10	Calshot	1+
Yateley Common South (MOD)	15	Needs Ore	4
Yateley Heath Wood	1	Normandy/Pennington/Keyhaven Marsh	3+
Wealden Heaths		Barton on Sea GC	1
Bramshott Common	2	**Other Sites**	
Broxhead Common (HCC/MOD)	5	Ringwood Forest	nc

[1] nc = no count of known breeding site

Records at presumed non-breeding localities are listed below:

Farlington Marshes : 1, Jan 1st-Mar 3rd; 1+, Sep 1st-Dec 31st (3-4 individuals involved).
Brownwich: 1, Feb 10th.
Titchfield Haven: 1/2, Jan 1st-Apr 3rd; 1/2, Oct 9th-Dec 31st.
Hook-with-Warsash: 1, Jan 1st-Mar 23rd; juv, June 26th/27th (not reared there); 2 (1 singing), July
    6th; then 1/2 to year's end.
Dibden Bay: 2, Nov 28th and Dec 8th.
Fawley Refinery: 1, Oct 17th.
Lepe: 1, Jan/Feb; 1-3, July-Dec.
Milford on Sea cliffs: 1, Sep 3rd and 28th.
Hordle: 1, Nov 29th.

Lesser Whitethroat   *Sylvia curruca*

**A moderately common but declining summer visitor and passage migrant; recorded
four times in winter.**

The first arrivals were two at Farlington Marshes on Apr 16th. Subsequently, birds were
seen at 13 further coastal locations between Apr 20th and 25th, the latter date coinciding
with the first sightings inland - at Itchen Valley CP and Casbrook Common. Heavier
passage occurred in the first week of May with the highest counts coming from the Hayling
Billyline route with six on 1st and Farlington Marshes with ten on 6th.

Records during the breeding season do not necessarily indicate the difference between
established territories and isolated sightings of singing males. Taking the most positive
interpretation, there were a total of at least 37 pairs/singing males at 25 widespread sites,
figures that continue to show the steady decline year on year. The only positive feature in
2002 was that there were nine reports from the north-east of the county compared with
only two in 2001.

The largest count in the autumn was of 15 at Farlington Marshes on Aug 23rd, with ten there on Aug 29th and six on Sep 7th. Otherwise, there were reports from a further 11 sites, mostly on the coast, with single birds inland at Broadlands Estate on the 15th Sep and Slufters Inclosure on the 16th Sep. The last record was a single bird at Farlington on Sep 28th, a comparatively early date.

Whitethroat   *Sylvia communis*

A numerous summer visitor and passage migrant; recorded three times in winter.

The first of the year was very early, on Mar 21st at Titchfield Haven. The normal arrival pattern resumed in the first week of April with a scattering of records along the coast, while the first inland record was on Apr 6th from Eversley GP. The first major overnight arrival was on Apr 22nd when 40 were found at Sinah on Hayling and 40 were also seen the next day in the Lymington/Hurst area.

The varied breeding sites reported show the ubiquitous nature of this common warbler. During May Eversley GP held 28 pairs and there were at least 30 pairs on the coast in the Lymington/Hurst area. June survey reports were as follows: in the Itchen Valley from Mansbridge to Allbrook there were 35 territories on 1st; the heathland of Longmoor Inclosure had 56 on the same date (48 in 2001); while a tour of 'the chalk' between Crondall and Upton Grey produced 24 singing males on 18th.

Whitethroat (Dan Powell)

Autumn reports came from 11 locations, with peak counts being 20 at Farlington Marshes on Aug 29th and 20 in the Lymington/Hurst area on Sep 7th. A total of 108 was ringed at Titchfield Haven in the autumn period. There were three October records, the last being one at Milton Reclamation on Oct 10th.

Garden Warbler
Sylvia borin

A common summer visitor and passage migrant.

A notable feature of this species is that there is no coastal bias in spring. The first of the year was on Apr 13th at Crab Wood, then of the 14 further reports in April, ten were from inland breeding sites, mostly in the period 23rd to 25th.

The largest count of breeding territories came from Eversley GP with 19 (up on the 13 of 2001).

During autumn passage 44 were ringed at Titchfield Haven, where the last bird of the year occurred on Oct 5th. There were eight additional September records, all of single birds at other coastal sites.

Blackcap
Sylvia atricapilla

A numerous summer visitor and passage migrant; moderately common in winter.

With 68 records received for January it is clear that wintering Blackcaps in Hampshire have become an almost commonplace sighting as a garden species. There was a minimum of 66, with males and females equally represented, reported from 52 locations. Reports continued through February and the first recorded song was on 15th from the Hayling Billyline route. Thereafter, from Mar 21st until the end of the month there were reports from 25 locations of apparent arrivals. The last reported 'garden' bird was Mar 26th in Stubbington, earlier than several previous years.

Substantial return was obvious by the last third of April and breeding records included 17 at Yateley GP, 34 in Itchen Valley CP and 53 at Lower Test Marshes (51 in 2001).

Autumn passage started comparatively early, with 12 bird-days in July at IBM Lake, followed by 28 in August and 27 in September. At Itchen Valley CP peak numbers occurred in the first week of September with 29 on 3rd; then 20 on 22nd. There were 53 at Titchfield Haven on Sep 22nd. October records came from only three locations: IBM Lake, Sandy Point and Farlington Marshes . The last apparent passage migrant was at this latter location on Nov 3rd, a day later than the first of the returning 'garden' birds – at Petersfield. Wintering birds built-up as normal and there were reports during December of 41 birds from 26 locations which were split 2:1 male to female, for the 30 birds where gender was established.

Yellow-browed Warbler
Phylloscopus inornatus

A rare autumn passage migrant, recorded twice in winter (0,23,1).

One was with Goldcrests in a garden at Shedfield Common on Oct 24th (WW); the 24th record for the county. The species has been recorded every year in the last ten except in 1997 and 2001.

Wood Warbler   *Phylloscopus sibilatrix*

A scarce summer visitor (principally to the New Forest) and passage migrant.

There was better reporting than in 2001, with nearly 50 records submitted, but they came almost exclusively as breeding reports from the New Forest totalling 45 presumed territories based on singing males from 24 locations (33 from 11 in 2001). These included the first of the year, one at Berry Wood on Apr 24th. Breeding reports from outside the Forest came only from Liss, Waggoners Wells and Bramshott Chase.

Outside the breeding sites there was just one spring record: this was at the former breeding site of Bourley, with one on Apr 28th but not seen again. A juvenile was tape lured at Fareham on July 29th and two late birds seen in September: one in Morgaston Wood on 1st and one at Beaulieu Road on 2nd.

Chiffchaff   *Phylloscopus collybita*

A numerous summer visitor and passage migrant; moderately common in winter.

The strong showing at the end of 2001 continued into the early year with 34 seen at 27 locations in January.

Spring migration started early with a report from IBM Lake of a possible migrant on Feb 24th, then from Nursling, Meon Valley and Eversley GP between Mar 3rd and 5th. The major arrival was in the week starting Mar 13th, with records received from 34 sites including ten at Lower Test Marshes on 16th.

Among the counts of breeding territories were 30 from Lower Test Marshes (37 in 2001) and 27 from Morgaston Woods. Apart from double-figure counts through September from Itchen Valley CP, there were few inland autumn records and the significant counts all came from the coast. A total of 461 was trapped at Titchfield Haven between August and October including 57 on Sep 21st and 71 on Sep 22nd. The October maxima were 19 at Barton on Sea and 13 at Itchen Valley CP, both on 12th; the last known migrant was one at Hurst Castle on Nov 12th.

Second winter period reports were similar to those in recent years with 42 seen in December from 24 different locations. The largest count, however, was just three at Itchen Valley CP on Dec 31st.

Siberian Chiffchaff *(P. c. tristis)*

A very scarce winter visitor.

There were four records of birds showing characteristics of this race. Single birds (possibly the same individual) were at Eastleigh SF on Jan 2nd (MR) and 10th (BG). In the following winter single birds were seen at Lower Test Marshes on Nov 11th (PCo per SSK) and at Mill Lane, Langstone Harbour on Dec 10th (JCr).

Willow Warbler   *Phylloscopus trochilus*

An abundant summer visitor and passage migrant.

This year's data indicate the species is both arriving and leaving early. The first for the year was one at Set Thorns Inclosure, NF on Mar 17th, a day later than the earliest county record set last year. Thereafter, there were 14 further records in March, mostly along the coast.

Passage records continued through April and the largest count was of 30 at Barton on Sea on May 4th.

During the breeding season noteworthy numbers of singing males/territories included 57 at Longmoor Inclosure (67 in 2001) and 36 at Morgaston Wood.

In the autumn, 119 were trapped during ringing activities at Titchfield Haven but the numbers along the coast were otherwise light. Better figures came from inland with 32 in Denny Wood on Aug 31st and 50 at Bourley on Sep 8th. During the rest of September records came from only eight locations, the last being one at Hook-with-Warsash on the 23rd, a date two weeks earlier than average.

Goldcrest   *Regulus regulus*
A numerous resident, passage migrant and winter visitor.

As with a number of common species, few records were submitted and in the absence of long term survey data, no trends can be determined. There was an insignificant spring passage, but bird-day totals for the last four months of the year (20, 93, 69 and 32) at Lakeside CP, Eastleigh showed the expected October influx. A breeding survey at Longmoor Inclosure on June 1st recorded 36 singing males over seven km squares.

Firecrest   *Regulus ignicapilla*
A scarce resident, passage migrant and winter visitor.

What started as an average year for this species went on to produce record numbers of breeding pairs and autumn passage bird-days. There was a sighting in every month of the year. The monthly totals of non-breeding (and post breeding dispersal) birds are shown in the table below:

	J	F	M	A	M	J	J	A	S	O	N	D
Coastal	5	3	6	6	1	0	0	1	3	8	15	9
Inland	2	1	2	4	0	0	0	0	2	4	4	3

In the early part of the year single birds were seen regularly at three locations (West Wellow, IBM Lake and Lower Test Marshes). Other records of single bird-days came from Sinah GP (Jan 8th), Bedhampton (Jan 9th), Bishopstoke (Jan 12th), Old Basing (Jan 12th), Keyhaven reedbed (Jan 21st), Victoria Park Portsmouth (Feb 15th) and Eastleigh SF (Feb 16th). The first passage birds were two at Sandy Point on Mar 11th.

As usual, breeding centred on the New Forest with a minimum of 39 singing males reported from 18 locations, one site held 13 birds. In the north-east of the county there were ten singing males in five locations and elsewhere four were reported from two locations.

Annual totals of breeding pairs 1993-2002 follow:

Breeding pairs	1993	1994	1995	1996	1997	1998	1999	2000	2001	2002
Firecrest	6	21	16	17	17	18	30	50	47	53

The first autumn record came from Titchfield Haven on Aug 31st when a juvenile male was ringed. Thereafter, September was quiet and included birds at Warsash on 10th, Woolmer Forest on 23rd, Farlington Marshes on 27th and Lower Test Marshes on 28th.

The latter location was one of the 27 sites with subsequent passage and/or (later) wintering birds. October was unremarkable, but in November three were found at Holly Hill Park Warsash; (9th), a further 11 single birds were reported, mainly in the south-east of the county from 10th to 20th; and one was found at Titchfield Haven (28th) and recorded subsequently to the end of the year. Presumed wintering birds into December were one at Farlington Marshes , two at Morgaston Woods (22nd) and up to five in the Warsash area.

Spotted Flycatcher   *Muscicapa striata*

A moderately common summer visitor and passage migrant.

There were 187 reports received from 132 sites. The first record of arrival was at Farlington Marshes on May 14th, followed by two there and a pair at Itchen Abbas the next day. A minimum of 73 birds was seen on spring passage.

A total of 24 singing males/pairs was recorded in 18 locations and breeding confirmed at 11 of these.

In the autumn 291 were reported with peak passage occurring during the last two weeks of August. Double-figure counts included ten at Liss on Aug 13th, ten at Danebury on Aug 18th, 25 at Beacon Hill, Warnford on Aug 24th and 17 at Beaulieu Road on Sep 2nd. Records of autumn sightings were received from over 65 sites. The last sighting for the year was a single at Old Winchester Hill on Oct 3rd. The autumn total was less than in 2001 but showed an increase on previous years

Minimum half-monthly totals of all autumn records are tabled below:

Aug 1-15	Aug 16-31	Sep 1-15	Sep 16-30	Oct 1-15
23	148	107	16	3

Pied Flycatcher   *Ficedula hypoleuca*

A scarce passage migrant; rarely breeds.

It was a poor year for this species with only 12 recorded. The only spring record was a male at Kings Somborne on Apr 18th.

A minimum of 11 was seen on autumn passage with singles at Wickham on Aug 4th, Northney on 6th, Warsash on 9th and 15/16th, Hordle on 27th, Portsmouth on 28th, Farlington Marshes on 31st and Sep 10th, Keyhaven and West Wellow on Sep 5th and IBM Lake from 5th-7th.

The annual totals for the last ten years are as follows:

	1993	1994	1995	1996	1997	1998	1999	2000	2001	2002
Spring	8	21	5	25	2	9	8	3	6	1
Autumn	18	14	63	25	31	9	11	10	27	11

Bearded Tit   *Panurus biarmicus*

A scarce resident, passage migrant and winter visitor.

Records came from nine coastal sites with no inland records. In the early winter, records of up to six came from Farlington Marshes , Titchfield Haven, Calshot/Fawley and Keyhaven

Marsh.

As part of a national breeding survey the following were recorded: eight territories at Farlington Marshes ; up to eight pairs at Titchfield Haven; two territories at Lower Test Marshes and two pairs at Keyhaven. A peak of 21 juveniles was seen at Farlington Marshes on June 14th. A juvenile was ringed at Lymington River on Aug 2nd, although it was not thought to have been reared there.

As usual, the September to October period produced visible movements to and from the main sites including: 14 flying high at Farlington Marshes on Oct 4th; four west at Hill Head on Sep 29th and eight west on Oct 6th; and ten east and 14 west at Keyhaven Marsh on Sep 30th.

In November and December numbers appeared to be higher that in recent years with records of 20 at Farlington Marshes , 15 at Titchfield Haven, six at Hook-with-Warsash, one at Lower Test Marshes, five at Fawley Refinery and five at Needs Ore

Monthly maxima at the key sites are summarised below:

	J	F	M	A	M	J	J	A	S	O	N	D
Farlington Marshes	4	6	17	-	18	38	20	-	-	14	20	-
Titchfield Haven	3	-	-	-	-	-	-	-	15	15	15	5
Hook-with-Warsash	-	-	-	-	-	-	-	-	-	7	6	-
Lower Test Marshes	-	-	-	2	1	-	-	-	-	-	-	1
Calshot/Fawley	-	-	2	-	2	-	-	2	5	5	1	1
Needs Ore	-	-	-	-	-	-	-	-	-	2	4	5
Keyhaven Marsh	-	-	6	4	4	7	7	-	32	22	-	-

Long-tailed Tit   *Aegithalos caudatus*

A numerous resident.

Although this is a common species only 17 records were received and more are required to establish any recent changes in the county population. During the winter months Long-tailed Tits are usually found in flocks of up to 35 with other tits and small woodland birds and they have recently become a regular visitor to garden feeding stations.

Breeding territories were reported from six sites; the highest number was 15 at Lower Test Marshes NR CBC plots.

Marsh Tit   *Parus palustris*

A common resident.

About 140 records were received from 85 sites, mainly from the well-wooded eastern side of the county and the New Forest. Usually seen singly or in pairs, the maxima were eight at Botley Wood on Mar 12th and six at Eyeworth Wood, NF on Feb 5th and six at Morgaston Wood on Dec 22nd. Of interest were four records of birds visiting feeders in gardens during both the winter periods.

Only thirteen singing males/breeding pairs were reported from nine sites during the breeding season. There were reports from 28 further sites between March and July that could suggest additional breeding areas. This represents only a tiny fraction of the 3-4000 pairs estimated for the county in BoH.

Willow Tit
Parus montanus

A local and declining resident.

A total of 39 records, mostly of ones and twos, was received from 29 sites.

Successful breeding was confirmed from Ewhurst Park (1 pair with three juveniles) and breeding behaviour noted from a further three sites, namely Warnford, Micheldever and Church Moor, NF. With the exception of Ewhurst these are all different from the sites identified in 2001.

Outside the breeding season, further records came from Appleshaw, Botley Wood, Broadlands (Romsey), Brockenhurst, Buriton, Casbrook Common, Easton, Ellisfield, Emmetts Down, Eyeworth Pond, Hannington, Longwater Lawn, Morgaston Wood, Mottisfont, Roydon Woods, Petersfield, Pitt Down, Saddlers Mill (Romsey), Selborne (Combe Wood), Sheet, Springhead (Greywell), Straits Inclosure (Alice Holt Forest) and Whitley Woods.

Coal Tit
Parus ater

A numerous resident.

About twenty records were received of this common species. The highest total of breeding territories was 24 at Longmoor Inclosure.

Peak winter counts were 50 at Morgaston Wood on Jan 13th and 20 at Woolmer Forest on Jan 6th.

Blue Tit
Parus caeruleus

An abundant resident and passage migrant.

Only seven records were received, all relating to breeding season counts. The highest counts were 82 territories on the Basingstoke Canal and 45 territories at Lower Test Marshes NR (48 in 2001).

Great Tit
Parus major

An abundant resident.

Only nine records were received, all relating to breeding season counts. The highest counts were 79 territories at Basingstoke Canal, 45 territories in Lower Test Marshes NR CBC plots and 40 territories in Botley Wood.

Nuthatch
Sitta europaea

A numerous resident.

Ten records were submitted. During the breeding season counts of territories came from Hook-with-Warsash (2), Lower Test Marshes NR (2), Longstock (1), Basingstoke Canal (7), Deadwater Valley, Bordon (2) and Longmoor Inclosure (3).

Treecreeper   *Certhia familiaris*

A numerous resident.

Only eleven records were submitted. During the breeding season counts of territories came from Hook-with-Warsash (4), Lower Test Marshes NR (5), Longstock (2), Basingstoke Canal (4), Salter's Heath (2) and Longmoor Inclosure (4). Unusually one was trapped and ringed at Winchester SF on July 21st.

Red-backed Shrike   *Lanius collurio*

A very scarce passage migrant, formerly a moderately common but local summer visitor.

There was just one spring record and three in autumn. In spring a male was watched for four hours at Eelmoor Marsh on May 25th (RC).

During the autumn a juvenile male was seen at Farlington Marshes on Aug 22nd (JCr, JRDS) and a different juvenile was seen later on Sep 1st (JCr). A juvenile was also present at Sandy Point from Sep 13th-16th (TAL et al).

Annual totals of bird-months for 1993-2002 follow:

Annual bird-months	1993	1994	1995	1996	1997	1998	1999	2000	2001	2002
Red-backed Shrike	3	1	2	5	1	3	0	2	5	4

Great Grey Shrike   *Lanius excubitor*

A very scarce winter visitor and passage migrant.

A total of 80 records was submitted, and included for the first time a coordinated *Wintering Great Grey Shrike Survey* of the New Forest which was conducted at monthly intervals in the second winter period by 30 observers. The only early year reports were of one in the Ashley Walk area from Feb 13th-17th.

The first autumn record was of one at Broomy Plain on Oct 22nd. A considerable arrival occurred during late October and November, with birds reported from nine areas of the New Forest.during the Survey. On November 17th a total of seven wintering birds were counted, but December returned only four. Elsewhere single birds were at Old Winchester Hill on five dates between Nov 29th and Dec 16th, at Eelmoor Marsh on Dec 6th and Woolmer Forest on Dec 23rd. The latter two were not seen again despite being searched for.

Annual totals of bird-months for 1993-2002 follow:

Annual bird-months	92/93	93/94	94/95	95/96	96/97	97/98	98/99	99/00	00/01	01/02
Great Grey Shrike	7	6	8	3	4	4	13	3	1	1

The minimum of ten reported in the late winter period represents the highest total since the winter of 1998/99, when 12 were recorded.

Woodchat Shrike
Lanius Senator

A rare passage migrant. (0,3,1)

A female was in the meadows at Titchfield Haven on the evening of June 14th (MJP *et al*). This is the fourth county record and the first since one at Dibden Bay on June 14th, 1981.

Golden Oriole
Oriolus oriolus

A rare passage migrant; has bred (?,54,0).

2001 addition: one was heard singing at West End Down from May 20th-22nd (GH-D).

Jay
Garrulus glandarius

A numerous resident and passage migrant.

Counts of breeding pairs came from Bricksbury/Bourley (15), Basingstoke Canal (10), Lower Test Marshes NR (7), Longmoor Inclosure (8) and Longstock (2).

The only specific record indicative of autumn movement was of five (including three high-flying birds) at Sandy Point on Oct 2nd, but autumn migration (and presumably post-breeding dispersal) was well illustrated by the monthly bird-day totals at Lakeside CP:

J	F	M	A	M	J	J	A	S	O	N	D
1	1	5	5	3	5	31	27	25	11	4	2

Magpie
Pica pica

A numerous resident.

In contrast to previous years no three-figure counts were reported, the largest roost was 65 at Fleet Pond on Jan 16th.

Jackdaw
Corvus monedula

A numerous resident.

The largest numbers were reported from roosting counts. In the early year, a pre-roost gathering of 2000 was at Five Lanes End, Greywell on Jan 1st and 2700 flying north to roost over Allington GP on Jan 12th. At the end of the year 3000 were found roosting at Springhead (Greywell) on Nov 4th and 1200 were at South Warnborough on Dec 22nd.

Rook
Corvus frugilegus

A numerous resident and probable winter visitor.

A total of about 912 nests was counted at 24 rookeries across the county, including 193 at two sites at Compton, 133 at three sites at Odiham Airfield (123 in 2001), 92 at Widley (103 in 2001) and 72 at Brambridge (76 in 2001).

Four-figure flocks reported were: 2000 to roost at Old Winchester Hill on Nov 1st; 1000 roosting at Springhead (Greywell) on Nov 4th and 3000 at South Warnborough on Dec 22nd.

Carrion Crow

Corvus corone

A numerous resident.

The highest count was of 240 at Darby Green on Mar 2nd and 150+ at Weston Shore on Nov 20th. Of the few breeding records, a pair again held territory on the Langstone Harbour Islands, but no young were fledged.

Hooded Crow

Corvus cornix

A rare visitor, usually in winter (?,42,1).

One bird was reported at Appleyards, near Fordingbridge, on Jan 16th (CP), and is the 43rd record since 1951.

Raven

Corvus corax

A regular visitor from neighbouring counties in increasing numbers; probably a scarce resident.

A similar year to 2001, with 165 reports received, although as most were fly-overs the actual number involved is very difficult to assess. There were sightings in every month with no clear peak and it is now clear that birds are resident in the south-west of the county and probably elsewhere. Added to this there is some mixing of birds at coastal sites with breeding birds on the Isle of Wight, it is surely a short time before breeding is finally reported in Hampshire. A pair raised two young in the Avon valley just over the county border. The records are summarised below followed by the county bird-month totals for ten years:

South-east of the county
Holbrook, Gosport: 1, June 13th.
Hook-with-Warsash: 2, June 6th.
Warnford: 2, Aug 17th; 2, Nov 4th.
Buriton: 2, Oct 21st-31st.
Exton: 2, Mar 12th.
Long Down: 2, Mar 3rd; 1, Mar 19th; 1, Nov 7th.
Eastleigh: 1, Feb 8th.
Old Winchester Hill: 1, bird present throughout year, 2, Oct 23rd-Nov 20th.

South-west of the county
Southampton Water/Waterside: 2, Mar 3rd-8th; 2, Aug 16th; 1, Sep 8th; 2, Nov 29th; 2, Dec 13th.
Beaulieu Estuary/Needs Ore: 1, irregularly throughout the year; 2, Sep 19th.
Lymington/Hurst area: Up to four/five seen regularly throughout.
Sway area: 1-2 seen regularly throughout.
SE NF: 4, Feb 22nd; 2, regularly to year-end.
SW NF: 2, Mar 3rd; 2, May 5th-8th; 2, July 19th; 1, Oct 10th; 2, Nov 13th.
NW NF: up to 2, regularly throughout the year; 3, June 11th.
Martin Down: 1, Feb 25th; 1, Mar 11th; 1, Apr 20th.
Avon valley: A pair seen regularly in the early part of the year. They nested just over the border in Dorset and raised two young. At least three stayed in the area until the end of the year.

North-west of the county
Appleshaw, Andover: 1-3 present from Apr 13th to the end of the year, 3 noted on June 19th.
Highclere Park: 2, July17th.

Centre of the county
Testwood Lakes: 1, Sep 30th; 1 S, Nov 3rd.
Timsbury: 1, Aug 4th.
West Wellow: 2, Aug 6th.
Gander Down: 2, Mar 12th.

Annual totals of bird-months for 1993-2002 follow indicating the dramatic increase in sightings over the past four years:

Annual bird-months	1993	1994	1995	1996	1997	1998	1999	2000	2001	2002
Raven	1	4	23	10	12	24	52	91	127	258

Starling   *Sturnus vulgaris*
An abundant resident, passage migrant and winter visitor.

About 80 records were submitted. Roost counts in the first quarter included 3500 in the reeds at Keyhaven on Jan 6th. Indications of possible spring passage were the large pre-roost gatherings reported on Mar 17th both at Farlington Marshes , with up to 2500, and 700 at Titchfield Haven.

Post-breeding concentrations, presumably with high numbers of juveniles, reported from Farlington Marshes varied from 1000-2000 feeding on various dates from May to July, although roosting numbers peaked at 5000 on June 16th. Other large counts included 1700 roosting at Keyhaven on June 21st, 1500 circling over Portsmouth on Aug 5th and 1500 at Southseaon Sep 9th.

In the last quarter Farlington Marshes recorded 2000 on Oct 25th reducing to 800 on Nov 1st, while at Keyhaven Marsh there was an increase from 2500 on Nov 4th to 5000 on Nov 16th. Other large counts included 1500 feeding in a weedy field near Tundry Pond on Nov 7th, 1000 at Paulsgrove Reclamation on Nov 19th and Dec 7th and 2000 roosting at Ibsley Water on Nov 24th.

Rose-coloured Starling   *Sturnus roseus*
A rare vagrant (0,14,2).

There were two records. An adult was in a garden in Eastleigh on July 14th (SI) and another was in a Petersfield garden on July 23rd (MS). These sightings followed a significant irruption of the species into western Europe with about 150 being seen in the UK during June and July.

House Sparrow   *Passer domesticus*
An abundant resident.

About 20 records were submitted. The largest flock in the first quarter was 104 at Upper Hamble CP on Mar 27th - the only three-figure count for this period. Notable counts reported in the second half of the year were:

East Tisted: 75, Aug 10th; 105, Aug 25th.
Duck Island Lane, Ringwood: 106, Aug 11th; 85 Oct 20th.
Hilton Hotel, Farlington: 73, Aug 28th;
Upper Hamble CP: 107, Oct 17th.

Fleet: 60 roosting, Dec 18th.

The scarcity of the species in some areas is indicated by an observer from Chandlers Ford who reported a single at a garden bird table on Dec 2nd as being the first for several years and another noting that a single at IBM Lake on May 26th was the only sighting of the year there.

House Sparrows (Rosemary Watts/Powell)

Tree Sparrow   *Passer montanus*

A scarce resident, passage migrant and winter visitor. A considerable decline has occurred in the last 15 years.

Birds were present again at a farmland site in the north-east of the county with up to eight in January, six in February, ten in March and four in April. Birds were not seen after Apr 28th. They were present in the same area from Nov 23rd with four being seen then and again on Dec 21st, with just two on Dec 27th. Pheasants are reared in this area and for this reason there are seed hoppers around the site that they use for feeding. Observers are encouraged to search areas of game cover and small copses where these feeding stations exist as this would appear to be an important factor in the species survival in southern England. Despite 30 nest boxes being erected in small groups in the immediate area, these simply boosted the local population of Blue Tits!

The only other sightings were of a single in an Alton garden on Nov 11th and a nearby farm on Dec 5th (MED). County annual bird-month totals for the last ten years are as follows:

Annual bird-months	1993	1994	1995	1996	1997	1998	1999	2000	2001	2002
Tree Sparrow	10	39	17	22	14	14	7	5	30	36

Chaffinch   *Fringilla coelebs*

An abundant resident, passage migrant and winter visitor.

In the early year flocks in excess of 50 were recorded up to Apr 18th with a maximum of 2000 at 13 sites, of which 360 were at Bakers Bridge, Elvetham on Feb 3rd.

During the breeding season 109 territories were found along the Basingstoke Canal, 29 at Lower Test Marshes (CBC sites) and 130 were estimated at Longmoor Inclosure.

Apart from 51 flying north-west in half an hour at Fleet Pond on Nov 5th, little autumn diurnal movement was noted. Flocks in excess of 50 on the ground were noted from Nov 1st with a low maximum of 489 at five sites, of which 130 were at Temple Valley on Dec 31st. This excludes those noted during the *Wintering Great Grey Shrike Survey* in the New Forest where a total of 147 at 14 sites was recorded on Nov 17th.

Brambling   *Fringilla montifringilla*

A moderately common winter visitor and passage migrant.

In the period up to Apr 29th, 81 records were submitted, with only 15 referring to flocks in excess of ten. Between January and early March the only flocks were 40 at Brookheath NR between Jan 6th and Feb 28th and 200 in a stubble field at Longwater Road, Eversley Cross on Jan 16th and Feb 1st, with 100 still present in the area on Mar 9th. Numbers were very low during the rest of March until 31st with 30 at Eversley Cross and increased slightly in early April, indicating passage, with 25 at Woolmer Pond on 1st and 14 at Dunmow Hill, Fleet on 2nd. The only other notable flock during April was 20 at Long Valley on 21st and the last was one at Petersfield on 29th.

There were very few autumn records with just four in October with the first west at Hill Head/Titchfield Haven on 6th, the next was not until 26th at Lower Test Marshes then one west at Titchfield Haven and another at Fleet Pond on 28th. Just three flocks exceeded four in the late year with 20 at Bolderwood on Nov 18th, 20 at St Cross on Nov 19th and 15 at Blackwater Arboretum, NF on Dec 24th.

The approximate monthly totals are tabulated below:

J	F	M	A	M	J	J	A	S	O	N	D
300	270	144	88	0	0	0	0	0	4	64	26

Greenfinch   *Carduelis chloris*

A numerous resident, passage migrant and winter visitor.

A total of 29 records was submitted with seven referring to three-figure flocks. Early in the year 140 were recorded in a pre-roost gathering at IBM Lake, Cosham on Jan 1st and 150 were feeding on black sunflower seeds in a Petersfield garden on Jan 20th.

During the breeding season 21 territories were found along Basingstoke Canal, 34 at Lower Test Marshes and 11 at Longmoor Inclosure.

The only autumn diurnal movement noted was 16 flying east at Taddiford Gap on Sep 28th. In the second half of the year there were 240 at Butser Hill on Dec 3rd and 310 feeding on black sunflower seeds in a Petersfield garden on Aug 27th, 200-250 were regular there up to the end of the year with 270 on Dec 10th.

Goldfinch
Carduelis carduelis

Present throughout the year. A numerous breeder and passage migrant with reduced numbers in winter.

In the early year flocks in excess of 80 were 100 at Ashley Warren on Jan 3rd, 80 in game strip stubble at East Meon on Feb 27th and 81 in a Petersfield garden on Mar 13th. Spring passage noted during April at Hurst Beach totalled 104 flying north/north-east. Passage elsewhere was very light but noted up to May 12th with 36 north/east at four sites.

During the breeding season 13 territories were found along the Basingstoke Canal and three at Lower Test Marshes.

Between August and October grounded flocks totalled 3535 at 41 sites, a marked increase on recent years. Flocks in excess of 150 were noted at four sites and 450 in a thistle field at Tundry Pond on Oct 16th was the largest recorded in Hampshire since 460 at Waltham Chase Meadows on Aug 13th 1984.

Significant flocks in the late year were 100 at Winchester SF on Nov 7th and 70 at Lakeside CP on Nov 11th.

Siskin
Carduelis spinus

Present throughout the year. A moderately common breeder (largely confined to the New Forest), common passage migrant and winter visitor.

A total of 207 records was submitted. Early and late year numbers were high, but autumn passage was very light.

During January and February, around 2300 were recorded at 31 sites. At Fleet Pond counts of 200 or more were made on nine dates up to Feb 12th, with 600 on Jan 8th and 12th. Elsewhere three-figure flocks were recorded at eight sites and included 102 at Broadlands Estate on Jan 13th and 200 at Eversley GP on Feb 16th. By March numbers were much reduced with a maximum of 73 at West Wellow on 12th. During April and early May only 24 were recorded at ten sites with no count above four.

There were eight reports during the breeding season involving three sites in the New Forest, four in the north-east and one in the Petersfield area. One flying east at Froxfield on June 19th could have indicated local breeding.

More than usual were recorded during the late summer with reports from four sites in July and six in August, the peak count was 30 at Millersford Bottom on Aug 15th. September saw 34 reported from five sites, with the only movement being six south at Dunmow Hill, Fleet on 20th. A very light coastal passage was noted between Oct 5th and Nov 21st with the largest movement being 43 east at Hurst Beach on Oct 24th.

Three-figure counts into the late year were as follows: 250 at Somerley Park on Oct 25th, with 150 there on 27th; 200 at Ovington on 28th; 100 at Testwood Lakes on Nov 10th, Dec 15th and 22nd; 320 at Rotherlands, Petersfield on Dec 6th; 100 at Bisterne on Dec 7th; 128 at Liss on Dec 14th and 675 at Yateley GP on Dec 29th.

Linnet

Carduelis cannabina

Present throughout the year. A numerous breeder and passage migrant, but numbers are usually much reduced in winter.

High numbers were recorded during January and February with maxima of 100 at Ashley Warren on Jan 3rd, 250 at Hartley Mauditt on Jan 6th and 300 at Winchfield Moor on Feb 5th.

Spring passage at Hurst Beach totalled 267 flying north/north-east between Mar 24th and Apr 27th with a day peak of 171 north on Apr 6th. Elsewhere during March and April counts included 140 at Hattingley (Medstead) on Mar 5th, 150 at West End Down on Mar 8th, 100 at Lodge Farm, Odiham on Mar 10th and 100 at Ibworth on Mar 28th and Apr 5th.

Survey work on the north-east heaths produced a total of 119 pairs/singing males at 14 sites, including the following: Blackbushe Airfield/Yateley Common, 29; Bricksbury Hill/Bourley Heath/Long Valley, 17; Hazeley Heath, 12; Longmoor Inclosure, 24; Woolmer Forest, 14 (incomplete count). Only two territories were found along the Basingstoke Canal compared to ten in 2000. Two large gatherings were noted in June with 100 in oil-seed rape at Noar Hill on 8th and 165 at Bisterne Common on 22nd (early post-breeding dispersal).

Considerable autumn passage was noted from July to October, with maxima of 275 at Barton on Sea GC on Sep 1st, 200 at Brownwich on Sep 30th and Oct 6th, 570 at Hoe Cross on Oct 6th, 300 at Milford on Sea on Oct 16th and 500 at Winters Down, Warnford on Oct 22nd. Three-figure flocks were recorded at a further 11 sites. The only coastal passage noted was 112 east at Hurst Beach during October.

Late year numbers were high with three-figure flocks noted at 11 sites with notable gatherings as follows: 250 at Gander Down on Nov 16th and Dec 25th; 250 at Ibworth and 230 at Newfound on Nov 28th and 250 at Old Winchester Hill on Dec 22nd, with 450 there on 28th.

Twite

Carduelis flavirostris

A very scarce winter visitor and passage migrant.

It was another poor showing with just three records, all in the late year. There were three at Hurst Beach on Nov 22nd (DR), three in gorse at Keyhaven Marsh on Nov 27th (BG) and three at Hurst Beach on Dec 20th (MPM) and almost certainly refer to the same three individuals. The county totals of overwintering birds in the ten years to 2001/02 follow but exclude the 2002 late winter period:

Overwintering	92/93	93/94	94/95	95/96	96/97	97/98	98/99	99/00	00/01	01/02
Twite	5	0	4	4	7	14	10	2	3	1

Lesser Redpoll

Carduelis cabaret

Present throughout the year. A scarce breeder, common passage migrant and winter visitor.

Although 68 reports of flocks of ten or more were received, numbers remained low throughout the year. During January, reported maxima were of 200 at Bishop's Dyke on

6th, 100 at Yateley Common on 10th, 100 at Denny Wood on 12th and 16th and 100 at Fleet Pond from 14th-18th. The largest flock in February was 80 at Black Gutter Bottom on 14th. Numbers continued to fall through March with 50 at Bishopstoke on 3rd and 70 at Eversley GP on 22nd being the only counts over 50. Apart from 29 flying north-east at Tweseldown on Apr 20th, reports of spring migration were negligible.

The only breeding season record received was of two pairs at Longslade Bottom; there were no other reports between May 8th and Sep 25th.

The first report of the autumn was of one at Itchen CP on Sep 25th. Autumn migration was very light with a total of 94 at nine sites (four coastal and five inland) between Oct 4th and Nov 18th, with 30 north-west at Pennington Marsh on Nov 4th the only significant movement. Grounded flocks during October were recorded at 15 sites, with 75 at Rowbarrow on 26th the only count above 20. During November and December, 18 sites held flocks of five or more with a maximum of 90 at Wellington CP on Dec 21st. In addition the New Forest *Wintering Great Grey Shrike Survey* located a total of 121 at nine sites on Nov 17th.

Common Redpoll   *Carduelis flammea*
A very scarce winter visitor.

Only one record was sufficiently detailed to be accepted, namely of a single female or first-winter at Lakeside CP on Feb 16th/17th (SI, DJU, MLE). Observers are required to provide detailed notes when claiming a Common Redpoll sighting (also widely referred to as Mealy Redpoll).

Crossbill   *Loxia curvirostra*
A scarce resident, whose numbers are periodically augmented by irruptions in late summer or autumn.

Numbers were low up to July with most records confined to the New Forest. During this period the only double-figure flocks were 12 at Bourley Reservoir on Jan 8th and 20 at Milkham Inclosure on Mar 10th. Although present at seven New Forest sites during the breeding season, there was no proof of breeding.

A large irruption occurred into the country in July but numbers remained low in the county until August. Numbers peaked in September and during this time there was a noticeable passage, mainly westerly. After a drop in numbers during October, a smaller influx occurred in November and December. All records of 40 or more are listed below followed by a table summarising all the records received:

North-east
Liss Forest: 40, Sep 8th.
Longmoor Inclosure: 42, Sep 19th.
Willows Green Inclosure, Alice Holt: 48, Nov 24th and Dec 9th.

New Forest
Pipers Wait: 40, Aug 31st.
Puckpits Inclosure/Acres Down: 60, Aug 31st.
Slufters Inclosure: 161, Sep 4th; 50, Sep 5th.
Holmsley Inclosure: 40, Oct 31st.
Bishop's Dyke/Beaulieu Road/Denny Lodge: 60, Nov 17th; 85, Dec 23rd; 70, Dec 31st.

Elsewhere
Somerley Park: 45, Oct 25th; 50, Dec 12th.
Morgaston Wood: 40, Dec 21st -30th.
Ampfield Wood: 50, Dec 25th.

All records	J	F	M	A	M	J	J	A	S	O	N	D
Grounded	23	12	31	7	5	5	25	237	369	169	255	397
Flying over	0	0	0	2	0	0	1	115	113	6	20	13
Total	23	12	31	9	5	5	26	412	482	175	255	430
Sites	2	2	6	4	2	1	6	25	25	11	23	18

Bullfinch   *Pyrrhula pyrrhula*

A numerous resident.

Only 50 records were received. At Farlington Marshes up to three were present between late February and mid March, with one on May 5th and June 30th, then up to two were present from mid November. Early year double-figure flocks were 12 at Shepherds Spring on Jan 30th and 12 at Dibden Bay on Feb 9th.

Survey work on the north-east heaths found 20 territories at seven sites including ten at Bricksbury Hill/Bourley Heath/Long Valley. Four territories were found along Basingstoke Canal. A four-hour walk around Liss found 22 on Aug 17th.

Autumn migration was suggested by three flying west at Casbrook Common on Nov 7th and four moving west at Titchfield Haven on Dec 5th. The only double-figure flock late in the year was ten at Elvetham Park on Dec 19th.

Hawfinch   *Coccothraustes coccothraustes*

A resident, moderately common in the New Forest but thinly distributed and elusive elsewhere.

Some 77 records were received with 20 away from the New Forest.

In the New Forest 57 were recorded at 11 sites in the first quarter with maxima of 15 at Blackwater Arboretum on Feb 24th and 22 at Pitts Wood Inclosure on Mar 3rd; no other site held more than three. Between April and June records suggestive of breeding came from 11 sites. These were all of one or two birds except for five at Acres Down on May 28th and three at Sloden Inclosure on June 2nd. Five were at Ocknell Plain on Sep 17th. From Nov 16th, a total of 26 was recorded at four sites with maxima of six at Pitts Wood Inclosure on Nov 30th and 12 at Blackwater Arboretum on Dec 28th.

At Romsey the species was recorded on 15 dates in the first quarter with a maximum of 20 on Jan 14th (Fishlake Meadows). One carrying nesting material on Apr 1st indicated local breeding. During the late year there were two on Nov 24th and four on Dec 20th. Elsewhere there were only five records with one at West Wellow on Feb 10th, two at Eling on Feb 17th, one at Sleaford Reservoir on Apr 1st, one on a garden feeder at Cosham on Apr 11th and a family party of five at Weston Common on Sep 17th.

Lapland Bunting
Calcarius lapponicus

A rare autumn passage migrant and winter visitor (1,66,2).

After a blank year in 2001 it was a return to the normal pattern of records – but sadly this species is rarely seen in the county. A single flew over Barton on Sea GC at 0712 hrs on Sep 21st (SGK). Another single was at Iley Point, Keyhaven on Dec 13th (MPM).

Snow Bunting
Plectrophenax nivalis

A very scarce autumn passage migrant and winter visitor.

A first-winter male, which was first seen in October 2001, remained in the Hurst Spit area until Jan 6th (MPM). A first-winter was at the Point on Farlington Marshes on Nov 18th (RAK, SK, JCr).

Yellowhammer
Emberiza citrinella

A numerous resident.

Male Yellowhammer, Ashley Warren (Mike Wall)

Some 110 records were received – almost twice the total for 2001. These were mainly for the breeding season and wintering flocks. In the first quarter counts exceeding 20 were received from 11 sites with maxima of 100 at Ashley Warren on Jan 6th with 120 there on Mar 5th and 100 at Hartley Mauditt on Jan 6th reducing to 50 by Mar 10th. By April most birds had returned to their breeding sites, although 40 were still at Cheesefoot Head on Apr 17th and 27 were at Bishops Waltham on May 4th.

In an incomplete survey of the north-east heaths a total of 44 pairs/singing males was located at nine sites, including the following (2001 for comparison): Bramshill Plantation, 6 (4); Bramshott Common, 1 (4); Hazeley Heath, 7 (10); Longmoor Inclosure, 24 (25); The Warren, Oakhanger, 2 (1); and Woolmer Forest, 5 (6). For the first time there were no territories in the Bricksbury Hill/Bourley Heath/Velmead/Tweseldown area, where numbers have declined steadily over the last five years. Other significant counts of territories from breeding areas included 20 between Martin Down and Tidpit Down, 18 between Crondall and Upton Grey and 16 in just half of Butser Hill.

In the last quarter there were counts exceeding 20 from nine sites. Monthly peaks were 40 at Butser Hill on Oct 11th, 30 at Hartley Mauditt on Nov 9th and 100 were at Toyd Down on Dec 14th.

Reed Bunting

Emberiza schoeniclus

A common resident, passage migrant and winter visitor.

In the opening quarter of the year the largest counts were 70 in a garden in New Alresford on Jan 1st, 57 at Springhead (Greywell) on Jan 13th and 42 in a garden at Duck Island Lane, Ringwood on Feb 15th.

Breeding counts on the coast included five pairs at Hook-with-Warsash and 15 pairs at Keyhaven/Normandy. A total of 37 territories was found at Lower Test Marshes (40 in 2001). In the Itchen Valley breeding totals included four pairs between Bishopstoke and Allbrook and nine pairs between Bishopstoke and Brambridge, 14 pairs between Mansbridge and Allbrook and 32 pairs estimated upstream from Winchester. There were two pairs on the Basingstoke Canal and four at Fleet Pond. Six pairs were on the Bourley Heath/Long Valley area (three pairs in 2001) and four pairs at Longmoor Inclosure.

Ringing at Sturt Pond (Hurst Beach) between mid-September and the end of October resulted in a total of 59 being trapped. The largest counts in the last quarter were 47 at Springhead (Greywell) on Nov 14th and 86 there on Dec 29th, 50 at Bourley Heath//Bricksbury Hill on Nov 14th and 97 there on Dec 27th - both counts being of a loose flock. The *Wintering Great Grey Shrike Survey* in the New Forest revealed 72 at 12 sites on Nov 17th but only 34 at seven sites on Dec 14th.

Corn Bunting

Miliaria calandra

A moderately common but declining resident.

About 75 records were submitted. In the first quarter flocks were reported from several sites including Cheesefoot Head/Gander Down, where a group of 20-30 was counted on several dates in Jan-Mar rising to 40 on Mar 29th. As the breeding season commenced a flock was still maintained at Hoe Cross, with 37 on Apr 6th, 29 on Apr 23rd, 47 on Apr 27th and 20 on May 4th.

During the breeding season a maximum total of 55 pairs/singing males was reported as follows: Hoe Cross 9, Toyd Down 8, Hambledon 8, Cheesefoot Head 5, Soberton 5, Windmill Hill 5, Fawley Down, Morestead 2, Whitsbury Down 2, Gander Down 2, with single territories at Chidden, Idsworth, Longwood Warren, Martin Down, Colemore, Crondall, Over Wallop, Sparsholt College and Upper Swanmore. This compares with 53 territories reported in 2001.

In the final quarter there were relatively few records however a flock at Toyd Down built up from 30 on Sep 22nd to 90 on Dec 14th. Movements were indicated by reports of single birds flying over Broadmarsh on Oct 24th and Needs Ore on Nov 5th.

APPENDIX ONE - ESCAPES

Black Swan
Cygnus atratus

Escape, although it is possible that breeding attempts have been made in the wild.
(*Australia*)

Records were received as follows: South Charford Farm, Avon valley: one (Feb 17th), two (Jun 23rd); Emsworth Mill Pond and Harbour: one from late 2001 until Mar 4th; Chilland: one, Feb 23rd; Arlebury Lakes: one, Feb 21st, Mar 25th-29th, presumed same as Ovington: one, Mar 30th; Eversley GP: three, Nov 28th; Fishlake Meadows: one, Sep 22nd; Southington Lane, Overton: pair, Oct 4th; Timsbury: one, Apr 14th.

Pink-footed Goose
Anser brachyrhynchus

A rare winter visitor to the county, although presumed feral birds have occurred in most months.

There was just one record of this species, during the year, involving a single bird present at Ewhurst Lake from Feb 10th to May 9th (MJW, PEH, NM).

Lesser White-fronted Goose
Anser erythropus

All records are presumed to relate to feral or escaped birds. (*A rare vagrant to Britain from Siberia*).

Four records were received, all of single birds in the Avon Valley: Bisterne (Feb 10th-Mar 3rd; Dec 12th); Sabines Farm (Nov 10th); Avon Causeway (Oct 28th).

Bar-headed Goose
Anser indicus

A small feral population has become established in the north-east of the county. (*Central Eurasia*)

Approximately 14 birds were reported around the county, the largest count being five at The Vyne Lake in October. There were no reports of any breeding attempts. Records, mostly ones and twos were received from Titchfield Haven, Avon Valley (various locations), Ewhurst Lake, Allbrook, Bere Mill, St. Mary Bourne, Wellington CP, Fleet Pond, Ashe Park Lake, Overton Lagoons, and Vyne Lake/Watermeadows.

Emperor Goose
Anser canagicus

Escape (*N E Siberia and Alaska*).

In the Southampton Water area, one was present intermittently at Langdown MOD base Feb - Aug; this, or another, was seen higher up the estuary at Bury Marshes on Nov 16th, Eling Nov 28th and at Cracknore Hard on Dec 15th. In the north-east, one was present at Lower Ashe Farm in Nov 2001, associating with the local Canada Goose flock, and it is likely that the same bird was responsible for the sightings at Anton Lakes on Jan 13th and in Andover Town Centre two days later, again in the company of Canada Geese.

Red-breasted Goose
Branta ruficollis

Most records are assumed to relate to escapes, although wild birds have been recorded in the county. (*Breeds western Siberia, closest wintering grounds Black Sea*)

There were two reports of single birds from the Itchen Valley: Northington (Oct 12th); Avington Lake (Dec 27th).

Wood Duck
Aix sponsa

Escape (*North America*).

A male was present throughout the year at King's Pond, Alton. Another male could be seen on a small pond in Sherborne St. John Feb - Apr, and it was presumably the same bird that occasionally wandered to the The Vyne watermeadows nearby; it reappeared at the latter site in November. A female was at Aldershot Park on Dec 14th.

Chiloe Wigeon
Anas sibilatrix

Escape (*Southern South America*).

One remained at Ibsley Water from 2001 and was reported on three dates: Mar 3rd, Sep 15th and Dec 28th.

Speckled Teal
Anas flavirostris

Escape (*South America*).

Five were in the Lymington/Hurst area on Jan 12th, but were not reported again until two were seen from Apr 1st – 5th, and again on May 19th. A male was at Farlington Marshes on Sep 14th. In the north-east, two were at Bramshill Police College on Nov 17th and Dec 8th.

Reeve's Pheasant
Syrmaticus reevesii

Presumed release for sport shooting (*Eastern Asia*)

2001 addition: A pair was seen in a field on the downs north of Whitchurch on Mar 31st.

Cockatiel
Nymphicus hollandicus

Escape (*Australia*).

The first of the year to exploit an open window was in Sway, on Jan 7th. Surprisingly there were only two records in summer, the normal peak time for this species, from New Milton on July 17th and North Baddesley July 20th. Farlington Marshes saw three records, relating to different birds, on Sep 15th, Oct 20th and 21st.

Budgerigar
Melopsittacus undulatus

Escape (*Australia*).

Two were reported, both from Farlington Marshes, on Mar 12th and Sep 17th.

Alexandrine Parakeet   *Psittacula eupatria*

Escape (*India and S E Asia*).

The bird regularly seen for a number of years in the Keyhaven/Pennington area, was recorded on three dates: Aug 27th, Sep 25th and Nov 9th.

Blue-crowned Conure   *Aratinga acuticaudata*

Escape (*South America*).

Up to seven were reported in the Lymington area from Sep - Dec.

Yellow-headed Amazon   *Amazona ochrocephala*

Escape. (*Central and northern South America*).

One at Sway on Feb 7th.

Red-vented Bulbul   *Pycnonotus cafer*

Escape (*India and S E Asia*)

One was seen at Bishopstoke on Apr 8th and sporadically thereafter.

APPENDIX TWO –
PENDING RECORDS / RECORDS NOT ACCEPTED

List of Records still under consideration by the *HOS Records Panel* or the *British Birds Rarities Committee*.

Montagu's Harrier: Old Basing, Aug 17th; **Wood Sandpiper**: Woolmer Pond, Oct 19th and 28th; **Yellow-legged Gull** of race *cachinnans* (**Caspian Gull**): Fleet Pond, Apr 28th and Oct 26th; Lower Test Marshes, Sep 19th; **Red-rumped Swallow** (*Hirundo daurica*): Pitts Wood, July 10th; **Whinchat**: Buriton, Mar 4th-6th; **Golden Oriole**: in off sea, Titchfield Haven, Apr 5th; **Common (Mealy) Redpoll**: Blackbushe Airfield, Mar 26th.

List of Records for which descriptions are still awaited for submission to the *British Birds Rarities Committee*.

Lesser Yellowlegs (*Tringa flavipes*): Eversley GP, June 13th 2001; **Ross's Gull** (*Rhodostethia rosea*): adult moving W, Hurst Castle, Jan 25th.

List of Records not accepted by the *HOS Records Panel* or the *British Birds Rarities Committee*.

In the vast majority of cases, the records below were not accepted because the relevant committee was not convinced that the identification was fully established; only in a very few cases was it believed that a mistake had been made.

Slavonian Grebe: off Pennington Marsh, Aug 29th; **Sooty Shearwater**: 1 E, Milford-on-Sea, June 9th; **Balearic Shearwater**: 2 off Hordle, July 9th; accepted as Shearwater *sp;* **Storm Petrel**: 2 SW off Hurst Beach, Oct 22nd; **Pygmy Cormorant** (*Phalacrocorax pygmeus*): Keyhaven, Feb 14th; **Night Heron** (*Nycticorax nycticorax*): 2, Southampton, May 13th 2001; Sowley Pond, Apr 13th; **White Stork**: Farley Mount, Nov 4th 2001; Frith End, April (exact date not available); **Goshawk**: Avon valley, Apr 8th; Five Lanes End, Aug 29th; **Gyr Falcon** (*Falco rusticolus*): Matley Wood, Oct 10th; **Black-winged Stilt**: Beaulieu, July 22nd; **Dotterel** (*Charadrius morinellus*): heard at night, Newlands Farm, Fareham, Nov 24th; **Sabine's Gull**: Milford on Sea, July 6th; **Iceland Gull**: second-summer, Woolston, Apr 10th/11th; **Great Reed Warbler** (*Acrocephalus arundinaceus*): Titchfield Haven, May 12th 2001; **Marsh Warbler** (*Acrocephalus palustris*): Lee, May 19th; **Rose-coloured Starling**: North Baddesley, Nov 19th; **Nutcracker** (*Nucifraga caryocatactes*): Lymington, Oct 28th 2001; **Common (Mealy) Redpoll**: Fleet Pond, Jan 26th.

List of Records from various media where details of observer could not be traced.

Purple Heron: Ibsley Water, Mar 29th; Itchen Valley CP, Apr 8th;Itchen Valley CP, May 30th; seen from IOW ferry near Sowley Shore, June 18th; **White Stork**: Hedge End, Apr 20th; Andover, Aug 4th; Hayling Island, Aug 7th; Southsea, Oct 6th; **Honey Buzzard**: 1 N, Farnborough, May 12th; Needs Ore, Sep 9th; Ashley Walk, Sep 14th; Blackbushe Airfield, Sep 19th; **Black Kite** (*Milvus migrans*): Fleet Pond, May 3rd; Titchfield Haven, July 27th; **Rough-legged Buzzard**: Pig Bush, Mar 28th; Holmsley Inclosure, Nov 10th; **Red-footed Falcon** (*Falco vespertinus*): Martin Down, July 6th; **Grey Phalarope**: Hayling Oysterbeds, Feb 10th; **Ring-billed Gull**: Hook-with-Warsash, Sep 28th; **Glaucous Gull**: Titchfield Haven, Mar 11th; **Little Auk**: Hill Head, Feb 25th; **Long-eared Owl** (*Asio otus*): Gosport, Feb 27th; **Serin** (*Serinus serinus*): Romsey, Apr 17th; **Twite**: 2, Ashley Walk, Dec 10th; **Common (Mealy) Redpoll**: 2, Baddesley Common, Mar 30th; 2, Beaulieu Road, Dec 23rd.

The *HOS Records Panel* would be pleased to receive details of any of the above observations for consideration for inclusion in the next *Hampshire Bird Report*.

GAZETTEER

The following place names are mentioned in the text of this report.

Abbots Worthy	SU4932	Beaulieu Lake, New Forest	SU3802
Abbotts Ann	SU3243	Beaulieu Road, New Forest	SU3406
Abbotts Barton	SU4831	Becton Bunny	SZ2592
Abbotts Wood Inclosure	SU8140	Bedhampton	SU7006
Abbottswood, Romsey	SU3723	Berry Wood	SU2105
Acres Down, New Forest	SU2609	Bickerley Common	SU1404
Aldershot	SU8749	Bickton	SU1512
Allbrook	SU4521	Bishop's Dyke, New Forest	SU3405
Allington Gravel Pit	SU4617	Bishops Waltham Moors	SU5516
Alresford	SU5731	Bishopstoke	SU4619
Alresford Pond	SU5933	Bisterne	SU1300
Alton	SU7239	Bisterne Common, New Forest	SU1801
Alverstoke	SZ6098	Black Dam Nature Reserve, Basingstoke	SU6551
Ampfield Wood	SU3723	Black Gutter Bottom, New Forest	SU2016
Anthony's Bee Bottom, New Forest	SU2201	Black Point, Hayling	SZ7599
Anton Lakes, Andover	SU3546	Blackbushe Airfield	SU8059
Applemore	SU3907	Blackfield	SU4402
Appleshaw	SU3048	Blackmoor	SU7833
Arlebury Lakes	SU5732	Blackwater Arboretum, New Forest	SU2604
Arlebury Mill	SU5833	Blashford Lakes	SU1508
Arlebury Park	SU5832	Bolderwood, New Forest	SU2408
Arlebury Water Meadows	SU5732	Botley Wood	SU5310
Ashe (source of Test)	SU5349	Bourley North/Long Valley	SU8350
Ashe Park Lake	SU5449	Bourley South/Bricksbury	SU8449
Ashford Hangers	SU7426	Brambridge	SU4721
Ashlett Creek	SU4603	Bramshill	SU7759
Ashley Walk, New Forest	SU1915	Bramshill Plantation	SU7461
Ashley Warren	SU4856	Bramshill Police College	SU7560
Avington Lake	SU5232	Bramshot Heath	SU8355
Avon Causeway	SZ1497	Bramshott Chase / Common	SU8633
Avon Water (Sway), New Forest	SZ2698	Breamore	SU1618
Awbridge	SU3324	Broadlands Estate / Lake, Romsey	SU3516
Baffins Pond	SU6601	Broadmarsh	SU7005
Barton on Sea	SZ2492	Brockenhurst, New Forest	SU2900
Barton on Sea Golf Course	SZ2592	Broom Channel, Langstone Harbour	SU6802
Barton's Mill (The Mill Field), Old Basing	SU6653	Broomy Plain, New Forest	SU2010
Basingstoke (Town Centre)	SU6352	Brown Candover	SU5738
Basingstoke Canal	SU7052	Brown Loaf, New Forest	SU1902
Basingstoke Canal, Aldershot	SU8851	Browndown	SZ5799
Basingstoke Canal, Crookham	SU7951	Brownwich	SU5103
Bassett, Southampton	SU4216	Broxhead Common	SU8037
Beachlands, Hayling	SZ7198	Budds Farm Sewage Farm	SU7005
Beacon Hill Warnford	SU6021	Bullington Cross	SU4641
Beaulieu, New Forest	SU3802	Burgate Meadows	SU1518
Beaulieu Estuary	SZ4298	Buriton	SU7421
Beaulieu Heath, New Forest	SU3500	Burrfields, Portsmouth	SU6602

Bury Marshes	SU3711	Droxford	SU6119
Burton Common	SZ1995	Dunmow Hill, Fleet	SU8154
Butser Hill	SU7120	Dunsbury, Havant	SU7009
Calmore	SU3314	Durngate, Winchester	SU4829
Calshot	SU4801	East Aston Common, Longparish	SU4344
Calthorpe Park, Fleet	SU7953	East Hayling	SZ7399
Camp Farm Gravel Pit/Sewage Farm	SU8852	East Meon	SU6821
Cams Bay	SU5905	East Tisted	SU7132
Carpenters Down Wood, Basingstoke	SU6455	East Wellow	SU3020
Casbrook Common	SU3625	East Worldham	SU7537
Castle Bottom	SU7959	Eastleigh	SU4417
Chandlers Ford	SU4321	Eastney	SU6800
Chappetts Copse, West Meon	SU2365	Easton	SU5132
Charity Down Farm	SU3438	Eelmoor Marsh, Pyestock	SU8353
Charlton Lakes	SU3446	Efford	SZ3192
Chawton	SU7036	Eling / Eling Marshes	SU3612
Chawton Park Wood	SU6736	Ellingham Lake	SU1407
Cheesefoot Head	SU5228	Ellingham	SU1408
Chessel Bay	SU4413	Ellisfield	SU6447
Chichester Harbour, Hampshire	SZ4096	Elvetham	SU7956
Chickenhall Lane, Eastleigh	SU4618	Emer Bog, North Baddesley	SU3921
Chidden	SU6619	Emery Down	SU2808
Chilcomb	SU5028	Emmetts Down	SU6622
Chilling/ Chilling Cliffs	SU5003	Empress Dock, Southampton	SU4210
Christchurch Bay	SZ2990	Empshott	SZ7531
Church Moor, New Forest	SU2406	Emsworth	SU7505
Clamp Kiln Farm, Wickham	SU6012	Emsworth Harbour	SU7704
Clanfield	SU6816	Emsworth Mill Pond	SU7405
Cliddesden	SU6349	Eversley	SU8062
Coldrey Park	SU7743	Eversley Common	SU7959
Colemore	SU7030	Eversley Cross	SU7961
Compton	SU4726	Eversley Gravel Pit (Berks side)	SU8162
Coombe	SU6620	Eversley Gravel Pit	SU8061
Coopers Hill	SU2014	Ewhurst Lake/Park	SU5757
Cosham	SU6606	Exton	SU6020
Cowplain	SU6910	Eyeworth Pond/Wood, New Forest	SU2214
Crab Wood	SU4329	Faccombe	SU3958
Cracknore Hard	SU4011	Fareham	SU5706
Crondall	SU7848	Fareham Creek	SU5805
Crookhorn, Waterlooville	SU6807	Farley Mount	SU4029
Cufaude Lane	SU6557	Farlington	SU6805
Curbridge	SU5211	Farlington Marshes	SU6804
Cutler's Farm	SU6609	Farnborough Airfield	SU8453
Danebury	SU3437	Fawley Down, Morestead	SU5127
Darby Green Sewage Farm	SU8360	Fawley Inclosure, New Forest	SU4205
Deadwater Valley, Bordon	SU8035	Fawley Refinery	SU4404
Denmead	SU6211	Fields Heath, New Forest	SU4502
Denny Wood, New Forest	SU3305	Fishlake Meadows, Romsey	SU3522
Dibden Bay	SU4008	Five Lanes End, Greywell	SU6950
Dibden Purlieu	SU4106	Fleet Pond	SU8255
Dogmersfield Lake/Park	SU7551	Fobdown, Alresford	SU5732
Drayton	SU6623	Foley Manor, Liphook	SU8230

Fordingbridge	SU1414	Hook-with-Warsash	SU4904
Fort Elson, Gosport	SU6001	Hook Valley, Warsash	SU5005
Fort Nelson	SU6007	Hordle	SZ2692
Four Lanes End	SU7248	Hordle Cliff	SZ2792
Frater	SU5904	Horndean	SU7012
Froxfield	SU7025	Horsea Island	SU6304
Fullerton	SU3739	Horsebridge	SU3430
Funtley	SU5508	Hounsdown, Totton	SU3511
Gander Down	SU5527	Hucklesbrook Lakes	SU1511
Gilkicker Point	SZ6097	Hucklesbrook Water Meadows	SU1411
Gosport	SU6100	Hurst Beach	SZ2990
Great Litchfield Down	SU4755	Hurst Castle	SZ3189
Great Thorney Deep, Thorney Island	SU7403	Hythe	SU4207
Greywell	SU7151	IBM Lake (Cosham)	SU6404
Hale	SU1718	Ibsley	SU1409
Hamble Common	SU4806	Ibsley Water (Blashford)	SU1508
Hamble Estuary	SU4805	Ibworth	SU5754
Hambledon	SU6417	Idsworth	SU7414
Hamer Warren	SU1310	Iley Point, Keyhaven	SZ3091
Hammer Common	SU8632	Inchmery	SZ4498
Hampton Ridge, New Forest	SU1913	Islands Thorns Inclosure, New Forest	SU2115
Hannington	SU5357	Itchen Abbas	SU5332
Harbridge	SU1410	Itchen Stoke	SU5532
Hartley Mauditt	SU7436	Itchen Valley	SU4617
Hartley Wintney	SU7756	Ivy Lake	SU1507
Hatchet Pond, New Forest	SU3601	Jacks Bush, Porton	SU2736
Havant Thicket	SU7110	Janesmoor Pond, New Forest	SU2413
Hawley Common	SU8560	Keyhaven / Keyhaven Harbour	SZ3292
Hawley Lake	SU8457	Keyhaven Marsh	SZ3192
Hayling Bay	SZ7198	Keyhaven Reed-beds	SZ3091
Hayling Billy Trail	SU7103	Kilmeston	SU5824
Hayling Oysterbeds	SU7103	Kingfisher Lake	SU1506
Hazeley Heath	SU7558	King's Pond, Alton	SU7239
Headbourne Worthy	SU4832	Kings Worthy	SU4932
Headley Mill Pond	SU8135	Kings Somborne	SU3529
Heath Warren	SU7660	Kingsclere	SU5457
Hermitage Stream, Bedhampton	SU7006	Kingston	SU1502
Highclere Park	SU4360	Knightwood Oak Inclosure, New Forest	SU2506
Hill Head	SU5302	Lakeside CP, Eastleigh	SU4417
Hillside, Odiham	SU7550	Langdown	SU4306
Hinchelsea Bog, New Forest	SU2601	Langley	SU8028
Hipley	SU6211	Langstone	SU7105
HMS Daedalus	SU5103	Langstone Bridge	SU7204
Hoe Cross	SU6314	Langstone Channel	SU6901
Holbrook, Gosport	SU5902	Langstone Harbour	SU6904
Holly Hill Park, Warsash	SU4481	Langstone Harbour entrance	SZ6899
Holmsley Bog, New Forest	SU2201	Langstone Harbour Islands	SU6903
Holmsley Walk/Inclosure, New Forest	SZ2198	Langstone South Moor	SU7104
Holt Pound Inclosure	SU4481	Latchmore Bottom, New Forest	SU1812
Hook Lake, Warsash	SU4905	Leckford	SU3737
Hook Links, Warsash	SU4904	Lee	SU3617
Hook Spit, Warsash	SU4805	Lee-on-the-Solent	SU5501

Lepe	SZ4598	Mottisfont	SU3326
Lichett Plain	SU8056	Needs Ore (Beaulieu Estuary)	SZ4297
Linbrook Lake	SU1507	Netley	SU4508
Liphook	SU8230	New Alresford	SU5832
Liss	SU7827	Newfound	SU5851
Liss Forest	SU7828	Newlands Farm, Fareham	SU5604
Liss Nurseries	SU7928	Newlands Farm, Purbrook	SU6608
Lockerley	SU2826	Noar Hill Nature Reserve	SU7331
Lodge Farm, Odiham	SU7452	Normandy Lagoon	SZ3394
Lodge Inclosure, Alice Holt Forest	SU8142	North Baddesley	SU3719
Long Down	SU6619	North Binness Island, Langstoke Harbour	SU6904
Long Sutton	SU7445	North End Farm, Harbridge	SU1411
Longmoor Inclosure, Wealden	SU7930	North Hayling	SU7303
Longslade Bottom, New Forest	SU2600	North Somerley Lakes	SU1408
Longstock	SU3839	Northington	SU5736
Longwater Bridge	SU5508	Northney	SU7304
Longwater Lawn	SU3208	Oakford Coppice	SU1402
Longwood Warren	SU5226	Oakhanger (The Warren)	SU7734
Lower Ashe Farm	SU5349	Oakley	SU5650
Lower Test Marshes Nature Reserve	SU3613	Ocknell Plain, New Forest	SU2211
Ludshott Common	SU8535	Odiham	SU7550
Lye Heath	SU6408	Odiham Airfield	SU7348
Lyeways Farm, Ropley	SU6731	Old Basing	SU6652
Lymington	SZ3394	Old Winchester Hill	SU6420
Lymington River	SZ3296	Oliver's Battery	SU4527
Lymore Lane, Pennington	SZ2992	Over Wallop	SU2738
Lyndhurst	SU2908	Overton	SU5149
Magdalen Hill Down	SU5029	Overton Lagoons	SU5150
Malthouse Farm, Sleaford	SU7938	Ovington	SU5632
Mansbridge	SU4516	Ower, Romsey	SU3216
Mapledurwell Cressbeds	SU6852	Oxey Lake	SZ3393
Marchwood	SU3810	Oxey Marsh / Barn Fields	SZ3293
Markway Inclosure, New Forest	SU2403	Pale Lane, Winchfield	SU7854
Martin Down	SU0419	Park Farm	SZ4096
Marwell Zoo	SU5021	Park Shore	SZ4096
Matley Wood, New Forest	SU3307	Passfield Pond	SU8233
Meadow Lake	SU3416	Paulsgrove Reclamation	SU6404
Medstead	SU6337	Pennington Marsh	SZ3292
Meon Valley	SU6118	Petersfield	SU7622
Micheldever	SU5244	Petersfield Heath Pond	SU7522
Midgham Wood	SU1412	Pig Bush, New Forest	SU3604
Milford on Sea	SZ2891	Pipers Wait, New Forest	SU2416
Milford on Sea Cliffs	SZ2891	Pittleworth	SU3839
Milkham Inclosure, New Forest	SU2110	Pitt Down	SU4129
Millersford Bottom, New Forest	SU1816	Pitts Deep	SZ3795
Milton Reclamation/Playing Fields	SU6700	Pitts Wood Inclosure, New Forest	SU2014
Minley	SU8258	Plaitford Common, New Forest	SU2718
Mockbeggar Lake (Blashford)	SU1508	Polhampton	SU5250
Mockbeggar, New Forest	SU1609	Pond House, Liss Forest	SU7829
Monxton	SU3144	Popham	SU5244
Morestead	SU5125	Port Solent	SU6305
Morgaston Wood	SU6257	Portchester	SU6205

Portsmouth	SZ6497	South Warnborough	SU7247
Portsmouth Dockyards	SU6300	South Wonston	SU4635
Portsmouth Harbour	SU6104	Southampton	SU4311
Portsmouth Outdoor Centre	SU6703	Southampton Airport	SU4517
Posbrook Lane, Titchfield	SU5304	Southampton Common	SU4114
Prince's Marsh, Liss	SU7726	Southampton Old Docks	SU4210
Puckpits Inclosure, New Forest	SU2509	Southington Lane, Overton	SU5049
Pylewell Lake	SZ3594	Southsea	SZ6498
Pylewell Saltings	SZ3494	Southsea Beach	SZ6598
Ramridge Copse, Weyhill	SU3148	Southsea Castle	SZ6498
Redbridge	SU3613	Southsea Cricket Pitch	SZ6698
Rhinefield Inclosure, New Forest	SU2504	Southwick	SU6308
Ringwood	SU1405	Sowley Marsh / Shore	SZ3795
Ringwood Forest	SU1210	Sowley Pond	SZ3796
Riverside Park, Southampton	SU4314	Sparsholt	SU4232
Romsey	SU3521	Sparsholt College	SU4231
Romsey Water Meadows	SU3421	Spinnaker (Blashford)	SU1507
Rookesbury Mill	SU3544	Springhead, Greywell	SU7150
Ropley	SU6231	St Cross, Winchester	SU4728
Rotherlands, Petersfield	SU7623	St John's College Playing Fields	SU6805
Rowbarrow, New Forest	SU3504	St Lucia Woods, Bordon	SU8036
Rowland's Castle	SU7310	St Mary Bourne	SU4250
Roydon Woods, New Forest	SU3100	Steep	SU7225
Sabines Farm, Avon Valley	SZ1499	Stockbridge	SU3534
Saddlers Mill, Romsey	SU3420	Stokes Bay	SZ5898
Salter's Heath, Monk Sherborne	SU6156	Stoney Cross Plain, New Forest	SU2512
Sandleheath	SU1216	Straits Inclosure, Alice Holt Forest	SU8039
Sandy Point	SZ7498	Stratfield Saye Park	SU7062
Sarisbury Green	SU4908	Strodgemoor Bottom	SU1903
Selborne	SU7333	Stubbington	SU5402
Setley Plain, New Forest	SU2900	Stubbs Farm Ponds	SU7640
Set Thorns Inclosure, New Forest	SZ2699	Sturt Pond, Milford on Sea	SZ2991
Shedfield Common	SU5613	Sway, New Forest	SZ2997
Sheepwash Farm	SU6509	Taddiford Gap	SZ2692
Sheet	SU7625	Tadley Common	SU6061
Shepherds Spring Lakes	SU3546	Tanners Lane	SZ3695
Sherborne St John	SU6255	Teglease Down	SU6519
Sherfield-on-Loddon	SU6758	Temple Manor	SU7533
Silchester Common	SU6262	Testbourne (River Test)	SU4445
Sinah Common/Gravel Pit/Warren	SZ6999	Testwood Lakes	SU3415
Sleaford Malt House	SU7938	The Kench, Hayling	SZ6999
Sleaford Reservoir	SU8038	The Solent	SZ2987
Sloden Inclosure, New Forest	SU2012	The Vyne	SU6356
Slufters Inclosure, New Forest	SU2210	Tidgrove Airstrip	SU5254
Snails Lake	SU1507	Tidpit Down	SU0617
Soberton	SU6217	Timsbury Gravel Pit	SU3424
Solent Breezes	SU5003	Tipner Lake	SU6504
Somerley Lakes	SU1407	Titchfield Haven	SU5302
Somerley Park	SU1406	Tournerbury, Hayling Island	SZ7399
Sopley	SZ1596	Toyd Down	SU0819
South Boarhunt	SU6008	Trotts Wood, Marchwood	SU3711
South Hayling	SZ7299	Tundry Pond	SU7752

Tunworth	SU6848	Whitsbury Down	SU1219
Tweseldown	SU8252	Wickham	SU5911
Upper Hamble Country Park	SU4911	Wickham Common	SU5810
Upper Hamble Estuary	SU5010	Wickham Hundred Acres	SU5910
Upper Swanmore	SU5817	Wide Lane Playing Fields, Eastleigh	SU4417
Upton Grey	SU6948	Widley	SU6607
Velmead Common	SU8253	Willows Green Inclosure, Alice Holt	SU8141
Victoria Park, Portsmouth	SU6300	Wilverley Plain	SU2501
Wade Court, Havant	SU7205	Winchester	SU4829
Waggoners Wells	SU8534	Winchester College Meadows	SU4828
Wallington	SU5808	Winchester Sewage Farm	SU4927
Waltham Chase Meadows	SU5615	Winchfield	SU7655
Warblington	SU7205	Winchfield Moor	SU7655
Warnford	SU6223	Windmill Hill	SU7115
Warren Heath, Bramshill	SU7759	Winklebury, Basingstoke	SU6153
Warren Hill, Liss	SU7829	Winkton	SZ1696
Warsash	SU4906	Winnall Moors	SU4830
Waterlooville	SU6710	Winsor	SU3114
Wattons Ford	SU1301	Winters Down, Warnford	SU5822
Wellington Country Park	SU7362	Woodgreen	SU1616
West End Down	SU6318	Woodmill, Southampton	SU4415
West Green	SU7557	Woolmer Forest	SU7932
West Hayling Shore	SU7101	Woolmer Pond	SU7831
West Lane, Hayling	SU7100	Woolston	SU4409
West Walk	SU6013	Wootton Coppice Inclosure, New Forest	SZ2499
West Wellow	SU2819	Wootton St Lawrence	SU5953
Western Court	SU6032	Wyck Pond	SU7639
Weston Common	SU6944	Yateley Common	SU8259
Weston Shore	SU4409	Yateley Gravel Pits	SU8261
Whitchurch	SU4648	Yateley Heath Wood	SU8058
White Hill, Overton	SU5147	Yew Tree Heath, New Forest	SU3606
Whitley Woods, New Forest	SU2905	Zions Hill Pond	SU4220

Arrival and Departure Dates of Summer Visitors

	Earliest Ever	Average 1971-2002	Earliest 2002	Latest Ever	Average 1971-2002	Latest 2002	Wintering Records
Garganey	4/3/54	20/3*	27/3	29/11/53	27/9*	12/9	5 (Dec-Mar)
Honey Buzzard	21/4/96	n/a	8/5	30/10/76	n/a	13/9	2 (Dec)
Montagu's Harrier	8/4/79	1/5*	24/4	2/11/60	2/9*	26/8	
Osprey	6/3/54	11/4*	17/3	11/12/99	13/10*	5/10	1 (Feb/Mar)
Hobby	16/3/02	15/4	16/3	6/11/01	9/10	23/10	6 (Dec/Jan)
Quail	9/4/91	17/5*	7/5	19/11/58	24/8*	17/9	
Stone Curlew	25/2/38	31/3*	26/3	6/11/66	5/10*	-	
Little Ringed Plover	5/3/97	20/3	15/3	11/10/80	18/9	19/9	9 (Dec/Jan)
Wood Sandpiper	4/4/83	6/5*	4/5	26/10/75	23/9	19/9	14 (Dec-Feb)
Pomarine Skua	9/3/95	26/4*	7/4	17/11/63	19/10*	10/11	
Arctic Skua	20/3/79	11/4	2/4	25/11/00	26/10	20/11	
Sandwich Tern	10/3/90	22/3	17/3	26/11/98 & 03	26/10	26/11	
Roseate Tern	21/4/96	6/5*	24/4	10/10/99	9/9*	22/9	
Common Tern	17/3/03	7/4	17/3	30/11/73	25/10	23/10	3 (Dec)
Arctic Tern	29/3/58	23/4*	17/4	6/11/60	6/10*	17/10	
Little Tern	24/3/57	12/4	10/4	22/10/72	2/10	12/9	
Black Tern	11/4/79	24/4	21/4	15/11/67	9/10	2/10	1 (Jan)
Turtle Dove	25/3/70	17/4	21/4	7/11/70	6/10	22/9	
Cuckoo	15/3/89	4/4	21/3	11/10/86	15/9	21/9	4 (Dec-Feb)
Nightjar	26/4/95	7/5	9/5	13/10/74	9/9	13/9	
Swift	8/4/97 & 01	18/4	20/4	17/11/74	4/10	19/9	1 (Nov)
Wryneck	8/3/04	27/4*	13/4	18/10/90	23/9*	26/9	
Sand Martin	27/2/90	17/3	9/3	12/11/85	15/10	29/9	
Swallow	27/2/94	23/3	15/3	22/12/77	27/11	6/12	2 (Dec/Jan)
House Martin	2/3/90	31/3	17/3	22/12/82	21/11	27/10	6 (Jan)
Tree Pipit	16/03/92 & 03	31/3	16/3	25/10/79	3/10	6/10	1 (Jan/Feb)
Yellow Wagtail	10/3/68	2/4	29/3	20/11/76	21/10	16/10	
Nightingale	3/4/75	16/4	10/4	9/10/85	23/8*	-	5 (Dec-Feb)
Redstart	17/3/68	5/4	29/3	24/11/89	15/10	28/9	1 (Mar)
Whinchat	21/3/68	17/4	21/4	1/12/84	31/10	18/11	
Wheatear	6/2/89	12/3	11/3	31/12/94	9/11	2/11	5 (Jan/Feb)
Ring Ouzel	3/3/96	30/3	16/3	4/12/03	29/10	4/12	3 (Jan)
Grasshopper Warbler	1/4/97	14/4	7/4	20/10/01	16/9*	13/9	4 (Dec-Feb)
Sedge Warbler	17/3/63	9/4	30/3	9/11/63	12/10	8/10	1 (Dec)

Arrival and Departure Dates of Summer Visitors (continued)

	Earliest Ever	Average 1971-2002	Earliest 2002	Latest Ever	Average 1971-2002	Latest 2002	Wintering records
Reed Warbler	1/4/94	16/4	4/4	2/12/84	20/10	19/10	5 (Nov-Mar)
Lesser Whitethroat	1/4/89	18/4	16/4	31/10/82	3/10	28/9	4 (Dec/Jan)
Whitethroat	7/3/97	11/4	21/3	17/11/95	6/10	10/10	1 (Dec-Feb)
Garden Warbler	17/3/74	13/4	13/4	29/11/87	1/10	5/10	
Wood Warbler	9/4/88	22/4	24/4	29/9/64	25/8*	2/9	
Willow Warbler	16/3/01	26/3	17/3	1/12/90	8/10	23/9	
Spotted Flycatcher	8/4/00	29/4	14/5	29/10/61	3/10	3/10	
Pied Flycatcher	26/3/96	15/4	18/4	22/10/77	28/9	10/9	

* = average based on incomplete data set (i.e. data missing for one or more years)

Departure and Arrival Dates of Winter Visitors

	Latest Ever	Average 1971-2002	Latest 2002	Earliest Ever	Average 1971-2002	Earliest 2002	Summering Records
Black-throated Diver	2/6/87	5/5*	12/5	14/9/01	8/11*	20/10	1 (May-Aug)
Great Northern Diver	27/5/01	9/5*	28/5	4/10/60	11/11*	3/11	1 (Aug)
Red-necked Grebe	9/5/68	1/4*	16/3	24/8/94	16/10*	21/9	
Slavonian Grebe	22/5/59	9/4*	23/4	25/9/88	29/10	22/10	2 (Aug)
Bewick's Swan	24/3/76	16/3*	6/3	19/10/89	2/11*	17/11	9 (Apr/May, Sep)
White-fronted Goose	20/5/84	30/3	17/3	5/10/52	15/11*	-	5 (Jun-Sep)
Scaup	19/5/77	10/4	28/2	9/9/00	28/10	15/10	3 (Jun-Aug)
Long-tailed Duck	27/5/00	6/5*	26/5	23/9/61	6/11*	8/11	2 (Jun-Aug)
Velvet Scoter	26/6/97	3/5*	16/5	29/9/91	1/11*	22/10	
Hen Harrier	10/6/86	9/5	2/6	29/8/79	27/9	16/9	
Merlin	24/5/03	23/4	24/5	2/8/89	28/8	22/8	1 (July)
Purple Sandpiper	31/5/61	23/4	30/4	7/7/69	9/10	8/9	2 (July)
Jack Snipe	9/5/77	17/4	23/4	5/9/90	30/9	19/9	
Water Pipit	6/5/98	17/4	13/4	26/9/93	16/10	2/10	
Fieldfare	23/5/80	1/5	21/4	6/9/81	2/10	27/9	3 (June, Aug)
Redwing	12/5/81	24/4	18/4	11/9/99	28/9	21/9	1 (June)
Great Grey Shrike	8/5/83	6/4	17/2	4/10/72	20/10	22/10	
Brambling	13/5/92	19/4	29/4	22/9/96	6/10	6/10	1 (July)

* = average based on incomplete data set (i.e. data missing for one or more years)

GUIDELINES FOR THE SUBMISSION OF RECORDS

All observers birding in Hampshire are urged to submit records to the Recorder on Hampshire Ornithological Society record forms. The form is available on the society web site at http://www.hants.org.uk/hos. Records can be entered on line and e-mailed to the Recorder at johnclark@cygnetcourt.demon.co.uk. Records can also be submitted in an Excel spreadsheet or Word file by e-mail or on disk by post. It would be of great assistance if observers would comply with the following points when submitting records.

- Records should be listed either by species (in the order used in the *Hampshire Bird Report*) or by date.

- Please submit your sightings to the Recorder quarterly and at the latest by Jan 31st of the following year.

- Information on the records required for species occurring **annually** is tabulated below.

A = All records; details of age, plumage, time, direction of movement etc should be included as appropriate, especially for birds seen in places where not usually recorded or out of season.

B = All breeding records, with type of evidence obtained: confirmed, probable or possible.

CB = Counts of breeding pairs/singing males/territories in clearly defined areas.

F = Flocks, roosts and falls: minimum number required is given in parentheses.

F&L = First and last dates of summer and winter visitors.

M = Observations of birds moving on migration: give each day's count separately, with time of observation and direction the birds were moving.

MM = Dated monthly maxima from localities you regularly watch, counts may be below the threshold in F when submitting a complete year's data.

R = All records from localities where not normally recorded.

S = All summer records.

W = All winter records.

N = Brief notes of diagnostic identification features observed should be written on the record form.

Red-throated Diver	A, inland & summer N	Brent Goose	F (100), MM, F&L, M, R, inland A
Black-throated Diver	A, inland & summer N		
Great Northern Diver	A, inland & summer N	Brent Goose (Pale-bellied)	A
Little Grebe	B, F (5), MM, R	Egyptian Goose	A
Great Crested Grebe	B, F (10), MM, R	Ruddy Shelduck	A
Red-necked Grebe	A, inland & summer N	Shelduck	coast: B, F (50), MM, inland: A
Slavonian Grebe	A, inland & summer N		
Black-necked Grebe	A, inland N	Mandarin	B, F (10), MM, R
Fulmar	A, inland N	Wigeon	F coast & Avon valley(100), elsewhere (25), MM, F&L, R
Manx Shearwater	A, N		
Gannet	A, inland N	Gadwall	B, F (25), MM, F&L, R
Cormorant	Coast: F (20), MM Inland: F (5), MM, R	Teal	B, F coast & Avon valley (100),elsewhere (25), MM, F&L, R
Shag	A, inland N		
Bittern	A	Mallard	CB, F (100), MM
Little Egret	B, F (10), MM, M, inland A	Pintail	main coastal sites F (20), MM, F&L, S, elsewhere A
Grey Heron	B, F (10), MM, M		
Mute Swan	B, F (20), MM	Garganey	A
Bewick's Swan	A, away from Avon valley & summer N	Shoveler	B, F (10), MM, F&L, R
		Red-crested Pochard	A
White-fronted Goose	A	Pochard	B, F (25), MM, F&L, R
Greylag Goose	B, F (10), MM, R	Tufted Duck	B, F (25), MM, F&L, R
Snow Goose	A	Scaup	A, inland & summer N
Bar-headed Goose	A	Eider	A, inland N
Canada Goose	B, F(100), MM	Long-tailed Duck	A, inland & summer N
Barnacle Goose	A	Common Scoter	A

Velvet Scoter	A, inland N
Goldeneye	main coastal sites F (10), MM, F&L, S, elsewhere A
Smew	A
Red-breasted Merganser	main coastal sites F (20), MM, F&L, S, elsewhere A
Goosander	A
Ruddy Duck	A
Honey Buzzard	A, away from New Forest N
Red Kite	A
Marsh Harrier	A
Hen Harrier	A
Montagu's Harrier	N
Sparrowhawk	B, M
Buzzard	B, F (5), M, R
Osprey	A
Kestrel	B, M
Merlin	A
Hobby	B, F&L, M, R
Peregrine	A
Red-legged Partridge	B, F (5), R
Grey Partridge	B, F (5), R
Quail	A
Pheasant	CB, R
Golden Pheasant	A
Water Rail	A
Spotted Crake	N
Moorhen	CB, F (20), MM
Coot	CB, F (20), MM
Oystercatcher	B, F (100), MM, M, inland A
Avocet	A
Stone Curlew	A
Little Ringed Plover	A
Ringed Plover	B, F (50), MM, M, inland A
Golden Plover	F (20), F&L, S, R
Grey Plover	F (50), F&L, S, R, inland A
Lapwing	B, F (100), MM, M, R
Knot	A
Sanderling	A
Little Stint	A
Curlew Sandpiper	A
Purple Sandpiper	A
Dunlin	F (100), MM, M, S, inland A
Ruff	A
Jack Snipe	A
Snipe	B, F (5), MM, F&L, R
Woodcock	CB, R, W
Black-tailed Godwit	F (50), F&L, S, R, inland A
Bar-tailed Godwit	F (50), F&L, M, S, R, inland A
Whimbrel	F (10), F&L, M, W, R, inland A
Curlew	B, F (100), MM, M, inland A
Spotted Redshank	A
Redshank	B, F (100), MM, M, inland A
Greenshank	A
Green Sandpiper	A
Wood Sandpiper	A
Common Sandpiper	A
Turnstone	F (20), F&L, M, S, R, inland A
Pomarine Skua	A, other than coast in spring N
Arctic Skua	A, inland N
Great Skua	A, inland N
Mediterranean Gull	A - include age/plumage
Little Gull	A - include age/plumage

Black-headed Gull	B, F (500), MM, S
Common Gull	B, F (50), MM, S
Lesser Black-backed Gull	B, F (50), MM, S
Herring Gull	B, F (50), MM, S
Yellow-legged Gull	A - include age/plumage
Great Black-backed Gull	B, F (20), MM, S, inland A
Kittiwake	A - include age/plumage
Sandwich Tern	B, F (50), F&L, M, R
Roseate Tern	A, inland N - include age/plumage
Common Tern	B, F (50), F&L, M, R, inland A
Arctic Tern	A - include age/plumage
Little Tern	B, F (25), F&L, M, R
Black Tern	A
Guillemot	A
Razorbill	A
Little Auk	N
Puffin	A, N
Feral Pigeon	CB, F (100)
Stock Dove	CB, F (25), M
Woodpigeon	CB, F (500), M
Collared Dove	CB, F (50), M
Turtle Dove	A
Cuckoo	CB, M, F&L
Ring-necked Parakeet	A
Barn Owl	A especially B
Little Owl	A especially B
Tawny Owl	B, R
Long-eared Owl	A
Short-eared Owl	A
Nightjar	A
Swift	CB, F (100), MM, F&L, M
Kingfisher	A especially B
Hoopoe	A
Wryneck	A
Green Woodpecker	CB, M, R
Great Spotted Woodpecker	CB, M, R
Lesser Spotted Woodpecker	A especially B
Woodlark	A especially B, M, W
Skylark	CB, F (50), M
Sand Martin	B, F (100), F&L, M
Swallow	CB, F (100), F&L, M
House Martin	CB, F (100), F&L, M
Tree Pipit	A especially CB, F&L, M
Meadow Pipit	B, F (25), M
Rock Pipit	A
Water Pipit	A
Yellow Wagtail	A, except coast in autumn F (10)
variant Yellow Wagtails	A, other than Blue-headed N
Grey Wagtail	A especially B
Pied Wagtail	CB, F (50), M
White Wagtail	A, autumn N
Dipper	A
Waxwing	A
Wren	CB, F (25)
Dunnock	CB, F (10)
Robin	CB, F (25)
Nightingale	A
Black Redstart	A
Redstart	A especially CB, F&L
Whinchat	A
Stonechat	A especially CB, F (5), W
Wheatear	A
Ring Ouzel	A

Species	Code	Species	Code
Blackbird	CB, F (25), M	Red-backed Shrike	A
Fieldfare	F (25), M, F&L	Great Grey Shrike	A
Song Thrush	CB, F (10), M	Jay	CB, F (10), M
Redwing	F (25), M, F&L	Magpie	CB, F (50), M
Mistle Thrush	CB, F (25), M	Jackdaw	CB, F (500), M
Cetti's Warbler	A especially CB, R	Rook	CB, F (500), M
Grasshopper Warbler	A	Carrion Crow	CB, F (50), M
Sedge Warbler	A especially CB, F&L, R	Hooded Crow	A, N
Reed Warbler	A especially CB, F&L, R	Raven	A
Dartford Warbler	A except New Forest CB	Starling	CB, F (250), M
Lesser Whitethroat	A especially CB, F&L	House Sparrow	CB, F (50), M
Whitethroat	CB, F (10), F&L	Tree Sparrow	A
Garden Warbler	CB, F (5), F&L	Chaffinch	CB, F (50), M
Blackcap	CB, F (10), W	Brambling	A
Wood Warbler	A	Greenfinch	CB, F (50), M
Chiffchaff	CB, F (10), W	Goldfinch	CB, F (20), M
Willow Warbler	CB, F (10), F&L	Siskin	B, F (10), M, S
Goldcrest	CB, F (10)	Linnet	CB, F (50), M
Firecrest	A	Twite	A, inland N
Spotted Flycatcher	A especially CB, F (5), F&L,	Redpoll	B, F (5), M, S
Pied Flycatcher	A	Crossbill	A
Bearded Tit	A	Bullfinch	CB, F (10), M
Long-tailed Tit	CB, F (20), M	Hawfinch	A
Marsh Tit	A especially B	Lapland Bunting	N
Willow Tit	A especially B	Snow Bunting	A
Coal Tit	CB, F (20), M	Yellowhammer	CB, F (10), M,
Blue Tit	CB, F (50), M	Reed Bunting	CB, F (10), M
Great Tit	CB, F (20), M	Corn Bunting	A
Treecreeper	CB, F (10)		
Nuthatch	CB, F (10)		
Golden Oriole	A		

- For the following scarcer species, records should be submitted on Unusual Record Forms which are available from the Recorder.

Sooty, Cory's and Balearic Shearwaters, European and Leach's Storm Petrels, Purple Heron, White Stork, Whooper Swan, Tundra Bean, Taiga Bean and Pink-footed Geese, Green-winged Teal, Ring-necked Duck, Surf Scoter, Goshawk, Rough-legged Buzzard, Lady Amherst's Pheasant, Corncrake, Kentish Plover, Dotterel, Temminck's Stint, Pectoral Sandpiper, Buff-breasted Sandpiper, Grey and Red-necked Phalaropes, Long-tailed Skua, Sabine's, Ring-billed, Caspian, Iceland and Glaucous Gulls, Black Guillemot, Bee-eater, Short-toed Lark, Shore Lark, Richard's Pipit, Tawny Pipit, Bluethroat, Aquatic, Marsh, Icterine, Melodious, Barred, Yellow-browed and Pallas's Warblers, Red-breasted Flycatcher, Woodchat Shrike, Serin, Mealy Redpoll, Scarlet Rosefinch, Cirl, Ortolan and Little Buntings

All exceptionally early or late migrants.

- Records of the above will not be published unless they have been accepted by the *HOS Records Panel.*

Records of rarer species are dealt with by the *British Birds Rarities Committees*. Space does not permit a full listing of these species although it should be noted that Ferruginous Duck and Savi's Warbler have been added to the list with effect from 1998. *BBRC* record forms are available from the Recorder.

John Clark
County Recorder
4 Cygnet Court
Old Cove Road
Fleet
Hampshire
GU13 8RL

Tel: 01252 623397
e-mail: johnclark@cygnetcourt.demon.co.uk

HAMPSHIRE BIRD RINGING REPORT 2002

Duncan A. Bell

Introduction

This Report records data gathered from the studies of bird ringers working in Hampshire during 2002. Its purpose is to record information on the migration and movements of Hampshire birds and also to increase the awareness of the many ringing activities that occur in the county.

Following this introduction a summary outlines the results of the year's ringing projects and **Table l** below lists the species ringed in Hampshire and their respective totals. Finally, the bulk of the report lists, in systematic order, recoveries and controls of birds ringed in, or reported from Hampshire during 2002.

Summary of Bird Ringing

In 2002 the number of birds ringed in the county totalled 18503 of 108 species, this is a 16% increase compared to 2001. The overall numbers of birds caught and ringed in Hampshire increased for the third year in succession. The reasons for this continued increase can be attributed to a number of factors including, standardised netting and the use of tape lures at coastal migration stations, ringing of *pullus* Gulls and Terns, Sand Martin studies at several Hampshire colonies and also the much publicised European study of Swallows.

All records presented in this report are a reflection of the time and effort invested in the field by individuals and groups involved with ringing studies in Hampshire.

Nestlings

The year's total of 3204 nestlings is an increase over 2001 by a massive 73%. Several Hampshire workers now concentrate on ringing birds in the nest The information gained when birds are subsequently recovered is especially valuable when the natal site is known precisely.

Brian Dudley ringed 679 birds mainly in the new forest, where he concentrates on birds of prey, included in his totals this year were 78 Sparrowhawk, eight Buzzard, nine Kestrel and two Hobby. Brian also rings other species and made the comment that Swallow, Spotted Flycatcher and Pied Flycatcher were in better numbers than 2001 but Lapwing were sadly down.

Graham Giddens continued his work at the gull and tern colony near Lymington by ringing 1217 Black-headed Gull, three Mediterranean Gull, 82 Sandwich Tern and 102 Common Tern.

In the north of the county, Tony Davis ringed 72 birds on the Heaths and Commons, birds ringed included one Woodlark, 17 Tree Pipit, three Stonechat, four Dartford Warbler and 35 Willow Warbler.

A considerable amount of effort was expended by a number of ringers recording Swallows at their nest sites. A total 557 were ringed in the county. Ruth Croger working the Bishops Waltham area was rewarded with an interesting early recovery from Morocco.

No ringing details were confirmed by the RSPB in connection with their studies of Stone–curlew but the number ringed is thought to have been 8.

Full grown

The number of full-grown birds ringed in 2002 was 15299, which is 8% more than in 2001.

It was the first year of the European Swallow project co-ordinated in Britain & Ireland by the British Trust for Ornithology. The total number of sites registered under the scheme now totals 36. Three of which are in Hampshire, namely Farlington Marsh, Titchfield Haven and Winchester Sewage Works. The project has fuelled much interest in Swallow roosting behaviour and habitats. Unfortunately, the first year of the project proved disappointing because large roosts did not form at the Hampshire registered sites and only 1352 birds were ringed.

Two Aquatic Warblers were ringed at Titchfield Haven during 2002 (Trevor Codlin)

Wader ringing totals were low compared to recent years with only 196 birds of 14 species ringed. Cannon net sessions for Black-tailed Godwit and Greenshank proved unsuccessful in Hampshire therefore attention was turned to near-by Thorney Island in West Sussex, where a catch of 73 Greenshank were taken and colour-ringed, these birds will no doubt be seen at Farlington Marsh in future seasons as there is considerable interaction between these roost / moulting sites.

Tim Walker monitored the Sand Martin colonies at Kimbridge and Fair Oak. A total of 643 birds were ringed and a number of inter-colony movements recorded. Birds leaving the colony were found using roost sites at Titchfield Haven and Icklesham

Reed bed and marshland sites at Farlington, Lymington and Titchfield were worked in the late summer and autumn passage period. At Titchfield Haven the ringing effort was extended to include the northern fields, which were worked by Pete Carr from late June until September. It was here that a juvenile Bluethroat was caught at the end of August. Overall it proved to be record year at Titchfield, with large warbler movements recorded during netting sessions in late August and September, birds caught included 97 Cetti's Warbler, 232 Grasshopper Warbler, two Aquatic Warbler, 1356 Sedge Warbler, 760 Reed Warbler, one Dartford Warbler, nine Lesser Whitethroat, 109 Whitethroat, 44 Garden Warbler, 484 Blackcap, 461 Chiffchaff and 119 Willow Warbler. In contrast at Farlington Marshes the numbers of Sedge (72) and Reed Warbler (51) were down, so ringing effort ceased before the end of August. In hindsight this may have been premature as both species had a heavy passage period at Titchfield during the last week of August and first two weeks of September.

Cetti's Warbler is a common resident at Titchfield Haven, where 103 adult birds were rung in 2002, and is expanding its range in the county (Trevor Codlin)

The Pied Wagtail roost in the DERA buildings in Farnborough was monitored again throughout the winter months by Alan Martin's Group with 438 birds ringed.

In the west of the county, Graham Giddens acquired a new coastal wetland site at Sturt Pond, Milford-on-Sea, which proved good for Snipe (12), Jack Snipe (1), Meadow Pipit (91) and Reed Bunting (66). The Meadow Pipits were caught using tape lures, positioned within a triangle of nets, during days of heavy migration in late September and early October.

Nigel Jones caught large numbers of Finch species in his garden in Romsey, where overall ringing totals for both Brambling and Siskin now exceeded one thousand. For 2002 his totals included 164 Chaffinch, 397 Brambling, 121 Greenfinch, 100 Goldfinch, 598 Siskin and five Lesser Redpoll. Elsewhere average numbers of Greenfinch, Goldfinch and Siskin were attracted and caught at garden feeding stations in Fareham, Fleet and Winchester.

Andy Welsh ringed 792 birds in the year. The majority were at the Hawthorns on Southampton Common, including 81 Robin, 46 Blackbird, 27 Song Thrush, six Garden Warbler, 128 Blackcap, 71 Chiffchaff, 51 Goldcrest and five Firecrest. His colour-ringing project work in the New Forest produced 41 Stonechat.

Colour Ringing

Conventional metal rings usually require birds to be recaptured to allow re-identification. With colour rings and other marking techniques it is possible to correctly identify individual birds in the field without recapture.

The success of any colour marking scheme, as part of a research project, requires an enormous input of time by the organiser. It also relies heavily on the accuracy and quantity of the reported observations.

The Farlington Ringing Group are currently studying Waders and Shore birds in the Solent. When captured, birds are marked with a combination of metal ring and four plastic colour-rings to make it possible to identify them as individuals in the field. A huge number of sightings have been reported to date and a large database has been put together. The selection of sightings and movements reproduced in the recoveries section of this report is surely testimony to the value of colour ringing. This unique dataset is of considerable conservation value. It has been possible to demonstrate how long individual birds stay in the Solent and how they use different parts of the estuary both within and between winters, showing how separate feeding and roosting areas are of importance to the Solent. Also being undertaken is the analysis of data to allow estimates of adult survival rates and the collection of sightings to record migration routes and dates.

Members of the Black-tailed Godwit Study Group, which includes members of Farlington Ringing Group journeyed to Iceland twice in 2002, in April and July. Several colour-marked Black-tailed Godwits from both the Solent and Wash were located at pre-breeding roosts and at nest sites.

Several passerines studies also use colour rings, there are currently projects being conducted affecting Pied Wagtail, Nightingale and Stonechat.

What to do with records of ringed and colour marked birds

Birds found with metal rings should be reported to the Ringing Unit of the BTO or for birds ringed outside the UK, reported direct to the address of the scheme shown on the ring. All finders will receive a report of the original ringing details and confirmation of the finding details direct from the appropriate Ringing Unit. Reported information should include ring number, date, time and place of sighting, species involved and condition of the bird when found.

When reporting colour-marked birds, great care is required in reading colour rings or other colour marks in the field. The information gained can be essential to the success of a project and the organisers of these schemes rely on your accurate records. Waders for example are fitted with four colour rings that can be on the upper leg (tibia) as well as the lower leg (tarsus) therefore a thorough check of both legs is needed. Records of colour marked birds should be reported to the organiser or group listed below. All sightings will be fully acknowledged.

Brent Geese, Wigeon, Oystercatcher, Grey Plover, Dunlin, Curlew, Redshank and Turnstone have been marked in Southampton Water as part of the environmental impact assessment into the use of the estuary and particularly Dibden Bay by shorebirds.

Black-tailed Godwit, Greenshank and Grey Plover samples have been marked in Langstone and Chichester Harbours as part of a long term population study of how the species use the Solent and also to understand migration routes in more detail.

Farlington Ringing Group: c/o Pete Potts, Solent Court Cottage, Hook Lane, Warsash, Southampton, SO31 9HF.

Nightingale with colour rings: Trevor Codlin, 37 Roebuck Avenue, Funtley, PO15 6TN

Pied Wagtail with colour rings: This study has been completed, but observations of colour-ringed birds should still be forwarded to: Graham Giddens, 104 Samber Close,

Lymington. SO41 9LF

Stonechat with colour rings: Andy Welch, 15 Wiltshire Road, Chandler's Ford, Eastleigh. SO53 3FB   e-mail MandandAnd@tinyworld.co.uk.

Recoveries

Details of ringing recoveries reported during 2002 are presented in the following pages. As in previous years these include sightings of colour marked birds reported by birders. Special acknowledgement is given to John Clark, Stuart Ruscoe, David Unsworth, Simon Wright and Russell Wynn who submitted species finder records or colour sightings for inclusion in this report.

Acknowledgements

On behalf of Hampshire ringers I would like to thank all public bodies and individuals that gave access to reserves, farms, woodland, gardens, etc. It is not possible to list all involved but without their continued support and understanding ringing, in Hampshire would not be possible

Thanks go to all ringers who submitted records for use in this report. The ringers concerned were: G. Alexander, K.B. Briggs, P Carr, Dr. R.A. Cheke, A.M. Davis, B. Dudley (J. Arnold, M.G. Holland, A. Page and R. Colin-Stokes), Farlington R.G. (D.A. Bell, A. Carter, R.E. Croger, P.J. Lymbery, P.M. Potts, Dr. E.T, G.C.M. and Dr. M.T.M. Roberts), M. R Fletcher, G.S. Giddens, Itchen R.G. (A.A. Browning, C.R. Cuthbert and W.F. Simcox), N.R. Jones, S. Lane, A. Martin, the Royal Air Force Ornithological Society (C. Wearn and J.N. Wells.) T.H. Walker, Titchfield Haven (B. S. Duffin and T. D. Codlin), Dr. A.B. Watson (London Gull Study Group) and A.J. Welch.

In preparing this report reference has been made to the paper on Bird Ringing in Britain and Ireland published in the Journal *Ringing and Migration* Volume 21 Part 2 (December 2002) and Wernham C.V. et al 2002, *The Migration Atlas: movements of the birds of Britain and Ireland*

Duncan A. Bell,
38 Holly Grove,
Fareham,
Hampshire,
PO16 7UP.

Table 1: Hampshire Ringing Totals 2002

Species	f.g.	pullus	total	Species	f.g.	pullus	total
Mute Swan	1	0	1	Yellow Wagtail	26	0	26
Teal	1	0	1	Grey Wagtail	7	14	21
Mallard	2	0	2	Pied Wagtail	526	64	590
Sparrowhawk	9	79	88	Wren	253	2	255
Buzzard	1	11	12	Dunnock	248	2	250
Kestrel	2	42	44	Robin	376	42	418
Hobby	0	2	2	Nightingale	8	0	8
Water Rail	8	0	8	Bluethroat	1	0	1
Moorhen	2	0	2	Redstart	7	0	7
Oystercatcher	0	1	1	Whinchat	4	0	4
Avocet	0	2	2	Stonechat	42	10	52
Little Ringed Plover	0	1	1	Blackbird	377	59	436
Ringed Plover	6	1	7	Fieldfare	4	0	4
Grey Plover	3	0	3	Song Thrush	115	5	120
Knot	1	0	1	Redwing	42	0	42
Curlew Sandpiper	3	0	3	Mistle Thrush	1	6	7
Lapwing	0	38	38	Cetti's Warbler	103	2	105
Dunlin	123	0	123	Grasshopper Warbler	239	0	239
Jack Snipe	1	0	1	AquaticWarbler	2	0	2
Common Snipe	16	0	16	Sedge Warbler	1533	0	1533
Woodcock	1	0	1	Reed Warbler	987	16	1003
Black-tailed Godwit	7	0	7	Dartford Warbler	2	4	6
Curlew	1	0	1	Lesser Whitethroat	19	0	19
Redshank	22	3	25	Whitethroat	174	5	179
Greenshank	7	0	7	Garden Warbler	65	0	65
Green Sandpiper	2	0	2	Blackcap	773	5	778
Common Sandpiper	3	0	3	Wood Warbler	1	0	1
Mediterranean Gull	0	3	3	Chiffchaff	816	21	837
Black-headed Gull	3	1217	1220	Willow Warbler	167	35	202
Sandwich Tern	0	82	82	Goldcrest	438	0	438
Common Tern	0	104	104	Firecrest	12	0	12
Stock Dove	5	21	26	Spotted Flycatcher	4	46	50
Wood Pigeon	25	2	27	Bearded Tit	47	2	49
Collared Dove	7	4	11	Long-tailed Tit	298	0	298
Barn Owl	1	12	13	Marsh Tit	5	0	5
Little Owl	0	13	13	Coal Tit	88	17	105
Tawny Owl	1	9	10	Blue Tit	1100	299	1399
Nightjar	5	0	5	Great Tit	529	222	751
Swift	1	5	6	Nuthatch	21	6	27
Kingfisher	28	0	28	Treecreeper	19	0	19
Green Woodpecker	10	0	10	Jay	10	3	13
Great Spotted Woodpecker	14	0	14	Magpie	3	0	3
Lesser Spotted Woodpecker	1	0	1	Jackdaw	15	8	23
Woodlark	0	1	1	Rook	14	0	14
Sand Martin	779	49	828	Carrion Crow	0	1	1
Swallow	1352	557	1909	Starling	19	0	19
House Martin	76	0	76	House Sparrow	183	4	187
Tree Pipit	1	17	18	Chaffinch	282	12	294
Meadow Pipit	106	3	109	Brambling	397	0	397
Rock Pipit	1	0	1	Greenfinch	981	2	983

Table 1: Hampshire Ringing Totals 2002 (continued)

Species	f.g.	pullus	total	Species	f.g.	pullus	total
Goldfinch	216	3	219	Crossbill	1	0	1
Siskin	752	0	752	Bullfinch	80	0	80
Lesser Redpoll	7	0	7	Yellow Hammer	22	0	22
Linnet	36	3	39	Reed Bunting	164	5	169
				GRAND TOTALS	**15299**	**3204**	**18503**

f.g. = Full Grown.

Table 2: Selected list of Recoveries for 2002.

This section of the report deals with recoveries. The recoveries are arranged by species with the ringing information on the first line and recovery data below (NB a few recoveries are multiple records with two or more lines of recovery information). The symbols and conventions used are listed below.

Age when ringed   This is given according to the EURING code. The figures do not represent years. Interpretation is as follows:

1   nestling or chick not yet able to fly
2   fully grown, year of hatching quite unknown
3   definitely hatched during current calendar year
4   hatched before current calendar year, exact year unknown
5   definitely hatched during last calendar year
6   hatched before last calendar year of ringing, exact year unknown
7   definitely hatched two calendar years before ringing
8   hatched more than two calendar years before ringing

Sex   M = male, F = female

Condition at recovery
X   found dead
XF found freshly dead or dying
XL found dead (not recent)
+   shot or intentionally killed by man
S   sick or injured - not known to have been released
VV alive and probably healthy, ring or colour marks read in field
R   caught and released by ringer
/?/ condition on finding wholly unknown
AC alive and probably healthy - now captive

Date of recovery   Where this is unknown, the date of the reporting letter is given in brackets

Shag *Phalacrocorax aristotelis*

1375461	1	20.06.01.	Isle of May, (Fife)
Green D11	VV	13.12.01.	West Mersea, (Essex)
	VV	06.01.02.	Brighton Marina, (Sussex)
	VV	28.08.02.	Langstone Harbour 608 km SSE

Bewick's Swan *Cygnus columbianus*

An individual bearing Darvic ring TPY was seen at Ibsley on Jan 5th/6th; first noted as as a first-winter in 1996/97 at Slimbridge, it was relocated there on Jan 11th.

Mute Swan *Cygnus olor*

JET	7	24.01.81.	Keyhaven
	VV	08.03.81.	Keyhaven
	VV	02.09.81.	Christchurch Harbour
	VV	28.09.81.	Keyhaven
	VV	12.12.81.	Keyhaven
	VV	18.07.82.	Christchurch Harbour
	VV	09.01.83.	Keyhaven
	VV	05.01.87.	Lymington
	VV = M	16.08.87.	Lymington
	VV	23.09.90.	Lymington
	VV	05.05.94.	Pennington Marsh, Lymington
	VV	13.07.98.	Christchurch Harbour
	VV	29.10.98.	Christchurch Harbour
	VV	02.10.02.	Milford on Sea
	XF	15.11.02.	Keyhaven
X1948		18.07.99.	Christchurch Harbour
KLL	VV	08.10.00.	Walpole Park, Gosport
	VV	24.09.02.	Walpole Park
	XF	16.10.02.	Whiteley, Fareham
KLD	3	07.99.	Christchurch Harbour
	VV	23.03.02.	Allbrook, near Eastleigh, River Itchen

Dave Stone who co-ordinates swan ringing in Christchurch Harbour stated that given the number of swans ringed at Christchurch reach year, very few are reported from the Itchen. Most birds from Christchurch Harbour disperse, after the moult, up the Avon or Stour or make small coastal movements including to the IOW.

X1948 was obviously a regular at Walpole Park, Gosport having been reported on a further seventeen dates between October 2000 & September 2002.

Canada Goose *Branta canadensis*

5196822	4M	09.07.98.	Richmond, (Greater London)
	+ Shot	02.10.99.	Woolmer Park, near Bordon 58 km SW
5208564	4	24.06.00.	Charlton, (Surrey)
	+ Shot	01.09.01.	Bordon 43 km SW

5220431	4	02.07.01.	Laleham, (Surrey)
	+ Shot	02.09.02.	near Fleet 28 km SW
Orange CIJ	?	20.07.01.	Laleham, (Surrey)
	VV	28.08.02.	Winchester Sewage Farm, Winchester

Three further colour ringed birds were reported as follows: *Orange ring* DYN: Titchfield Haven, Oct 28th, ringed Wraysbury (West London) June 25th 2002. *Orange ring* CII: Titchfield Haven, Dec 11th, ringed Laleham (Surrey) July 11th 2001. *Orange ring* BIP: Kings Pond, Dec 21st-25th, ringed Battersea Park (London) July 1st 2001.

These recoveries all suggest that Canada Geese arrive in Hampshire from West London.

Wigeon *Anas penelope*

FP45816	5F	04.02.01.	Dibden, Hythe, Southampton Water
	VV	29.12.02.	Slimbridge, (Gloucestershire) 118 km NW
FP45822	5M	04.02.01.	Dibden, Hythe, Southampton Water
	+ Shot	29.09.02.	Steene, (Nord) 50 57N 02 20E,
			France 264 km E

Honey Buzzard *Pernis apivorus*

| GH91445 | 1 | 31.07.95. | *Site Confidential,* Wales 52 30N 03 19W |
| | S | 19.10.95. | Winchester 212 km SE |

Details of earlier Honey Buzzard recoveries were not published previously, due to site sensitivity at the time.

Sparrowhawk *Accipiter nisus*

| EF80696 | 1F | 28.07.82. | Mitchelldever |
| | XF | 08.09.99. | Pennington, Lymington 48 km SSW |

This is a new longevity record for Sparrowhawk from BTO ringing.

Kestrel *Falco tinnunculus*

ER61968	1M (3/3)	04.07.95.	Titchfield, near Fareham
	X	14.08.01.	Stansted Forest, Rowlands Castle
			(Sussex) 23 km ENE

The finding details that came with this recovery suggest that ER61968 was taken by a predatory bird.

Oystercatcher *Haematopus ostralegus*

BLB	1	10.05.98.	Kallo, (Oost-Vlaanderen)
L80303			51 15N 04 17E, **Belgium**
	R	23.02.01.	near Dibden, Southampton Water 400 km W
FA72610	6	29.01.00.	Cracknore Hard, Southampton Water
	VV	10.05.02.	Uitkerke, (West-Vlaanderen)
			51 18N 03 08E, **Belgium** 322 km ENE

FP36821	3	30.12.00.	Cracknore Hard, Southampton Water
	VV	30.06.02.	van Haaftenpolder, Oosterschelde, (Noord-Brabant)
			51 36N 04 09E, **Netherlands** 396 km ENE

FP36827	8	30.12.00.	Cracknore Hard, Southampton Water
	VV	28.02.01.	Barnegat, Holysloot, (Noord-Holland)
			52 25N 05 03E, **The Netherlands** 478 km ENE
	VV	03.03.01.	Barnegat, Holysloot, (Noord-Holland)
	VV	19.04.02.	Uitdam, Opeprwold, (Noord-Holland) 480 km ENE
			also seen 05.07 to 13.07.02 with chick

FP36837	3	30.12.00.	Cracknore Hard, Southampton Water
	VV	26.05.02.	Lytham St Anne's, near Blackpool
			(Lancashire) 334 km NNW
	VV	25.07.02.	Lytham St Anne's, near Blackpool

FP36848	6	30.12.00.	Cracknore Hard, Southampton Water
	VV	18.08.02.	Red Nab, Heysham, (Lancashire)
			362 km NNW

FP00638	5	27.01.01.	Dibden Bay, Southampton Water
	VV	29.07.02.	Starrevaart, Leidschendam, (Zuid-Holland)
			52 06N 04 26E, **The Netherlands** 427 km ENE

Large numbers of Oystercatchers visit Britain & Ireland outside the breeding season. Recoveries of birds ringed in southern Britain, found in the breeding season, have been recorded as far as Iceland in the north and Estonia to the east, but the majority have been recorded from the Low Countries and Norway.

Grey Plover *Pluvialis squatarola*

DB34651	6	20.01.01.	Weston Shore, Southampton Water
	VV	10.04.02.	Bettringharder Koog, (Schleswig-Holstein)
			54 34N 08 53E, **F. R. Germany** 803 km ENE

| DB34885 | 4 | 15.11.00. | near Dibden, Southampton Water |
| | VV | 03.10.02. | near Cliff Marshes, (Kent) 146 km ENE |

Knot *Calidris canutus*

DFH	5	19.05.88.	Norderheverkoog, Schleswig-Holstein
7696406			54 25N 08 47E, **The Netherlands**
	R	20.01.01.	Sinah, Hayling Island 774 km SW

Dunlin *Calidris alpina*

NT26481	3	07.08.98.	Farlington Marshes
	X	25.05.02.	Kilnave, Loch Gruinart, Isle of Islay
			(Strathclyde) 659 km NW

NLA	0	31.07.00.	De Richel, (Friesland), 53 17 N 05 08E
H227468			**The Netherlands**
	R	16.11.01.	Farlington Marshes 501 km SW

NT65042	3	23.08.02.	Farlington Marshes
	R	05.09.02.	Lagoa de Santo Andre, Setubal, (Estremadura)
			38 05N 08 47W, **Portugal** 1543 km SSW

Black-tailed Godwit *Limosa limosa*

ER61978	4M	29.08.95.	Farlington Marshes
	VV	23.04.96.	Wombwell Ings, (South Yorkshire)
	VV	08.04.00.	near Camperduin, near Schoorl, (Noord-Holland)
			52 44N 04 29E, **The Netherlands** 434 km NE

ER90882	4	01.11.97.	Farlington Marshes
	VV	26.07.01.	Cley Marshes, (Norfolk) 275 km NE
	VV	30.07.02.	North Killingholme Haven, near Immingham
			(Humberside) 317 km N

ER90778	4	16.11.98.	Farlington Marshes
	VV	01.05.99.	Alftafjordur, near Djupivogir,
			64 35N 14 55W, **Iceland** 1730 km NW
	VV	14.04.02.	Belfast Harbour, (Down), Northern Ireland 534 km NW

ES74716	4	16.11.98.	Farlington Marshes
	VV	27.06.02.	Sjavarborg, Saudarkrokur, 65 44N 19 38W
			Iceland 1969 km NW
	VV	10.07.02.	Sjavarborg, Saudarkrokur,

| ES74712 | 4 | 16.11.98. | Farlington Marshes |
| | VV | 29.09.02. | Pin Mill, Orwell Estuary, (Suffolk) 202 km NE |

ES74717	4F	16.11.98.	Farlington Marshes
	VV	06.09.99.	Maldon, Blackwater Estuary, (Essex) 155 km NE
	VV	01.03.00.	Jacques Bay, near Stour Lodge, (Essex)
	VV	29.03.00.	Jacques Bay 193 km NE
	VV	12.06.01.	Floi, Svi-ugar-or/Vorsabaer
			63 51N 20 51W, **Iceland** 1862 km NW
	VV	28.06.02.	Floi, **Iceland**

ES42497	4M	16.11.98.	Farlington Marshes
	VV	22.03.02.	Western Haven, Newton Harbour,
			(Isle of Wight) 31 km SW
	VV	11.07.02.	Efra-Hagarnes, 66 04N 19 06W, **Iceland** 1981 km NW

The Black-tailed Godwit colour-ringing project is being extended to sites in France and Ireland, this will provide additional information on the birds movements and life history.

Multiple observations of colour-ringed birds are continuing to provide uniquely valuable information on the links between passage, wintering and breeding sites. A good species account, written by Jennifer Gill, Les Hatton and Peter Potts appears in the recently published BTO Migration Atlas (2002)

Greenshank *Tringa nebularia*

| DN86741 | 4 | 06.10.91. | Farlington Marshes |
| | R | 24.08.02. | Thorney Island, Chichester Harbour, 7 km E |

DN86945	3	17.09.97.	Farlington Marshes
	VV	23.04.02.	Lake of Burano, Capalbio (Grosseto)
			42 24N 11 23E, **Italy** 1331 km SE

DB00666	4	01.08.99.	Farlington Marshes
	R	06.08.01.	Farlington Marshes
	R	01.12.01.	Farlington Marshes
	VV	24.04.02.	River Esk, Musselburgh, (Lothian) 584 km NNW

DB34671	4	06.08.01.	Farlington Marshes
	VV	05.05.02.	Reserve Naturelle du Marais d'Yves, near La Rochelle
			(Charente-Maritime), 46 01N 01 03W, **France**

DB34579	3	15.09.01.	Farlington Marshes
	VV	06.09.02.	Santona, Colindres, (Santander)
			43 30N 03 28W, **Spain**

DB34644	4	20.09.02.	Farlington Marshes
	VV	27.12.02.	Isley Marsh, Yelland, near Bideford
			(Devon) 220 km SE

Due to on-going colour ringing studies of Greenshank by Farlington Ringing Group the passage, moulting and wintering sites of this species are becoming understood. To date we have been unable to identify their precise breeding localities in Scandinavia (Scotland ?).

Turnstone *Arenaria interpres*

| SV35542 | 6 | 20.03.01. | Weston Shore, Southampton Water |
| | XL | 15.11.02. | Calshot, Southampton 9 km SSW |

Black-headed Gull *Larus ridibundus*

EH42635	6	14.01.87.	Drayton, Portsmouth
	VV	13.12.95.	Hyde Park
	VV	05.02.00.	Hyde Park
	VV	07.08.00.	St James's Park
	VV	16.01.02.	Hyde Park, London, (Greater London)
			95 km NE

| ES47882 | 1 | 28.06.00. | Pylewell Lake, near Lymington |
| | XF | 11.10.02. | Stokes Bay Golf Course, Gosport 26 km E |

| ES47996 | 1 | 28.06.00. | Pylewell Lake, near Lymington |
| | XF | 17.12.00. | West Sedge Moor, Taunton, (Somerset) 105 km WNW |

| EG43150 | 1 | 12.07.00. | Pylewell Lake, near Lymington |
| | VV | 11.08.02. | Radipole Lake, Weymouth, (Dorset) 68 km WSW |

ES74771	4	14.10.00.	near Dibden, Southampton Water
	R	20.05.02.	Gdynia-Lezyce, Pomorskie (Gdansk),
			54 32N 18 23E, **Poland** 1392 km ENE
	R	10.06.02.	Gdynia-Lezyce, Pomorskie (Gdansk),

Herring Gull *Larus argentatus*

Two colour-ringed birds were recorded at Keyhaven rubbish tip, one had been ringed as a pullus in Bristol (Avon) and the other ringed as an immature at a tip near Newton Abbott, (Devon).

Nightjar *Caprimulgus europaeus*

RE95548	1	03.07.99.	Bramshill Warren Heath, near Eversley
	AC	26.05.01.	El Harrach, (Alger)
			36 39N 03 17E, **Algeria** 1663 km SSE

This is only the 14th overseas recovery of a BTO-ringed Nightjar and the first in Algeria. Nightjars winter in eastern and southern Africa (Cresswell 2002 in Migration Atlas) and this bird was probably on return passage when captured in Africa.

Sand Martin *Riparia riparia*

ESI AX5400	3	20.09.00.	Las Minas, San Martin de la Vega, (Madrid)
			40 14N 03 33W, **Spain**
	R = M	27.08.02.	Kimbridge, near Romsey 1208 km N
P903343	3J	31.07.01.	Kimbridge, near Romsey
	R = F	06.06.02.	near Rainworth, (Nottinghamshire) 235 km N
P727354	3	31.08.01.	Pylewell Lake, near Lymington
	R = F	08.06.02.	Rectory Farm, The Bryn, (Gwent) 151 km NW
P537467	3	31.08.01.	Icklesham, (Sussex)
	R = F	27.08.02.	Kimbridge, near Romsey 156 km W
ESI BF5981	3	27.09.01.	Las Minas, San Martin de la Vega, (Madrid)
			40 14N 03 33W, **Spain**
	R = F	31.07.02.	Kimbridge, near Romsey 1208 km N
R275025	4M	29.06.02.	East Horton Farm, Fair Oak
	R	23.08.02.	Titchfield Haven, Hill Head, Fareham 15 km SSE
P502932	4F	17.07.02.	Whittington, Kirkby Lonsdale, (Lancashire)
	R	29.07.02.	Titchfield Haven, Hill Head, Fareham 385 km SSE
R275211	3J	16.07.02.	Kimbridge, near Romsey
	R	06.09.02	Las Minas, San Martin de la Vega, (Madrid)
			40 14N 03 33W, **Spain** 1208 km S
R275592	3J	22.08.02.	East Horton Farm, Fair Oak
	R	25.09.02.	Penon de Zapata, Alhaurin de la Torre, (Malaga)
			36 39N 04 34W, **Spain** 1610 km S
P625549	3J	27.08.02.	Kimbridge, near Romsey
	R	28.09.02.	Las Minas, San Martin de la Vega, (Madrid)
			40 14N 03 33W, **Spain** 1208 km S

| P625570 | 3J | 27.08.02. | Kimbridge, near Romsey |
| | R | 18.09.02. | Icklesham, (Sussex) 156 km E |

R080660	3	21.08.02.	Pylewell Lake, near Lymington
	R	15.09.02.	Las Minas, San Martin de la Vega, (Madrid)
			40 14N 03 33W, **Spain** 1179 km S

P431138	3	28.08.02.	Titchfield Haven, Hill Head, Fareham
	R	17.09.02.	Las Minas, San Martin de la Vega, (Madrid)
			40 14N 03 33W, **Spain** 1189 km S

R080825	3	29.08.02.	Pylewell Lake, near Lymington
	R	18.09.02.	Las Minas, San Martin de la Vega, (Madrid)
			40 14N 03 33W, **Spain** 1179 km S

| R281390 | 4 | 07.09.02. | Chelmarsh Reservoir, Bridgenorth, (Shropshire) |
| | R | 10.09.02. | Titchfield Haven, Hill Head, Fareham 201 km SSE |

In late summer and autumn, British Sand Martins cross the channel then move along the west coast of France skirting the western end of the Pyrenees, they then cross the Ebro Valley to follow a central or eastern coast route across Spain, finally crossing into Africa by the short route at or near Gibraltar. Las Minas de la Vega is located 22 km south east of Madrid, it is the site of an International Theme Park and a regular roost/feeding site for Hampshire Sand Martins.

Swallow *Hirundo rustica*

| P625009 | 1 (5/5) | 08.06.02. | Cross Lane Farm, Bishop's Waltham |
| | /?/ | 26.09.02. | near Oujda, 34 41N 01 45W, **Morocco** |

| P245516 | 1 (5/5) | 15.06.02. | Chilling, Warsash, Southampton |
| | R | 25.08.02. | Pylewell Lake, Lisle Court 19 km WSW |

The September recovery in north Africa is an early date as most Swallows leave Britain in late August through September. Analysis of recovery information suggests 12% of Swallow recoveries from Africa had been hunted by man.

Yellow Wagtail *Motacilla flava*

| P117305 | 3M | 17.09.00. | Titchfield Haven, Hill Head, Fareham |
| | XF | 10.05.02. | Abbotsley, (Cambridgeshire) 168 km NNE |

Pied Wagtail *Motacilla alba*

| P692986 | 3F | 13.10.01. | Farnborough |
| | XF | 09.01.02. | Peterborough, (Cambridgeshire) 146 km NNE |

This is the longest recovery todate from more than 2,500 ringed at the Farnborough roost. Two other birds notified during the year were local movements to Church Crookham (3 km) and Fleet (1 km).

Wren *Troglodytes troglodytes*

| 2M8249 | 3 | 03.10.00. | Icklesham, (Sussex) |
| | XF | 20.01.01. | Hayling Island 119 km W |

| 7Z2380 | 3 | 28.09.02. | Titchfield Haven, Hill Head, Fareham |
| | XF | 10.12.02. | Shoreham-by-Sea, (Sussex) 68 km E |

British & Irish Wrens are mostly sedentary, movements over 20 km are uncommon (21%) and those over 100 km unusual. Initial movements in Autumn usually occur in October, following completion of moult and increased territorial activity.

Sedge Warbler *Acrocephalus schoenobaenus*

| P970363 | 3 | 22.07.02. | Powgavie, Inchture, (Tayside Region) |
| | R | 11.08.02. | Titchfield Haven, Hill Head, Fareham 635 km SSE |

| P430098 | 3 | 07.08.02. | Titchfield Haven, Hill Head, Fareham |
| | XF | 08.08.02. | Plumstead, (Greater London) 119 km NE |

| R282141 | 3 | 15.08.02. | Farlington Marshes |
| | R | 22.08.02. | Icklesham, (Sussex) 119 km E |

| P834731 | 3J | 17.08.02. | Llangorse Lake, (Powys) |
| | R | 28.08.02. | Titchfield Haven, Hill Head, Fareham 187 km SE |

P430875	3	23.08.02.	Titchfield Haven, Hill Head, Fareham
	R	25.08.02.	Icklesham, (Sussex)
	R	28.08.02.	Icklesham, (Sussex) 135 km E

| R035492 | 3J | 27.08.02. | Oxmoor Wood, Runcorn, (Cheshire) |
| | R | 04.09.02, | Titchfield Haven, Hill Head, Fareham 298 km SSE |

P431939	3	31.08.02.	Titchfield Haven, Hill Head, Fareham
	R	07.09.02.	Rye Meads, Hoddesdon, (Hertfordshire)
	R	08.09.02.	Rye Meads, Hoddesdon, (Hertfordshire) 137 km NE

P877177	3	11.09.02.	Titchfield Haven, Hill Head, Fareham
	R	24.09.02.	Villeton, (Lot-et-Garonne), 44 21N 00 16E
			France 727 km S

2002 was an unusual year for the Sedge Warbler as autumn migration peaked in late August and the first two weeks of September, this was two to three weeks later than normal. Could this have resulted from bad weather and losses of early nests and broods followed by successful re-lays

Reed Warbler *Acrocephalus scirpaceus*

| N703740 | 3J | 24.07.99. | Redbridge, Totton, Southampton |
| | R = F | 30.07.02. | Pylewell Lake, near Lymington 19 km SSW |

| N622226 | 3J | 22.08.99. | Titchfield Haven, Hill Head, Fareham |
| | R | 05.05.02. | Brandon Marsh, Coventry, (Warwickshire) 175 km N |

| P225997 | 3 | 22.08.00. | Farlington Marshes |
| | R | 12.05.02. | Hazelwood, near Ham Creek, (Suffolk) 231 km NE |

| P727945 | 3 | 16.07.02. | Pylewell Lake, near Lymington |
| | R | 06.08.02. | Icklesham, (Sussex) 154 km E |

| P283763 | 3J | 29.06.02. | Titchfield Haven, Hill Head, Fareham |
| | R | 02.08.02. | Icklesham, (Sussex) 135 km E |

| P283778 | 3J | 29.06.02. | Titchfield Haven, Hill Head, Fareham |
| | R | 03.08.02. | Chew Valley Lake, (Avon) 111 km WNW |

| R226571 | 3 | 08.09.02. | Allerthorpe, (Humberside) |
| | R | 22.09.02. | Titchfield Haven, Hill Head, Fareham 346 km S |

Blackcap *Sylvia atricapilla*

| K660409 | 5F | 09.05.01. | Botley Wood, Tapnage |
| | R | 10.07.01. | Winchester Sewage Farm 19 km NW |

| P118358 | 3JF | 03.09.01. | Titchfield Haven, Hill Head, Fareham |
| | R | 19.04.02. | Southampton Common 16 km NW |

| R113036 | 3J | 22.06.02. | Winchester College, Winchester |
| | R = F | 05.09.02. | Beachy Head, (Sussex) 115 km ESE |

| P283920 | 3J | 14.07.02. | Titchfield Haven, Hill Head, Fareham |
| | R | 17.08.02. | South Stoke, near Goring, (Oxfordshire) 80 km N |

| P897059 | 3F | 11.08.02. | Cottam Power Station, (Nottingham) |
| | R | 04.09.02. | Titchfield Haven, Hill Head, Fareham 278 km S |

K660409 was caught at Botley Wood with a fully developed brood patch, however it relocated to Winchester were it was thought to have bred.

Chiffchaff *Phylloscopus collybita*

| 5B1441 | 3J | 24.06.02. | Loughton, (Essex) |
| | R | 18.09.02. | Titchfield Haven, Hill Head, Fareham 130 km SW |

| 3Z1919 | 3J | 16.07.02. | Isle of Grain, (Kent) |
| | R | 28.09.02. | Titchfield Haven, Hill Head, Fareham 152 km WSW |

The Migration Atlas 2002 suggests British Chiffchaff orientate to the south east and take advantage of a short sea crossing to the continent. Clearly these two British born birds were moving to the south west. There were record numbers of Chiffchaff caught at Titchfield Haven during Autumn 2002.

Long-Tailed Tit *Aegithalos caudatus*

| 6D4262 | 4 | 08.01.02. | Windlesham, (Surrey) |
| | R | 17.02.02. | Fleet 17 km SW |

Great Tit *Parus major*

| H696868 | 4M | 06.12.98. | Bramley |
| | R | 02.11.01. | Fleet 17 km ESE |

Treecreeper *Certhia familiaris*

| 7Z2307 | 3 | 20.07.02. | Titchfield Haven, Hill Head, Fareham |
| | XF | 24.07.02. | Gosport 7km ESE |

Jackdaw *Corvus monedula*

| EJ69954 | 6 | 22.05.85. | Twyford, near Winchester |
| | XF | 08.05.01. | Twyford, near Winchester   0 km Local |

This is a new longevity record for Jackdaw from BTO-ringing

Greenfinch *Carduelis chloris*

| VR37800 | 4M | 25.03.02. | Temple End, (Hertfordshire) |
| | R | 24.12.02. | St Cross, Winchester 121 km SW |

Goldfinch *Carduelis carduelis*

| P582943 | 6M | 29.03.01. | Fareham |
| | R | 28.09.02. | Wood Lane, Colemere, (Shropshire) 252 km NW |

This bird was caught in a Fareham garden, one of a small party of four birds that stopped a couple of hours when apparently on migration.

Birds returning from France and Iberia pass through Hampshire in March and April.

Siskin *Carduelis spinus*

| P903809 | 5F | 24.03.02. | West Wellow |
| | R | 03.04.02. | Ae Village, (Dumfries & Galloway) 487 km NNW |

This is a typical recovery, a Scottish Siskin returning to its breeding area having wintered in the south.

CURRENT BIRD SURVEYS IN HAMPSHIRE

G C Evans

Introduction

We are often asked how county bird surveys arise, and how they fit in to the wider picture. Things have changed over the years, but this short paper attempts to explain the background to current surveys, and to summarise what is going on at the moment.

National context

Nationally, Hampshire Ornithological Society (HOS) is a member of the British Trust for Ornithology's (BTO) Bird Clubs Partnership. HOS collaborates with the BTO and other organisations such as the Royal Society for the Protection of Birds (RSPB) and the Wildfowl and Wetlands Trust (WWT) on national bird surveys within the county. The programme of national surveys is influenced by national Biodiversity Action Plan (BAP) priorities and by the Birds of Conservation Concern (BoCC) list, and is usually a result of discussion between the national bodies (RSPB, BTO, WWT, and the government's Joint Nature Conservation Committee – JNCC). Where relevant, other government departments such as the Department of Environment, Food, and Rural Affairs (DEFRA), and other organisations such as the Game Conservancy Trust (GCT), may also be involved. The timing of national surveys is then often dependent on the necessary funding being available.

County context

HOS has, for many years, also organised local surveys. There have been a number of species surveys, but the Society's most ambitious project was a Tetrad Atlas distribution survey that ran from 1986 to 1991 in conjunction with the last BTO national atlas project. The county results were published by the Society in the *Birds of Hampshire* book.

In recent years, much effort has been made to link local surveys to local conservation priorities, and HOS has had significant involvement in the formation of a group that rejoices in the title of *Joint Hampshire (Biodiversity Action Plans) Bird Monitoring Group* (JHG). The group includes representatives from Hampshire & Isle of Wight Wildlife Trust (HWT), Hampshire Biodiversity Information Centre (HBIC), RSPB, BTO, and GCT, and is formally responsible for coordinating and reviewing actions arising from the county's bird-related Species and Habitat Action Plans (SAPs and HAPs). Many of these actions include population monitoring and surveys, and HOS involvement on the group ensures that HOS continues in its lead role for actually organising and carrying out Hampshire bird surveys.

The Surveys

Here is a brief summary of some of our current bird survey work.

Breeding Birds Survey (BBS): The BBS is an ongoing national survey running since 1994, and involves breeding season transect counts in a randomly selected sample of 1-km squares. The BBS superseded the Common Bird Census (CBC) as the primary means of monitoring the populations of common species. In the county context, the survey is valuable in providing systematic and objective monitoring of relatively numerous species that are of conservation concern (for example

Yellowhammer, Bullfinch, Song Thrush, Spotted Flycatcher). In Hampshire, there are 80 randomly selected squares (about 2% of the county) and, in recent years, 60 or 70 squares have been completed each year. The survey goes online from 2004, and we hope to involve more observers covering more squares. We anticipate publishing a ten-year review of the Hampshire BBS data in the not too distant future.

Wetland Birds Survey (WebS): WebS is an ongoing national survey for population monitoring of wetland birds (waders, wildfowl, and other water birds). The survey is based on systematic coastal and inland counts of non-breeding wetland birds on fixed dates. All estuaries and major inland waters are covered. In the county context, the WeBS survey is especially important in providing a long-running dataset on our shore birds throughout the Solent (see, for example, the paper elsewhere in this *Hampshire Bird Report*). High-tide counts at roosts provide a good indication on population trends for most species, although in recent years, additional effort has been made to undertake low-tide counts that provide important information on preferred feeding areas.

Winter Farmland Birds Survey (WFBS): This survey, concluded in March 2003, was part of a three-year BTO national survey to investigate relationships between winter farmland land-use and management, and the numbers of each species. The survey involved field-by-field survey of randomly selected 1-km squares, and was important in establishing factors that may be affecting farmland birds in winter. In Hampshire, it was very relevant to the seed-eating farmland birds SAP (one of three Species Action Plans written by HOS), which covers species such as Yellowhammer and Linnet. After discussion with the JHG, we therefore doubled the national sample-rate so as to have sufficient sample size to compare with national results. We have at least two winter's worth of data from over 60 1-km squares (about 3% of the county's agricultural land), and we hope soon to be analysing the results, with a view to publishing a summary in the 2003 Hampshire Bird Report (HBR).

River Valley Survey: Our most ambitious survey in 2002 was of the main river valleys (Avon, Test, Itchen, and Meon). Discussion at JHG, led us to use the opportunity of the national Breeding Waders of Wet Meadows (BWWM) project, to survey a number of other important wetland species and to cover far more than just the national sample sites. The river valleys were divided into 70 sections for the purposes of the survey, and volunteers successfully completed three survey visits to 55 of these sections (80% coverage). The results gave us no big surprises, but have provided important quantitative and objective evidence to confirm previously anecdotal impressions of the changes in our river valley bird populations. Since similar surveys twenty-five years ago, birds such as Snipe and Yellow Wagtail have almost disappeared, and Redshank have declined considerably. During the same period though, Cetti's Warbler and Gadwall have built up to significant populations, and of course Little Egrets are now seen frequently.

As part of the analysis, we are now making careful comparisons with surveys from the 1975 to 1982 period, with a view to publishing results in the 2003 HBR.

Garden BirdWatch (GBW): This is a popular BTO national survey collecting weekly counts from observers' gardens. There are now more than 600 gardens monitored in Hampshire, and the survey is increasingly important as a means of monitoring birds in this important habitat. The survey shows the growing use of gardens being made by species such as Goldfinch and Blackcap in response to increased use of different foods, and provides particularly useful information on BAP-priority species such as Song Thrush.

We expect to soon be analysing the Hampshire-specific data, and preparing a paper for a future bird report.

MigrationWatch: This is a relatively new national online survey that has been used during the past two years to collect information about the arrival of summer migrants. The project has been particularly successful in establishing the methods and practicality of online input of bird survey data; we are optimistic that it may provide a foundation for much wider use in the future.

As with Garden BirdWatch We are exploring the possibility of analysing the Hampshire-specific data, and preparing a future report.

Species surveys: Individual species have also been surveyed, often as part of national breeding surveys. During the last six years or so, species surveyed have included: Herons (ongoing full survey of heronries), Skylark (sample), Lapwing (sample), Nightingale (full survey), Sand Martin (full survey), House Martin (ongoing small sample), Little Egret (roost survey), Mute Swan (sample), Canada Goose (sample), Stone Curlew (ongoing full survey in conjunction with RSPB's national monitoring), Bearded Tit (full survey), Peregrine (full survey 2003), Woodcock (sample 2003).

The Nightingale survey was particularly important in confirming a major decline in the county population and in demonstrating, in conjunction with the national data, that Hampshire is now on the edge of the species' range.

Other Projects & Site Surveys: HOS/BTO members are also involved with a number of specialist projects and surveys. There are too many to mention them all here, but they include:

- detailed surveys of specific sites using *Common Bird Census (CBC)* mapping techniques,
- special studies of individual species (for example, Stonechat) or bird groups (for example, colour-ringing of shorebirds),
- Waterways Bird Survey (WBS) - similar to the CBC but along a river or canal, the Waterways Breeding Bird Survey (WBBS) – the waterways version of BBS, and the Winter River Bird Survey – an inland WeBS for rivers and streams,
- ringing projects - such as the Constant Effort ringing sites project (CES), Retrapping adults for survival (RAS), Europe-wide Swallow roost survey, Barn Owl monitoring programme,
- woodland resurvey project (resurvey of woodland CBC plots that were surveyed in the sixties),
- many Hampshire nest records are also submitted to the national *Nest Record Scheme.*

Future Surveys

Forthcoming national surveys will include a Gull Roost Survey (winter 2003/04), a breeding Nightjar survey (2004), a sample survey of feeding Swallows, and a Winter River Bird Survey. Locally, there will be a sample survey of breeding waders in the New Forest, and arising from the seed-eating birds SAP and JHG discussions, we will also soon be organising a county-wide sample survey of Yellowhammer and Corn Bunting.

Looking a bit further ahead, a major all-species distribution survey will be taking place in collaboration with the BTO national Atlas project, probably commencing in the winter of 2006/2007.

Acknowledgements

I would like to thank the many volunteers who so willingly contribute to our surveys, and the landowners and their managers who kindly grant permissions to access their land. I would also like to thank John Eyre and Norman Pratt for comments on an earlier draft of this paper.

Contacts & Further Information

To participate in any Hampshire bird surveys, in first instance contact Glynne Evans at hantsbto@hotmail.com. For further general information about BTO surveys and national results, see http://www.bto.org/.

As always, any records of unusual birds in Hampshire should be sent direct to the County Recorder johnclark@cygnetcourt.demon.co.uk

Glynne Evans,
Waverley,Station Road,
Chilbolton,Stockbridge,
Hampshire
SO20 6AL

SOLENT WATERBIRD POPULATION CHANGES[1]
1986/87 TO 2000/01

D J Unsworth

Introduction

The primary purpose of this paper is to provide a concise summary of the population changes shown by waterbirds in the Solent during the winter's 1986/87 to 2000/01. The data presented is based almost entirely on the counts carried out for the Wetland Bird Survey[2]. The information also supports initiatives associated with Hampshire biodiversity action plans (BAPs) and associated habitat and species actions plans (HAPs and SAPs) as they affect the Solent.

There is significant and accumulating evidence of movement by waterbirds between the component estuaries of the Solent, and it is increasingly recognised that taking a holistic approach to the Solent estuaries in terms of applied conservation is more appropriate.

Results

Table 1 provides a summary of waterbird totals in the Solent for the three separate five-year periods – 1986/7 to 1990/91, 1991/92 to 1995/96 and 1996/97 to 2000/01. The data presented for each period is the five-year peak mean treating the Solent as the "estuary". The peak mean is calculated by summing the peak counts for each species in each winter (taken as November to March), irrespective of the month in which the peak occurred, and then dividing by five to determine the mean.

The figures shown are not therefore, simply a summation of the peak counts from the constituent estuaries, since this will inflate the overall totals due to possible movement between estuaries. As such, they are quite likely to underestimate the true numbers present, although using this standardised method does give an idea of the trends. Those species with peak means of one or less have been excluded.

Unfortunately, information for a few species is either incomplete or not available, for example, Black-necked Grebe, Little Egret and Grey Heron.

An analysis of the information in Table 1 suggests that for the period concerned, the populations of Little Grebe, Mute Swan, Greylag Goose, Canada Goose, Wigeon, Gadwall, Teal, Pintail, Avocet, Golden Plover, Jack Snipe and

---

[1] For the purposes of this paper, the Solent is treated as the 12 estuaries as defined by the Wetland Bird Survey from Pagham Harbour to NW Solent on the north shore of the Solent and from the Yar to Brading Harbour on the north shore of the Isle of Wight.

[2] The Wetland Bird Survey is a joint scheme of the British Trust for Ornithology, Wildfowl and Wetlands Trust, Royal Society for the Protection of Birds and Joint Nature Conservation Committee (the last on behalf of English Nature, Countryside Council for Wales, Department of the Environment Northern Ireland and Scottish Natural Heritage).

Greenshank all show progressive increases. Similarly, progressive declines are shown by Shelduck, Goldeneye, Ringed Plover, Sanderling, Dunlin, Ruff, Redshank and Turnstone. For a number of important Solent species the population trends are less clear. For example, Brent Goose, Red-breasted Merganser, Oystercatcher, Grey Plover, Lapwing, Knot, Black-tailed Godwit and Bar-tailed Godwit all show variable trends and deserve further investigation.

For the national picture and longer term trends, reference should be made to the annual report of wildfowl and wader counts published by the Wildfowl and Wetlands Trust (WWT). Against the longer term background presented there, it is possible for example, to compare the peak in numbers shown by four high-Arctic breeding species (Brent Goose, Grey Plover, Knot and Bar-tailed Godwit) in the Solent during 1991-/92 to 1995/96, with the national (and longer term) position.

Table 2 provides more detail for the most important species in individual estuaries, showing peak means for the three separate five-year periods so that an indication of population changes on individual estuaries can be gauged. Note that the threshold levels for internationally and nationally important populations are regularly reviewed to reflect ongoing population changes. Hence, there may be some apparent discrepancies in Table 2. The latest population estimates can be found in Kershaw & Cranswick 2003, and Rehfisch et al 2003 and have been used to define important populations for 1996/97-2000/01 in Tables 1 and 2.

Discussion

*Although a familiar - and clearly numerous - bird in the Solent, Dark-bellied Brent Goose numbers mask how significant the Solent is for this important sub-species. Approximately 23% of the British wintering population currently occur in the Solent, **representing about 10% of the entire world population**. The Brent Goose is therefore of the highest conservation importance, and should feature prominently in any conservation programmes associated with the Solent. Likewise, any development proposals likely to have an impact on the species should take account of the importance of the Solent as a wintering site.*

Fortunately, the "Brent Goose Strategy for the South East Hampshire Coast" (Hampshire Brent Goose Strategy Group – of which HOS is a member – published by the Hampshire and Isle of Wight Wildlife Trust in July 2002) is already addressing these issues. A Species Action Plan for the Brent Goose is also in preparation. Also relevant is a recent assessment of the **national** trends, in the "State of the UK's Birds 2002" (published in July 2003), where the national long term (winters 1970/71 to 2000/01) and short term (winters 1990/91 to 2000/01) population changes are quoted as +228% and –16% respectively.

The Black-tailed Godwit is another familiar Solent bird, with approximately 11% of the Icelandic breeding population wintering here. This is typically a mobile species, moving between sites as the non-breeding season progresses, seemingly in response to changing feeding conditions. Black-tailed Godwits also regularly feed on flooded pasture, such as at Titchfield Haven and in the Avon Valley, so the numbers using the intertidal zone will be influenced by rainfall levels. Owing to the mobile nature of the species, a review of the numbers using the Solent, Avon Valley and Poole Harbour together, using techniques such as ringing, colour-ringing, plumage-dyeing and radio tracking could provide a valuable insight into the population dynamics of the species on the central south coast.

The Dunlin is the commonest shorebird, in numerical terms, occurring in the Solent, although during the period under review, they have shown a significant decline in numbers. The reasons for this decline are unclear although global warming has been suggested as a possible reason for this, and other wader species, because the centre of the wintering populations are shifting progressively further east (see for example, BTO News No. 248). However, a variety of other factors could be operating, such as pollution levels affecting prey densities, reduced nutrient levels from sewage outfalls, or the quality of roost sites may be declining due, for example, to increased disturbance from Peregrines or people.

Another issue worthy of further consideration around the Solent is the regularity of movement taking place between estuaries, particularly by waders, through the tidal cycle and how this changes through the winter period. Detailed analysis of ringing data, and more co-ordinated observations of tidal cycle movements would greatly increase our understanding of how shorebirds use the Solent.

Acknowledgements

The results presented here would not have been possible without the unstinting dedication shown by the network of voluntary WeBS counters around the Solent. To them, I would like to extend my personal thanks, and I hope that this paper goes some way to saying "thank you" for their efforts.

I would also like to thank Norman Pratt for providing comments on a draft of this paper. Finally, my thanks to Colette Hall at the WWT for providing the data used in this paper. Many of the results for 1996/97 to 2000/01 had to be calculated by me, based on raw data from the WWT. As such, any errors which have arisen are mine.

References

Kershaw, M & Cranswick, PA. 2003. Numbers of wintering waterbirds in Great Britain, 1994/95-1998/99: I. Wildfowl and selected species. *Biological Conservation* 111: 91-104.

Rehfisch, MM, Austin, GE, Armitage, M, Atkinson, P, Holloway, SJ, Musgrove, AJ and Pollitt, MS, 2003. Numbers of wintering waterbirds in Great Britain and the Isle of Man (1994/95-1998/99): II. Coastal waders (Charadrii). *Biological Conservation* 112: 329-341.

Table 1: Peak mean winter counts for the Solent 1986/87 to 2000/01

	Average Peak			1996/97 -2000/01	
	86/87 –90/91	91/92 –95/96	96/97–00/01	% GB	% Int.
Red Throated Diver			2		
Great Northern Diver			3		
Little Grebe	135	193	246	3.2	
Great Crested Grebe	212	178	230	1.4	
Black-necked Grebe			16		
Cormorant	413	510	382	1.7	
Mute Swan	209	296	342	0.9	
Bewick's Swan	4	16	0		
Pink-footed Goose	2	4	0		
White-fronted Goose	1	19	6		
Greylag Goose	28	180	327		
Canada Goose	619	965	1424		
Barnacle Goose	2	12	4		
Dark-bellied Brent Goose	25882	29878	22853	23.3	10.4
Pale-bellied Brent Goose			5		
Shelduck	5917	4266	3013	3.9	1.0
Wigeon	7710	8171	11405	2.8	
Mandarin	1	3	0		
Gadwall	91	128	174	1.0	
Teal	6314	6880	8510	4.4	2.1
Mallard	2589	2626	2276		
Pintail	814	1059	1216	4.4	
Shoveler	273	320	324	2.2	
Pochard	213	248	235		
Tufted Duck	260	192	207		
Scaup	7	4	12		
Eider	57	30	22		
Long-tailed Duck	5	6	2		
Common Scoter	9	13	8		
Goldeneye	248	241	217	0.9	
Smew	5	2	1		
Red-breasted Merganser	522	485	507	5.2	
Goosander	9	7	2		
Coot	620	497	497		
Moorhen			254		
Oystercatcher	4110	4112	4817	1.5	
Avocet	4	8	27		
Ringed Plover	2116	1427	1053	3.2	1.4
Golden Plover	2094	3031	3740	1.5	
Grey Plover	4375	5852	5062	9.6	2.0
Lapwing	6923	12905	11123		
Knot	2827	3049	1509		
Sanderling	296	237	145		
Little Stint	2	1	7		
Purple Sandpiper	0	2	1		
Dunlin	64172	60864	47835	8.5	3.6
Ruff	57	19	5		
Jack Snipe	4	12	26		
Snipe	455	426	372		
Woodcock	4	0	1		
Black-tailed Godwit	1709	1911	1651	11.0	4.7
Bar-tailed Godwit	1526	1715	1275	2.1	1.1
Whimbrel	2	4	3		
Curlew	3687	4130	4111	2.7	1.0
Spotted Redshank	14	15	11		
Redshank	3922	3870	3628	3.0	1.5
Greenshank	18	27	41		
Green Sandpiper	4	4	7		
Common Sandpiper	3	2	3		
Turnstone	1243	1147	819	1.6	0.8

Table 2: Species of key importance in the Solent estuaries

	1986/87 – 1990/91	1991/92 – 1995/96	1996/97 – 2000/01
Pagham Harbour			
Slavonian Grebe		35	25
Cormorant	52	171	217
Brent Goose	2741	2981	2034
Teal	452	1396	1401
Pintail	345	628	751
Avocet	1	6	19
Grey Plover	915	1117	1230
Black-tailed Godwit	186	180	165
Chichester Harbour			
Little Grebe	33	55	62
Slavonian Grebe			8
Brent Goose	9816	11133	8449
Shelduck	2755	1654	1146
Teal	1473	1332	1726
Red-breasted Merganser	131	139	168
Ringed Plover	1040	593	290
Grey Plover	2046	2944	1945
Sanderling	297	235	144
Dunlin	21194	21092	17014
Black-tailed Godwit	690	868	469
Bar-tailed Godwit	1094	1378	1005
Curlew	1194	1306	1382
Redshank	1670	1368	1557
Greenshank	2	14	27
Langstone Harbour			
Little Grebe	22	21	47
Black-necked Grebe*	32	26	18
Brent Goose	7474	7144	6020
Shelduck	1449	919	662
Red-breasted Merganser	190	202	161
Ringed Plover	482	368	560
Grey Plover	1455	1713	1550
Dunlin	31156	27048	24325
Black-tailed Godwit	779	300	234
Bar-tailed Godwit	630	413	380
Portsmouth Harbour			
Little Grebe	13	30	43
Brent Goose	2885	2955	2389
Black-tailed Godwit	70	30	169
Southampton Water			
Little Grebe	35	33	41
Great Crested Grebe	90	97	113
Cormorant	105	143	189
Canada Goose	344	486	783
Brent Goose	1661	2394	1947
Wigeon	2503	2544	3226
Teal	1379	1778	2200
Dunlin**	4485	4427	5690
Black-tailed Godwit	558	858	729
Beaulieu Estuary			
Greylag Goose	28	178	325
Brent Goose	696	1327	1847
Grey Plover	418	856	630
Black-tailed Godwit	254	55	272

Table 2: Species of key importance in the Solent estuaries (continued)

	1986/87 – 1990/91	1991/92 – 1995/96	1996/97 – 2000/01
N W Solent			
Slavonian Grebe		6	12
Brent Goose	**2251**	**3108**	**2296**
Gadwall	21	49	87
Shoveler	51	87	144
Black-tailed Godwit	**110**	**232**	**304**
Greenshank	8	7	11
Newtown Harbour			
Brent Goose	**1110**	**1524**	**1571**
Black-tailed Godwit	**135**	**227**	**156**

Notes: **Bold and underlined**   - internationally important
         Bold   - nationally important
         * Black-necked Grebe average peak counts have been calculated from the Hampshire Bird Reports 1986-2001.
         ** Dunlin numbers in Southampton Water 1996/97 to 2000/01 are based on low tide counts.

Dave Unsworth
5 Nelson Rd
Bishopstoke
Eastleigh
Hants
SO50 6BR

A SURVEY OF BREEDING BIRDS ALONG THE HAMPSHIRE SECTION OF THE BASINGSTOKE CANAL

G J S Rowland

Introduction.

Following my survey of the Hampshire section of the canal carried out in 1991, and that undertaken by Mick Scott and Spike Millington in 1978, I publish below the results of the 2002 survey. The 1991 survey was requested by Hampshire Wildlife Trust, as was this year's, indirectly.

The results of the 1978 & 1991 surveys were published in the 1991 Hampshire Bird Report (published in April 1993). In addition to the figures of breeding birds for the navigable section of the canal, from Greywell Tunnel East to the Hampshire/Surrey county boundary near Aldershot, I publish below, separately, the results of a survey of the non-navigable section from Greywell Tunnel West to the village of Up Nately. This section was not covered in the 1978 & 1991 surveys.

Methodology

The Hampshire section of the Basingstoke Canal is approximately 16 miles in length, excluding the isolated section from Greywell to Up Nately. Needless to say, no attempt was made to cover the whole of the Hampshire section in a day! Instead, the survey took place over several days, dividing up the length of the canal into manageable 'chunks' varying in length between three to five miles.

The first survey was carried out between the 20th & 30th April and involved a gentle stroll along the section chosen on any particular day. As well as water birds, pairs and/or singing males of passerine and non-passerine species were counted, up to approximately 40 yards either side of the canal. The presence of most of the passerine species was detected by sound rather than by sight.

The first survey concentrated on counting resident and early migrant species, such as waterfowl, Grey Wagtail, Wren, Robin, Blackcap and Chiffchaff

A second survey took place during early to mid-May, in order to include water birds missed the first time round but also to include later migrant passerine (and non-passerine) species, such as Turtle Dove, Garden Warbler and Spotted Flycatcher. Fortunately, the weather during the latter part of April and early May,2002, was warm and settled, which helped enormously in the attempt to produce a reasonably accurate survey.

Overleaf, the results of the survey are tabulated and discussed.

Results

Table 1. Water Birds
Breeding populations along the canal in 1978,1991 & 2002
(Number of pairs present unless otherwise stated.)

Species.	1978	1991	2002	Notes.
Little Grebe	34	9	2	
Mute Swan	1	2	4	At least 2 prs bred successfully, in 2002.
Canada Goose	1	1	1	No young seen in 2002.
Mandarin	1	1	1	Male only in 1978 & 1991. Pair in 2002. Two prs bred in 1998 & 2000.
Mallard	11	14	22	11 prs with broods in 2002.
Tufted Duck	3	2	nil	
Moorhen	111	34	20	
Coot	23	12	5	2 prs with broods; 3 prs nesting, May, 2002.

Table 2. Passerine and remaining non-passerines
Breeding populations in 1978, 1991 & 2002.
(Number of pairs or singing males.)

Species.	1978	1991	2002	Notes
Collared Dove	14	Present	Present	No count in 1991 & 2002
Turtle Dove	1	1	nil	
Cuckoo	12	4	2	
Kingfisher	nil	1	nil	
Green Woodpecker	3	5	6	
Great Spotted Woodpecker	5	9	11	
Swallow	nil	nil	1	Nesting in canal-side building.
Grey Wagtail	16	I	7	
Pied Wagtail	7	4	3	
Wren	217	144	153	
Dunnock	33	25	38	
Robin	77	98	143	
Nightingale	9	2	nil	
Blackbird	129	102	79	
Song Thrush	34	33	35	
Mistle Thrush	11	13	7	
Sedge Warbler	1	1	nil	
Lesser Whitethroat	2	2	2	
Whitethroat	13	4	7	
Garden Warbler	11	25	13	
Blackcap	29	31	40	
Wood Warbler	nil	1	nil	
Chiffchaff	43	30	43	
Willow Warbler	108	43	15	
Goldcrest		12	15	No count in 1978.
Spotted Flycatcher	3	5	nil	
Long-tailed Tit	12	13	8	

continued

Table 2 (continued)

Species.	1978	1991	2002	Notes
Marsh Tit	1	5	2	
Willow Tit	4	nil	nil	
Coal Tit	10	9	8	
Blue Tit	92	-	82	No count in 1991.
Great Tit	71	-	78	No count in 1991.
Nuthatch	8	17	7	
Treecreeper	5	6	4	
Jay	15	13	9	
Magpie	-	-	13	No count in 1978 & 1991.
Jackdaw	-	8	11	No count in 1978.
House Sparrow	-	-	4	No count 1978 & 1991. Apparently using holes in trees.
Tree Sparrow	3	nil	nil	
Chaffinch	95	-	99	No count in 1991.
Greenfinch	8	15	19	
Goldfinch	8	10	13	
Linnet	2	4	2	
Redpoll	2	1	nil	
Bullfinch	7	10	4	
Reed Bunting	7	5	2	

Table 3. Breeding populations along the non-navigable section of the Basingstoke Canal, between the village of Up Nately and the western entrance to the Greywell Tunnel. (2002 only)

Species	Pairs	Species	Pairs
Little Grebe	4	Blackcap	9
Mallard	5+	Chiffchaff	5
Moorhen	5	Goldcrest	2
Coot	6	Long-tailed Tit	2
Grey Wagtail.	1 pair/singing male(s)	Blue Tit	4
Wren	9	Great Tit	3
Dunnock	2	Jay	1
Robin	8	Chaffinch	10
Song Thrush	1	Greenfinch	2
Blackbird	8		

The following additional species were observed during the 2002 survey but were either difficult to census accurately or were not using the canal habitat for breeding purposes.

Grey Heron	Wood Pigeon	House Martin	Starling
Kestrel	Tawny Owl	Tree Pipit	Yellowhammer
Pheasant	Swift	Meadow Pipit	
Lapwing	Woodlark	Rook	
Common Sandpiper	Skylark	Carrion Crow	

A total of 61 species was seen/heard during the survey, twelve fewer than during the 1991 survey

Discussion.

In the 1991 report (published 1993), I commented on the decline in breeding numbers of Little Grebe, Moorhen and Coot. This year's survey confirms a continuing decline in these species' fortunes. Increased use of the canal by motorized boat traffic may be one reason for this state of affairs but this does not explain the decline that has taken place along the section from the river Whitewater to the eastern entrance to the Greywell Tunnel, which is forbidden to boat traffic. Another reason may be water quality, and this might be worthy of further investigation. Also worth considering is the level of predation by mink - not a single water vole was seen during the entire survey. Finally, as regards these three species, it is not always easy to see "into" the flashes, notably at Rushmoor, Claycart & Belmore, between Fleet and Aldershot, so I may have overlooked additional breeding pairs.

I failed to see or hear Kingfisher and Spotted Flycatcher, which was somewhat surprising. What was not a surprise, however, was that I failed to record any sightings of Turtle Dove, Nightingale, Willow Tit and Tree Sparrow. All four species are in decline, nationally. As regards the Nightingale, the habitat along the canal, once a stronghold of this species particularly between Aldershot and Fleet, is no longer suitable. On a more upbeat note, it was gratifying to see the former status of Grey Wagtail restored somewhat.

The Wren has shown a modest increase on the 1991 total whilst the Robin has almost doubled its representation since 1978.The now decidedly arboreal nature of the habitat along much of the canal emphatically favours Blackcap and Chiffchaff over Garden Warbler and Willow Warbler, as the figures reveal. In fact, the last-named species is probably at its lowest ever presence along the canal.

In the 24 years that have elapsed since Mick Scott and Spike Millington carried out their survey, there has been a remarkable consistency in the figures for some species, notably Dunnock, Song Thrush, Chiffchaff, Coal Tit, Blue Tit, Great Tit & Chaffinch. The figure for Nuthatch is surprisingly low, as it is for the easily overlooked Treecreeper, whereas that for Reed Bunting comes as no surprise.

Finally, the most remarkable event that I was fortunate enough to witness during this year's survey was the sight of a Mallard brood successfully emerging from its nest situated at least 15 feet up an oak tree near Broad Oak bridge and plopping onto the soft undergrowth, watched by "mum" who had flown down first!

My thanks to Andrew Branson for encouraging me to do this year's survey, and to my wife, Maureen, for ferrying me to and from various locations along the canal.

Gilbert Rowland
14, Dunmow Hill
Fleet
Hants.
GU5 13AN

STILT SANDPIPER
A NEW SPECIES FOR HAMPSHIRE

Dr Russell B Wynn

Introduction

At about 0750 hrs on Sunday July 21st, 2002, I was doing the usual circuit around my local patch at Pennington Marshes, Hampshire, when I noticed a medium-sized greyish wader feeding on the far side of the Butts Lagoon. At first glance I thought it was a Ruff but its greyish tone and overall jizz made me suspicious so I walked around to the bank adjacent to the bird for a better look. I managed to approach to within 50 metres, and an initial look through the 'scope revealed an elegant-looking wader with a long, decurved black bill, long greenish legs and lots of lovely dark barring extending all the way from the breast to the undertail coverts. Although I had never seen one before I knew straight away that I was dealing with an adult Stilt Sandpiper, however, doubting my own memory I scrabbled around in my bag for the *Collins Bird Guide* and quickly checked through all the key features. There was no doubt about it – it really was a Stilt Sandpiper!

I proceeded to spend the next two hours in a dream-like state writing a detailed set of notes and taking a series of digiscoped images. The bird was obviously in largely summer plumage, but the presence of some new

Stilt Sandpiper, Keyhaven (Russell Wynn)

feathers on the scapulars and wing coverts indicated that it was beginning its post-breeding moult into winter plumage. It remained faithful to a small area in the corner of the lagoon, where it fed in shallow water amongst emergent vegetation, much like a Ruff or a Wood Sandpiper. At 1000 hrs I saw another birder walking along the seawall with a mobile 'phone on his belt, so I rushed over and asked him if I could make a call. I contacted the reserve warden and a few local birders

Stilt Sandpiper, Keyhaven Marsh, July 21st 2002 – Dan Powell

who arrived within minutes in various states of disrepair. Once we were all happy that the identification was watertight and the site was ready for a big weekend twitch we 'phoned the news out at 1100 hrs.

I estimated that several hundred people proceeded to visit the site during the day; happily everyone saw the bird and there were no problems at all, although the bird did fall asleep for long periods for much of the afternoon. It was reported as flying off at dusk after I had gone home, but when I returned at dawn the following morning it was still present. It remained in the area until August 3rd, and was probably one of the most well-twitched birds of 2002. It is the 20th to be recorded in Britain and the first for Hampshire. An account of the bird and several photos can be found in *Birding World (v.15, No.7)* and *Birdwatch (No.123)*.

Size and structure

Size somewhere between Dunlin and female Ruff but more elegant, with longer legs, bill and neck. Structurally it recalled a lanky Curlew Sandpiper. Distinctive side-on profile noted at times with 'lumpy' front end due to prominent breast and lower belly.

Bare parts

Long all-black bill, gently decurved, about one-and-a-half times length of head, with distinct blunt tip. Long greenish legs, quite dull in tone, long tibiae lifted almost horizontal when wading.

Plumage

Head: Showed a distinctive pattern, with a slightly rufous brown crown and forehead with fine darker brown streaks, a pale greyish finely streaked nape and throat, and rufous ear coverts. The supercilium was whitish and well defined, widest behind the eye and roughly meeting above the bill base. This contrasted with a dark brown loral stripe. A small whitish patch was visible on the centre of the crown toward the rear.

Stilt Sandpiper, Keyhaven (Russell Wynn)

Upperparts: The base colour was brownish-grey, although at distance the flight feathers showed a coarsely patterned mix of grey and blackish chequering. Most of the

200

upperpart feathers were plain pale brownish-grey with darker shafts but without obvious fringes, however, some summer feathers remained on the mantle, scapulars and secondaries which were dark blackish with broad white fringes. The primaries and tertials were dark brownish-grey with thin buff edges, and the primaries extended about 2-3 cm beyond the tertials and just beyond the tip of the tail. The white rump was sometimes glimpsed when the bird was preening, contrasting with a broad, dark terminal band on the uppertail. One observer saw the upperwing and commented on its overall plain appearance without wingbars.

Underparts: Overall whitish with prominent black barring on the lower breast, belly, flanks and undertail coverts – only the region around the vent was totally unbarred. The upper breast was more finely barred with a few dark spots around the shoulder.

Call / Flight
No call heard, and not observed in flight.

Behaviour
Elegant movements, recalling Wood Sandpiper. Preferred knee-deep water when feeding on vegetated margin of lagoon. Fed actively up to late morning and then spent long periods sleeping. Fed by 'touch-probing'. Not shy, happily fed within 30-40 m of the assembled crowd.

Possible confusion species
Not really an issue in this case!

Dr Russell Wynn
Challenger Division,
Southampton Oceanography Centre,
European Way,
Southampton,
SO14 3ZH

AVOCETS BREEDING IN HAMPSHIRE 2002

Trevor Carpenter

In 2002, Avocet bred successfully in Hampshire for the first time. Two pairs nested at a site in the North-East Solent, both producing offspring. The site is referred to in this account as TNS (The Nesting Site).

For some years it has been an open question as to why, when so many Avocets winter in 'next door' Dorset, do we see so few in Hampshire? Both of our neighbouring coastal counties have also seen successful breeding, yet despite suitable habitat birds rarely hang around for more than a few days. The year 2002 started in much the same way as previous years with a small number of records of single birds in the first three months including a notable inland records of one at Lakeside Country Park, Eastleigh on March 15th.

On March 27th two Avocets were reported from Titchfield Haven. Birds were then regularly reported from the site throughout April with numbers having risen to five by April 5th. Daily counts varied from day to day but five were reported on 10th and there were at least two to four for the rest of the month. On April 17th, two Black-winged Stilts joined the Avocets, for one day only. Add a couple of Little Egrets and the scene on the south scrape was very continental.

Along the coast at TNS, two Avocets were seen on April 19th. Given the comings and goings at the Haven it seemed reasonable to assume that birds were moving between the sites. However, there is some doubt as to exactly how many birds were involved at this time and on 23rd, two birds were reported at the Haven between 0700 hrs and 0830 hrs while two birds were also reported from TNS at 0830 hrs. The birds at TNS were showing nesting behaviour in a manner that suggested that they hadn't just flown in. Two birds continued to be seen at TNS throughout April and on 28th, one observer noted a sitting bird. However, on the following day, there were three birds present, thought by the observer to be two females and a male all of which were very active with no sign of any of the birds sitting. A pair was seen copulating, and following this act, the male was very aggressive towards the second female. By the first few days in May one bird was permanently sitting.

It is assumed that birds were frequently moving between sites at this time and on April 30th one bird was seen to leave the Haven and fly south-west into the Solent in driving wind and rain. From this and other observation at both sites, it seemed that movement between sites was not flown in a straight line. Instead birds tended to leave both sites by flying out to sea and at some point turning back to the land and their destination. There were no records of birds following the coast. Throughout April and until at least May 19th birds were reported from other county sites to the west and to the east, with an estimated 26 birds being seen during spring passage. It is possible that some of these records related to birds from the Haven/TNS, e.g. .on April 14th, three birds were reported from Budds Farm SF, Bedhampton. This was at a time when numbers at the Haven had dropped from five to a fairly regular two. So it is possible that three of that group moved on. On May 4th two birds were seen from TNS, flying east mid channel while three birds had been seen on the reserve minutes before, thus giving cause to believe the two mid channel birds were new migrants.

Throughout May it was usual to find the TNS sitting bird in position with a mate in attendance or flying in. Numbers at the Haven fluctuated with four on May 17th and an unconfirmed report of six on May 19th. Given that one bird was always sitting at TNS throughout this time, maximum numbers at both sites must always be at least one more than the count at the Haven. On May 23rd four birds were seen at TNS for the first time. The sitting bird was 'spooked' from her position and went for a fly around. Very shortly afterwards, the mate stepped into to take her place on the nest. It is understood that at this time there was at least one chick present and that Avocets had bred in Hampshire for the first time. A day later on the 24th there were six birds present, four adults and four chicks, with the parent pair seen to be keeping gulls and other birds at bay.

Avocet chasing Black-tailed Godwits (Dennis Bright)

By May 27th the four chicks and their parents had moved base, initially to another island and within a few days to the back of the scrape in deep cover, making the chicks very difficult to see. At the same time the second pair, first seen on 23rd, were making themselves comfortable to the left of the original sitter's position and in subsequent days one bird was ever present and remained in the same position until at least Jun 19th. Occasional sighting of the original pair's chicks continued to be made but because of the cover it was difficult to confirm numbers. However sightings suggest that the four chicks had been reduced to three by early June. Birds continued to be recorded at the Haven and the assumption has to be that the majority of these sightings were TNS birds finding better feeding opportunities at the Haven.

It was June 22nd before there was any significant change to this scenario. On this day there were at least eight birds at TNS, four adults and three well-grown chicks with the original pair, and one young chick that was seen with the second pair. It is believed that the second pair also produced a total of four young. On 23rd the three well-grown chicks were seen with the mother and were joined by the adult male who flew in, presumably from the Haven. Because of the cover on the second island it was very difficult to see whether any chicks were present. It had been noticed before this day that some of the birds were discoloured and it could now be confirmed that the original pair were both looking very tatty with some brown discolouring especially on the female, while the second pair was pristine

On Monday 24th the second pair flew off north at around 0630 hrs with no sign of any young left around. The first pair, whilst still having three chicks in tow, which had swum towards the east bank, became very agitated around 0715 hrs and the birds were continually up in the air but the observer could see no reason for their concern. At 0800 hrs the Avocets' distress calls were getting louder. The pair of Avocets was then seen to fly to the eastern edge of the reserve and continued to flutter around. The cause of their distress was a Fox, which it was assumed had taken at least one of the chicks. The worst was feared and it was clearly possible that both pairs had lost all of their chicks.

Adult Avocet with two young, Titchfield Haven (Dennis Bright)

On Tuesday June 25th, a member of the public made a surprising discovery on the shore at Hill Head. The official release from Titchfield Haven management is shown below:

"The two Avocets on the south scrape have now been joined by a pair with two chicks. The chicks were rescued yesterday from the shore at Hill Head by staff after being discovered by a member of the public. Due to interference on the nesting site the family party had been displaced during the previous 24 hours. Fortunately the young were accompanied by the parent birds who remained in attendance whilst the assisted transfer from shore to the safety of south scrape took place. This is the first ever breeding of Avocets in Hampshire and hopefully the remainder of the period up to the chicks fledging will pass unhindered. An earlier wilful disturbance incident reported on the nesting site is now being investigated by the police"

It is assumed that the two chicks accompanied by their parents had walked (or swam) along the shore from TNS during the course of the day, a distance of some four or five kms. Unfortunately it would seem their surviving sibling and the second pair's offspring were almost certainly taken by the Fox. Avocets were recorded regularly until mid August including both of the adults and young and new migrant birds. The two chicks first flew sometime in early July.

At the time of writing it looks as if the 2002 occurrence may not be an isolated instance and that Avocets may become regular breeders in the county. Whether they colonise in the sort of numbers now common on the east coast remains to be seen.

Trevor Carpenter
28A Kiln Rd
Fareham
Hants
PO16 7UB

SAVI'S WARBLERS BREEDING IN HAMPSHIRE – A HISTORICAL PERSPECTIVE

Barry Duffin

Introduction

On the 11th May 1969 a Savi's Warbler *Locustella luscinioides* was found singing in riverside reeds on private land close to Upper Titchfield Haven Nature Reserve by R.J.Carpenter. In subsequent days the bird moved a short distance down river but continued to sing from reeds on the edge of the river until at least 21st June. During this period the bird was watched on occasions by D.Billett, M.Bryant and Dr.C.Suffern. A number of breeding Grasshopper Warblers *Locustella naevia* were present in the area and were often singing at the same time as the Savi's Warbler. There was no evidence to suggest more than one bird was present or that breeding took place. This was the first occurrence of this species in Hampshire.

Savi's Warblers breed in the Low Countries, Germany, Poland and central Russia, south to the Mediterranean, the Black Sea and Caspian region. Until the middle of the 19th century small numbers bred in the fens of Norfolk, Suffolk, Cambridgeshire and Huntingdonshire. The draining of the fens had a disastrous effect on the species which became extinct in England by 1856, and it was not until 1954 that it was recorded again in Cambridgeshire (Boston 1956). Breeding was subsequently proven firstly in Kent in 1960, and later at two sites in Suffolk in 1970-71 (Pitt 1967, Axell and Jobson 1972).

This short paper summarises the records of the occurrence of Savi's Warblers at Titchfield Haven National Nature Reserve year by year since 1969.

Annual Observations

Table 1. Summary of numbers and dates of Savi's Warblers *Locustella luscinioides* at Titchfield Haven National Nature Reserve 1969-1998

Year	First Date	Last Date	Singing Males	Probable Pairs Breeding	Confirmed Pairs Breeding
1969	11/05	21/06	1	-	-
1976	27/05	05/06	1	-	-
1978	05/05	18/07	6	3	2
1979	27/04	04/07	2	1	-
1980	22/04	06/07	3	1	-
1981	13/04	16/06	1	1	-
1982	14/04	26/06	2	1	1
1983	27/04	06/07	1	1	1
1987	24/04	08/05	1	-	-
1989	10/05	29/05	1	1	-
1990	27/04	13/07	2	1	-
1991	27/04	30/07	3	2	1
1992	26/04	23/06	2	2	1
1998	11/04	18/05	1	-	-

1976. On the evening of 27th May T.A.Lawman, D.Pearce and myself heard a Savi's Warbler singing from within a large inaccessible reed-bed within Titchfield Haven Nature Reserve. The bird could not be seen and a decision was taken not to investigate further for fear of disturbing a nesting pair of Bearded Tits *Panurus biarmicus*, the only breeding pair on the reserve at the time. The observers were at once aware of the difference of the Savi's Warbler song from that of the Grasshopper Warbler, of which several singing males were present in other localities of the site. The bird was noted singing on a further four occasions, the last being on 5th June. Song was only heard during warm still evenings, daytime checks proved negative. There was no evidence of this bird having been paired.

1977. A singing Savi's Warbler was located on the evening of 25th June in the vicinity of the 1976 site. Only short sporadic bursts of song were heard at 1715hrs but singing was much more frequent at 2000hrs. On the morning of the following day the bird was singing from the same location. During a subsequent evening visit later that day the bird was observed as it was singing from the top of dead reed stems. The bird continued to sing during the early morning each day until 29th June, but there was no evidence of breeding behaviour.

1978. Three singing males held territory for more than a month. A further three singing males were located at different sites but the period of song from these three birds was very short. At two of the main sites, including the 1976 site, food carrying was noted during the first week of July. During ringing activities in early July a male and female were trapped on 1st, the female showing a full brood patch. Later a newly fledged bird was trapped on 6th July. Successful breeding at the third of the main sites was not proven but was considered probable.

1979. Two sites were occupied by singing males, the first from 27th April, the second from 11th May. Coverage was much reduced this year, but when one of the two sites was visited on 4th July adult birds clearly showed signs of agitation, by giving regular alarm calls.

1980. A bird located close to the 1976 site on 22nd April continued singing daily until 6th May and then again from 29th June until 6th July. A second bird located on 15th May some 700 metres to the north of the first site, continued singing until 25th June and was observed acting in an agitated manner on 18th June suggesting a nesting site was nearby . A bird sang intermittently at a third location from 6th May until at least 26th May. Two of the sites were considered to hold paired birds.

1981. The 1980 site was occupied again from 13th April until at least 16th June. Although coverage of the site was very limited the singing male was considered to have been paired and nesting most probably took place.

1982. The 1976 site was occupied with a bird singing regularly from 14th April until 2nd June, and then again from 15th-26th June. Food carrying was observed at the site on 1st June. A second site was found to be occupied by a singing bird from 27th May until at least 6th June but there was no evidence here of nesting.

1983. A singing male was regularly reported from 27th April until 5th May, then intermittently from 20th May until 22nd June. On the 8th June an observer on the river watched this bird singing at a range of only five metres, the uttering of the ticking notes which often precede the reeling song were clearly audible. Food carrying was noted in early July. An adult was trapped on 6th July.

1987. A singing male arrived at the 1976 site on 24th April and was still present the next day. Strong north-westerly winds during the next two weeks prevented any observations being made. The only subsequent date when song was reported was on the evening of 8th May in calm conditions. Much of remainder of the month of May brought inclement weather, certainly not conditions for listening out for Savi's Warblers.

1989. A bird found singing on 10th May remained at this locality until at least the 29th May. Subsequent coverage of the site was not possible during June.

1990. A singing male occupied a newly created reed-bed site for the first time from 27th April until 7th May. Severe weather then interrupted observations until 19th May. The singing bird was then recorded intermittently until early June when once more bad weather prevailed. The last date on which this bird was recorded was 13th July. A pair was considered to have most probably bred at this site. A second site, the 1976 site, was occupied from 11th-13th July.

1991. A singing male was observed at one site regularly from 27th April until 5th May, and then again intermittently from 21st-30th May. A second bird discovered singing some 800 metres to the north of the first site on 10th May was in place until 31st May, and then sang again, intermittently from 17th-30th July. Two more sites in close proximity to the second bird's territory were frequented from 16th June until the last week in July. There is a possibility that there was some re-locating of birds during June. Food carrying was reported in June from one site and possibly from a second site.

1992. Two of the 1991 sites were occupied. A bird sang regularly at site one from 26th April until 23rd May, and then again on 22nd-23rd June. Site two was occupied by a singing bird from 20th-26th May and then again on 7th June. Evidence of nesting was noted at one of the sites.

1998. A singing male was reported at the 1976 site regularly from 11th-15th April, and again from 28th-30th April. A singing male discovered at another site 800 metres away on 8th May was last reported on 18th May. There was no evidence that either bird was paired and there was the possibility that only one bird was involved.

Field Notes

Behaviour

Once located by song Savi's Warblers were found to be very obliging birds to watch, often singing in very exposed positions. Birds would often react to the presence of an observer inquisitively, boldly climbing to the tops of reed stems. Early in the season when birds were establishing territories any presence of humans would often provoke bursts of song. Breeding birds when approached presented an agitated pose with much flicking of the tail and wings. Short scolding notes could be followed by harsh chatter when birds were alarmed.

Characteristics

Field notes taken by several observers agreed that Savi's Warblers differed from the closely resembled Reed Warbler *Acrocephalus scirpaceus* in being a larger, bulkier bird. The bird's broad, longish, rounded tail was a most obvious feature particularly when in flight.. The upperparts appeared a uniform dark reddish-brown, with the ear-coverts noticeably paler. The underparts were mainly off-white, with throat and chin being a conspicuous white. When observed at close quarters and in good light a pale supercilium was clearly noticeable. Details taken from trapped birds revealed fine, dark fault bars on the upper tail, warm buff under tail-coverts with pale tips, buff sides to lower breast and flanks. Upperparts distinctly rufous-brown in juvenile birds. Tarsus pinkish. Upper mandible black and lower mandible pale horn coloured.

Song

All records of Savi's Warblers at Titchfield Haven have referred to birds first being located by song. The high-pitched reeling song of the Grasshopper Warbler is distinctly different from the lower-pitched buzzing of the Savi's, but many observers find separation difficult. The 1998 Savi's Warbler sang in a reed-bed only fifty metres from an observation hide, but the majority of birdwatchers visiting this location mistakenly reported this bird as a Grasshopper Warbler. Detection of the ticking notes preceding the full song can only be detected when an observer is in close proximity to the bird. In calm, warm conditions, particularly in the evening, song has often been noted at ranges of at least 400 metres from the recorder. In over two decades of recording of Savi's Warblers at Titchfield Haven there have been few records of birds singing throughout the day, which could suggest that a high percentage of birds may have been paired.

Habitat

Almost all established territories at Titchfield Haven have been associated with extensive, inaccessible areas of reed *Phragmites communis*. The favoured reed-beds being those that were damp but not necessarily in standing water, and where there was often an appreciable build-up of litter. The presence of an undergrowth of sedges *Carex* or Reed Sweet-grass *Glyceria maxima* added to the preferred habitat. Prior to the mid-1980s all major reed-beds at Titchfield Haven were situated within the flood-plain of the River Meon, and as a consequence territories were very susceptible to flooding in wet springs and summers. In recent years additional large tracts of reed-bed have been created where water levels can be managed, and to these areas birds quickly took up residence.

Table 2. Numbers of Breeding Pairs of Savi's Warblers in UK 1969-2001

1969	1970	1971	1972	1973	1974	1975	1976	1977	1978	1979
12	8	7	14	13	8	3	9	26	28	30
1980	1981	1982	1983	1984	1985	1986	1987	1988	1989	1990
29	15	18	17	12	15	12	20	13	17	12
1991	1992	1993	1994	1995	1996	1997	1998	1999	2000	2001
19	24	8	10	3	3	5	3	9	2	9

Summary

The first occurrence of Savi's Warbler in Hampshire was of a singing male at Titchfield Haven in 1969. From 1976 to 2002 singing male Savi's Warblers were recorded in fourteen years, with confirmed breeding being noted in five of those years, and probable breeding in a further five years. Given that Savi's Warblers breed in habitat that is generally inaccessible without causing disturbance to the birds and associated species, the numbers of confirmed breeding pairs should be regarded as a minimum. Annual occurrences at Titchfield Haven have been summarised in this paper, and brief field notes have been presented on behaviour, characteristics, song and habitat. Numbers of singing males at Titchfield Haven have reflected the rise and fall of the United Kingdom breeding population, the peak years being from 1977 to 1980. Disappointingly low numbers have been reported breeding in the UK since 1993 (see Table 2), a period when only one singing male occurred at Titchfield Haven.

B S Duffin
Titchfield Haven Nature Reserve

References

Axell, H. E., and Jobson, G. J. 1972. 'Savi's Warbler breeding in Suffolk'. *Brit. Birds*, 65: 229-232.

Boston, F. M. 1956. 'Savi's Warbler in Cambridgeshire'. *Brit. Birds*, 49: 326-327.

Gibbons, D. W., Reid, J. B., and Chapman, R. A. 1993. *The New Atlas of Breeding Birds in Britain and Ireland*: 1988-1991. London.

Pitt, R. G. 1967. 'Savi's Warblers breeding in Kent'. *Brit. Birds*, 60: 349-355.

BREEDING GOSHAWK IN HAMPSHIRE - A FIRST?

W Percy, A Page, A Lucas

Introduction

The Goshawk (*Accipiter gentilis*) is firmly established as a resident breeding bird in Britain.

Sporadic breeding in the period up to the end 1960s was consolidated through the 70s and 80s, and had resulted in an estimate of 200 breeding pairs by 1988 (Gibbon *et al*). The *British Birds* Rare Breeding Birds in the UK report for 1998 (Ogilvie *et al*) gave at least 255 localities and 179-249 pairs throughout Britain, although it was noted that some observers were still withholding information. This assessment of the breeding population is considered a significant underestimate by some longstanding Goshawk fieldworkers who can list 40 breeding pairs in one study area alone. Further more it is considered common in many forests in Wales (Roberts, *pers. comm.*).

It remains a puzzle why Goshawks have not colonised the large forested areas of Hampshire, particularly the New Forest. The largely sedentary nature of the adults maybe a factor, though within the large commercial plantations of the north and west of Britain, the population has expanded, where unmolested, to densities in some areas of nests only 1.5 km apart (Anon.).

Ringing recoveries have shown that the dispersal of young Goshawks outside large forest blocks brings them into conflict with gamekeepers' interests (J. Lewis, *pers. comm.*), and, undoubtedly the young birds are attracted to pheasant release pens where the outcome can be less than favourable.

Although some areas have outstanding productivity, with one study area alone producing over 100 youngsters in a season, colonisation of new woodlands across game rearing country has been slow. This is considered the prime reason why isolated breeding attempts in the south during the 1990s have petered out after a few years (M. Cowlard, *pers. comm.*).

Records in Hampshire

Rumour and unsupported claims of breeding have persisted in the New Forest for many years, though seasoned raptor watchers, with decades of experience, have failed to confirm these rumours (J M Tubbs, D V and G B Westerhoff *pers. comm.*). The authors have had little difficulty confirming breeding once pairs have been located and it is difficult to imagine displaying Goshawks remaining undetected under intensive watching. We are therefore led to conclude that while genuine Goshawk sightings have occurred sporadically over the years that breeding has not been previously recorded in the Forest.

A review of HOS records also fails to authenticate breeding anywhere else in Hampshire.

It is hoped that this paper will bring forth genuine, supportable, but previously suppressed data to be archived for Hampshire birding.

2002 – First Successful Breeding Recorded in Hampshire

Since 2000, the authors have monitored Goshawks breeding close to the Hampshire border which were successful in rearing up to five young in a season.

Goshawk nestling during ringing (courtesy of Wayne Percy)

Intensive fieldwork by the authors has now led to the discovery of two pairs breeding in the New Forest and a subsequent slowly expanding population. In 2002 a pair, consisting of an immature male and an adult female, were observed displaying throughout February with the subsequent location of a nest in a Scots Pine on 2nd Mar. This nest fledged at least three young during June.

On 25th Mar a second nest was located 5¼ miles from the first. This nest, in a Douglas Fir, again fledged at least three young. Very unusually, both birds of this pair were immature, suggesting a colonising population. A pair of Goshawks breeding at less than a year old is worthy of note.

In another area of the Forest a single, immature male held territory. All nests were located under licence.

2003 - Update

At the time of writing (August 2003) the population in the New Forest has increased to three breeding pairs and a further two occupied territories. A BTO ringing scheme is now under way, which it is hoped may provide more information about population expansion.

With these three breeding pairs and a further three breeding pairs close to the border, it is hoped that the species will continue to consolidate and regularly breed in Hampshire, much to the pleasure and delight of county ornithologists.

Birding forays in early spring can only be enlivened by this handsome and powerful addition to the county's avifauna.

Acknowledgments.

We would like to thank the Forestry Commission and their agents for their invaluable assistance with fieldwork.

We would also like to thank Richard Jacobs and Steve Roberts for their support.

W.Percy, A.Page, A Lucas

References.

Gibbons, D W, Reid J B, & Chapman, R.A. 1993. *The New Atlas of Breeding Birds in Britain and Ireland*. 1998-1991. London.

Ogilvie, MA & the Rare Breeding Birds Panel, 2000. 'Rare breeding birds in the United Kingdom in 1998'. *British Birds 93: 372*

Anon. 'Goshawk breeding habitat in Lowland Britain'. *British Birds 82: 56-67.*

HAMPSHIRE ORNITHOLOGICAL SOCIETY

Honorary Officers, 2003-2004

President: Chris Packham

MANAGEMENT COMMITTEE

Chairman:	John Eyre	3 Dunmow Hill, Fleet, GU51 3AN
Secretary:	Peter Dudley	3 Copsewood Road, Hythe, Southampton, SO34 2TQ
Treasurer:	Nigel Peace	4 Wincanton Close, Alton, GU34 2TQ
Membership Secretary:	Alison Wall	11 Waterloo Avenue, Basingstoke, RG23 8DL
Membership Records Officer:	John Norton	215 Forton Road, Gosport PO12 3HB
County Recorder:	John Clark	4 Cygnet Court, Old Cove Road, Fleet, GU51 2RL

Chairman of Scientific Committee:	Glynne Evans
Chairman of Membership Committee & Meetings Co-ordinator:	Andrew Walmsley
Conservation Liaison Officer:	Norman Pratt
Bird Report *Editor:*	Alan Cox
Co-editor:	Martin Pitt
Production:	Mike Wall
Librarian:	Richard Jacobs
Newsletter Editor:	David Thelwell
Publicity Officer:	Keith Betton
Sales Officer:	Margaret Boswell
Ordinary Members:	John Collman, Mark Edgeller, Mike Wall, Brian Sharkey

MEMBERS OF SUB-COMMITTEES

Scientific:
Glynne Evans (Chairman), Kevin Briggs (Secretary), Duncan Bell, John Clark, John Collman, John Eyre, Norman Pratt, David Unsworth, Keith Wills and Russell Wynn.

Membership:
Andrew Walmsley (Chairman), Margaret Boswell, Judith Chawner, Richard Jacobs, Peter Morrison, Sue Morrison, John Norton and Alison Wall.

Membership enquiries should be addressed to the Membership Secretary,
subscription renewals and membership enquiries to the Membership Records Officer
and other general correspondence to the Secretary.

POLICY, MEMBERSHIP AND ORGANISATION OF THE HAMPSHIRE ORNITHOLOGICAL SOCIETY

The Society was founded in January 1979, following the winding-up of the Ornithological Section of the Hampshire Field Club. The objects of the Society are, within the County of Hampshire:

a.   To advance the education of the public in all aspects of ornithology.

b.   To promote research into ornithology and to publish the useful results of such study and in particular to publish reports, newsletters and other papers of ornithological interest or as may be deemed by the Management Committee suitable or desirable for promoting the Society's objects.

c.   To support and encourage the preservation and conservation of wild birds and places of ornithological interest.

Membership is available for the following subscriptions (effective after September 30th, 1994):

Ordinary Membership (including students)).......................... }	
Family Membership)... }	
(2 or more members at the same address)......................... }	£9.00
Corporate Membership (Schools, NHSs etc.)....................... }	
Junior Membership (Members under 18)	£3.00

Application should be made to the Membership Secretary. Subscriptions are renewable on January 1st each year, but the subscription of any new member joining after September 30th shall cover the succeeding calendar year, save that members so joining shall not be entitled to receive the Bird Report published in the year they are joining.

All members receive the annual Bird Report and quarterly newsletters, which give details of all indoor and outdoor meetings arranged on behalf of the Society.

The Newsletters contain Society news and views, articles on various aspects of Hampshire ornithology, recent reports, ringing news, and details of the organisation, progress and results of surveys organised by the Scientific sub-committee. These include wildfowl and wader counts, breeding censuses and migration watches. New surveys are started every year, and the newsletter serves as a medium to contact potential volunteers. All members are invited to take part in surveys and contribute articles to the newsletter.

Regular field meetings are arranged for all parts of the county throughout the year. Meetings are designed to introduce members to various habitats and to provide opportunity for novices of all ages to learn more about birds under field conditions.

Indoor meetings (usually illustrated lectures) are arranged in the winter months. Most of these will be of interest to all members, but some may cater particularly for specialist groups, e.g. survey workers' meetings.

There are two sub-committees:

(a) The Scientific sub-committee is responsible for organising surveys, for the collection of records and for the production of the Bird Report. It also handles liaison with the BTO, ringing groups, conservation bodies and similar organisations.

(b) The Membership sub-committee is responsible for the Newsletter, the Members' Day, conferences, indoor and outdoor meetings and the library."

Officers of all the committees are listed on page 213 of this report.

HAMPSHIRE BIRD REPORT

BACK NUMBERS

The following issues are still available

1990	-	**£1**
1991	-	**£1**
1992	-	**£1**
1993	-	**£1**
1994	-	**£1**
1995	-	**£2**
1996	-	**£3**
1997	-	**£3**
1998	-	**£3**
1999	-	**£5**
2000	-	**£5**
2001		**£8**

Please add 75p postage and packing for each report order (to 1992)
Please add £1.00 postage and packing for each report order (1993 and after).

CHECKLIST OF THE BIRDS OF HAMPSHIRE

Produced by John Eyre, the checklist gives a full list of all species ever reliably recorded in Hampshire with a month by month guide to their relative abundance.

Price £1.50 including P&P.

Cheques should be made payable to *HOS*

Orders to: Mrs. M. Boswell,
5 Clarence Road,
Lyndhurst
SO43 7AL